T0337747

# Korean Adoption and Inheritance

# Korean
# Adoption
# and
# Inheritance

*Case Studies
in the Creation of a
Classic Confucian Society*

Mark A. Peterson

East Asia Program
Cornell University
Ithaca, New York 14853

The Cornell East Asia Series is published by the Cornell University East Asia Program and is not affiliated with Cornell University Press. We are a small, non-profit press, publishing reasonably-priced books on a wide variety of scholarly topics relating to East Asia as a service to the academic community and the general public. We accept standing orders which may be cancelled at any time and which provide for automatic billing and shipping of each title in the series upon publication.

If after review by internal and external readers a manuscript is accepted for publication, it is published on the basis of camera-ready copy provided by the volume author. Each author is thus responsible for any necessary copy-editing and for manuscript formatting. Submission inquiries should be addressed to Editorial Board, East Asia Program, Cornell University, Ithaca, New York 14853-7601.

*The Cornell East Asia Program, with the generous support of Dr. Hen Suh Park, awards the $1000 Yeonam Prize annually for a book-length Korean work (any topic) submitted to the Cornell East Asia Series: Korea. The Yeonam Prize is named in memory of Ji-Won Park (1737-1805), pen name Yeonam, a leader of the Practical Learning* (Silhak) *movement and an ancestor of Dr. Hen Suh Park.*

Number 80 in the Cornell East Asia Series.
© 1996 by Mark Peterson. All rights reserved
ISSN 1050-2955
ISBN 1-885445-70-9 cloth
ISBN 1-885445-80-6 paper
Printed in the United States of America

For Laurel and Joy

# Contents

# List of Tables

# Preface

I began this work as part of a seminar paper in one of Ed Wagner's classes at Harvard back in 1972 when I noticed the absence of adoptions in the *chokpo* [genealogy] entries covering the early Chosŏn period. For the class paper, I set out to study adoption practices and then in 1973, in Seoul, the late Bill Shaw introduced me to the *Kyehu tŭngnok* (the register of adoptions), a government record kept by the Ministry of Rites in traditional times but preserved in the Kyujanggak collection [Chosŏn period government archive] of The Seoul National University library (only recently did I find two missing volumes have been kept separately in the Changsŏgak [royal archive], now at the Academy of Korean Studies). I gained access to the Kyujanggak library, again with the kind assistance of Bill Shaw who introduced me to Lee Man-gap (then the director of the library) and Yi Sang-un (who is still assisting researchers who come to use the collection). My debt to those who helped me get started on this work that I have begun, set aside, begun, set aside, and begun again, is immense.

In those days, the SNU campus was at its old site in Tongsung-dong. I remember meeting Martina Deuchler, a *sŏnbae* [senior classmate] who had already left Harvard before I began my studies there, but who I saw day after day in the reading room of the old Kyujanggak poring over Chosŏn-period documents, but who would take time to answer questions of a younger *hubae*.

Of course, the greatest debt I owe is to Professor Wagner who introduced me to the world of Korean social history and a whole fleet of reference works necessary for navigating through those largely unchartered waters (particularly as far as work in the English-speaking world was concerned). In those days it was correct to refer to the time period in question as the Yi dynasty; but now the term Chosŏn dynasty is correct. Professor Wagner's colleague in many research projects involving the organization of all kinds of primary sources—notably the examination rosters, but many other kinds of material, as well—was Prof. Song June-ho. During the years I lived in Seoul, 1977-83, I spent many pleasurable hours at the feet of Prof. Song, learning myriads of things from his years of extremely careful study. In Korean, I often use the word *Ŭnsa-nim* (beloved teacher) in reference to both Prof. Wagner and Prof. Song.

Prof. Song shared with me the first generation photocopies of the Puan Kim documents when they were first given to the Chŏnbuk University museum, a while before they were taken over by the Academy of Korean Studies and published. Those documents and many others would find their way into Prof. Song's hands and he would freely share them with me. Many of them are in this book in footnotes and in the bibliography with only simple bibliographic notation that does not reveal that they were introduced to my by Prof. Song.

From 1979 through 1983, and from time to time thereafter, I have studied classical Chinese from one of Korea's living masters, Na Kap-chu. Also known by his pen name, Sŏngjae, he is one of only a handful left of the generation that learned the classics in the traditional system and who has been able to both teach the classics and compose in classical Chinese. For five years, in the early morning we pored over various old documents, some printed and some in cursive script, including numerous passages from the *Shillok* [the annals of the Chosŏn court] as he patiently put up with my questions while he tried to teach me how to read that extremely difficult literature.

Much of the research for this book was done during the years I lived in Seoul and worked at the Fulbright office. I always appreciated the encouragement and support of the staff there, Shim Jai-ok, Mrs. Nam (Kim Chŏng-hŭi who is now teaching English literature at Sŏngshim Women's University), Im Pu-hŭi, Kim Sŏn-suk, An Myoung-hee, Han Yeh-hee, Mrs. Park (Im Ok-cha, now at UNICEF/Korea), Lee Han-sŏng, Fred Carriere, and others.

I also want to thank Pak Pyŏng-ho who helped me get a grant from the Korean Traders Scholarship Foundation for research on the *Kyehu tŭngnok*. And to Ch'oe Chae-sŏk and two of his graduate students, Pak Hye-in and Ch'oe Kwang-shik, who helped me to index and evaluate the data therein. I have appreciated the discussions and insights of Lee Kwang-gyu and Kim Kwang-ok of the SNU anthropology department, and Kim Chong-un, with whom I have worked in various capacities at SNU.

I gratefully acknowledge the Fulbright-Hays (Department of Education) doctoral dissertation research grant, under which I did the lion's share of the research for this book. And to the Asiatic Research Center of Korea University that provided me an affiliation when I was conducting the research on the Fulbright grant.

Numerous lineage associations were helpful to me and shared information about their lineage, its genealogy, and traditions. Among them, Yi Che-su in Kwangju has been encouraging for many years. Many of the office staff at lineage offices in Seoul and around the countryside, at *hyanggyo* [rural government schools], and at *sŏwŏn* [private academies] have been cordial and helpful in tracking down documents.

My colleagues at BYU have been a constant source of support; among them those that gave specific help at one stage or another of this project were Spencer Palmer, Rhee Honam, Kim Han-Kon, and Gary Williams. In the translation and revision of this work for the Korean edition three people have played essential roles. First is the translator, Kim Hyejŏng; she has diligently, persistently and carefully gone over the text again and again to prepare the text to be clear and accurate. She was introduced to me by Lee Hoon-sang of Donga University in Pusan, who since the time I lived in Pusan (1987-90) has helped me in numerous endeavors. And finally, and again, Prof. Song June-ho who made a thorough critique and several recommendations for revision for the Korean edition. Unfortunately, I was not able to accept all of his recommendations for revision because we have a radically different views on some aspects of the subject. But we have agreed to disagree and he has, as when we first met, continued to help and support me in numerous ways. It is inconsistent with Korean culture for someone my age to call someone his age (he is over twenty years my senior) a friend, but in western culture there is no higher compliment and truly he has been a great friend to me over the last twenty years.

I appreciate those at the Cornell East Asia series, David McCann, Joan Piggott, and Karen Smith who helped at various stages of preparing this book.

I also want to acknowledge those who have helped in such things as providing housing for me on numerous short trips to Seoul, including Jeff and Janae Jones, Dave and Diane Thompson. And in many ways Bruce Grant has helped me develop many of my ideas on Korea throughout my years of study.

Finally, I want to thank my wife, Randy, who has seen this work through the ups and downs, ons and offs, and has always been there to help—but she is the first to note that if it were not for modern word processors, she doubts she would have survived the revisions and retypings that are necessary to create a book. So finally, I thank Radio Shack (and first my TRS-80, Model III with its whopping 64K of RAM) and Macintosh for keeping me, my sanity, and my wife, together.

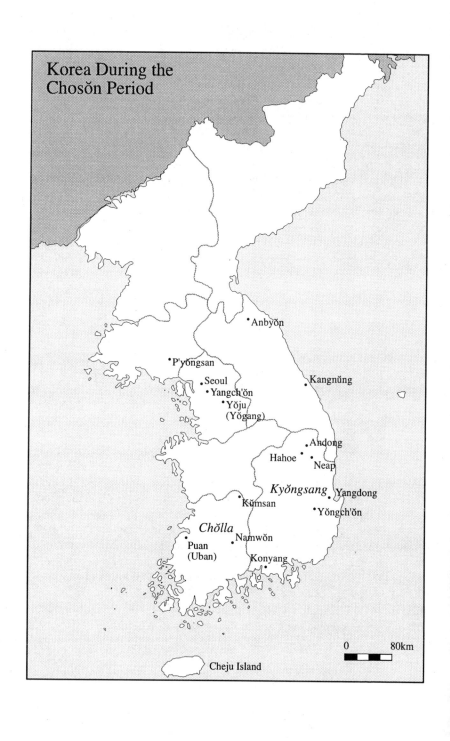

Korea During the
Chosŏn Period

Anbyŏn

P'yŏngsan

Seoul
Yangch'ŏn
Yŏju
(Yŏgang)

Kangnŭng

Andong
Hahoe
Neap

Kyŏngsang Yangdong

Kŭmsan
Yŏngch'ŏn

Chŏlla
Namwŏn
Puan
(Uban)
Konyang

0        80km

Cheju Island

# Introduction

## An Archetypical Case

Yi Ka-myŏng was born in the early 1890's. His immediate ancestors had all been military officers and his more distant ancestry was traced to early Chosŏn period (1392-1910), Yi dynasty royalty. His grandfather was one of the soldiers mobilized to put down the Tonghak Rebellion (1894-95) and became one of the fatalities. Yi Ka-myŏng's father was honored as the son of a martyred hero and was appointed to the prestigious palace guard in Seoul, but he no sooner left his village for the two-day trip than he contracted cholera; he died shortly after his arrival in Seoul. The unfortunate Yi Ka-myŏng was about ten when he lost his father and grandfather. Left in the care of his relatives, an early marriage was arranged for him when he was thirteen. His bride was fourteen. They never had children and both died in 1982 within months of each other in their late eighties.

When Mr. Yi had reached middle age, he began to seek a solution to his childless dilemma. He maintained his marriage with his first wife but over a period of time made informal marriages with other women for the purpose of bearing a son. None of the liaisons was successful. Finally, he heard of a widowed woman in a nearby village, a Mrs. An, who was somewhat destitute. Her husband had been killed in the Korean War; she and a young son needed support. Mr. Yi observed that since she was obviously fertile, perhaps she could bear a son for him. She and her son came to live in the household, although for such an arrangement there was no formal ceremony. She was young enough to be the daughter or daughter-in-law in the household, and in many ways she was treated that way, especially by the first wife. Mr. Yi referred to her as an "unfortunate woman" (*pulssanghan yŏja*) because she had to serve two old people. The first wife in the years before her death was senile and totally dependent on the second wife. Her son, however, was treated largely as if he were Mr. Yi's son. They called each other "father" and "son," and the young boy was sent to school and treated as if he had been born into the household.

1

Eventually Mrs. An bore two children; both were daughters. One daughter died in a childhood accident but the other grew to maturity, married, and has had a daughter of her own.

Thus, Mr. Yi had no children by his first wife, but after bringing a series of "informal wives" or *de facto* wives into the household, a young widow had given him a stepson, a surviving daughter and a granddaughter. But for the traditionally-minded Mr. Yi, the situation was not satisfactory. A few years before he died, Mr. Yi adopted the son of an agnatic cousin to be his heir, but in less than a year the adoption was dissolved. In fact, it had not yet been reported to the township office and was not entered on the household register. It was during an initial trial period that Mr. Yi decided the new son was not sufficiently attentive. The boy was the fourth of five sons. He was young (mid-twenties), unmarried, and maybe too modern to be concerned with the affairs of lineage and ceremony which Mr. Yi considered important. Several months later another adoption was arranged. This time the heir was the son of a much more distant cousin, was older (in his late forties), married, and, most importantly, already had a son of his own. He also needed financial assistance since he had five daughters before his only son was born. (A Korean saying has it that "a thief will not bother breaking into the home of a man with three daughters"; daughters are raised for others and cost a fortune to marry off.) The second adoption was registered and the two distant relatives served each other's needs very well.

### Agnatic Adoption

The above case illustrates several aspects of traditional Korean culture in general, and of lineage and family organization in particular. The overriding cultural value the case illustrates is that of a son as an heir. The man, as a young fatherless boy, was arranged to be married at an early age. He brought in extra wives, had a stepson, a daughter and granddaughter, and yet in the end he adopted a patrilineal cousin's son. The ever-present objective was to obtain a son. The early marriage and the extra marriages failed; the third method, adoption of a bloodline nephew, succeeded although two attempts were necessary.

The importance of the patrilineal lineage organization cannot be over emphasized. Mr. Yi had a stepson whom he has cared for and educated. He filled the financial and ceremonial role of the father at the boy's wedding. The young man now has a good job as an engineer, but the boy's surname is An, not Yi, and nothing can change that. He does not have the right blood, or in terms of Neo-Confucian ideology, they do not share the same "mind-matter" (*ki*, Ch. *ch'i*). The correct bloodline is the key, Mr. Yi asserted; and that is why the adopted son, a member of the patrilineage, will be his rightful and only heir.

The above case is unique only in that several ways of solving the sonless dilemma are demonstrated in one man's life. It illustrates the value, organization, and breadth of the lineage. As we examine cases in historical documents we will track the development of the kinship system and see the emergence of lineage and trace changes in the lineage system. Prior to the seventeenth century the kinship system will be called a cognatic system; during the seventeenth century (and a few decades before and thereafter) we will see the formation of a classic patrilineal lineage system.

## The Patrilineage

Korean society has been characterized as a classic patriarchal, patrilineal, patrilocal society. That is to say that political authority is in the hands of the males, that property is inherited through males, and that residence after marriage is in the males' homes. With men dominating society, what is the position of the woman? We have interesting insiders' views captured in common aphorisms. All Koreans know the saying, *namjon yŏbi*, ("men are exalted but women are lowly"). And the daughter, once she is married, is called a *ch'ulga oein*, ("one who left the household and became a stranger").

The Korean patrilineage can be described as "men related to men through men." Women are incidental. One resource for studying the lineage is the published genealogical tables (*chokpo*). Although it is difficult to measure, Korea may well have more printed genealogies per capita than any other country in the world. The printed genealogy is a listing of all the members of the lineage, members who obtain their status through birth. There is no provision for including others.[1] One could be expelled, however, for criminal conduct, for example. The genealogy marks the effective boundaries of the lineage.

What of the women? Are they members of their natal lineage or their husbands? They are more the latter than the former since they are buried with their husbands and are offered ancestor ceremonies with their husbands after they die, but they never take their husband's name and are always described as having come from their natal lineage, rather than being described as members of the husband's lineage. Daughters are listed in the

---

[1]The Korean lineage was much more strict than its similar counterparts in China or Japan. In both the other East Asian countries influenced by Confucianism there were ways for non-agnates to get into the genealogy and the lineage, but not in Korea.

genealogy as having married out and into another lineage; and wives are shown to have married in from another lineage.[2] The depth of a woman's ancestry in a genealogy is often only one or two generations, the woman and her father, although there are cases where the woman's grandfather or great grandfather or in some cases an illustrious remote ancestor is listed. Women appear in the genealogy only in reluctant recognition of the fact that men cannot bear children by themselves.

Only men belong to the lineage. When the lineage meets to revere its ancestors in the ancestor ceremony (*chesa*), it is only the men who meet. When contemporary genealogies are published, it is only the men whose lines continue down through time. And each man has the duty of seeing to it that his line is continued in order that he and his ancestors are served. Each man is responsible for assuring that the ancestor ceremonies will continue after he is gone—to "keep the incense burning." The only way this can be done is by providing a son.

## The Family before the Seventeenth Century

The above description is true of what might be called the traditional classic patrilineal lineage system and to a large degree it persists today despite the onslaught of the forces of modernization. It has not always been the case. As recently as the seventeenth century, the kinship system of Korea was radically different. In the early Chosŏn period, membership in a kinship group was not based on the principles of patrilineal descent. Inheritance was not passed on to the eldest son alone, but daughters shared equally with sons in the division of the property of the father and the mother. If a couple had daughters but did not have a son, they did not need to adopt; and if they had no children, they sometimes would adopt a relative of the wife or a non-relative and the child might be a daughter. Women were not excluded from the family organization but played an integral role in family affairs such as the ancestor ceremonies; they held the right to participate on a rotational basis (*yunhaeng*) as much as did any of the sons. And their posterity was recorded in the genealogy in as much detail as was that of their brothers.

---

[2]Unmarried daughters were not included in the genealogy. The genealogy served several purposes, one of which was to keep track of dates for performing ancestor ceremonies; this Confucian ceremony excluded unmarried women. But those excluded from the male-dominated, formal ancestor ceremonies, mostly women, would have alternative ceremonies performed by the local shaman when a perceived need arose. For this practice in the modern day see the work of Laurel Kendall, such as "Korean Ancestors: From the Woman's Side" in *Korean Women: View from the Inner Room*, edited by Laurel Kendall and Mark Peterson. (New Haven: East Rock Press, 1984.) See also Janelli and Janelli, *Ancestor Worship and Korean Society*. (Stanford: Stanford University Press, 1982) chap. 6.

This work will present significant cases that marked critical points along the way of the transition. The point of original for this study was adoption, which appears in section three (chapters seven through nine). I was first struck by the uniqueness of the Korean practice as it appeared in the lineage genealogies. My understanding of the topic grew as I realized that the word "adoption" might not adequately or accurately convey the meaning of what was going on and thus for a time I used the term intralineage adoption to show it was a case of continuation of lines or lineages by means of moving around the sons or nephews in the subsequent generation. Later, scholars began to use the term agnatic adoption to describe the phenomena in China and elsewhere. But to get to the point of understanding agnatic adoption, I found I had to first look at inheritance practices in general.

Section one (chapters one through three) treats the transformation of the inheritance system from an equilateral system to one wherein daughters were omitted and the eldest son received the lion's share—primogeniture.[3] This remarkable transformation of the inheritance system had ramifications throughout the kinship system, from patterns of marriage to performance of ancestor ceremonies.

Section two explores the role of women as daughters, wives, and mothers; and traces the loss of status that they suffered with the loss of inheritance rights. Therein we also examine the status of the *ch'ŏp*, the concubine or secondary wife, and her son, the *sŏja*, the "illegitimate" son or the child born of a father who was an aristocrat and a mother who was a *ch'ŏp*, who was, by definition, a non-aristocrat, either a commoner or a slave. In the record, the *sŏja* and those who took their part often compared Korea's situation to that of China where there were no institutionalize limitations imposed on the sons of concubines. Throughout the dynasty there were those who used their *sŏja* as heirs, but, as we shall see, the prejudice against such heirs was so deeply ingrained, that few were able to overcome the limitations placed upon them officially and unofficially. And thus as heirs, they were not often selected.

---

[3]In this work primogeniture will be defined as that system of inheritance that provides the largest portion of inheritance for the eldest son, with smaller portions for younger sons. The term can describe a system wherein all the property is given to the eldest with nothing for younger siblings, but that is not the case is Korea.

In Korean the problem is handled by using the term *changja sangsok* for true primogeniture, unigeniture total inheritance, by the eldest son; and *changja udae sangsok* for priority in inheritance for the eldest son, but minor portions for the other sons—the case in Korea.

## The Mid Chosŏn Period, The Seventeenth Century

One important issue in this work is a critique of the commonly accepted periodization. Most authors refer to the early Chosŏn period and the late Chosŏn period. The former covered the time from the founding of the dynasty until the Japanese invasion in the late sixteenth century. The latter covered the three hundred years after the wars. This work lends support to the argument that the periodization of the Chosŏn period ought to include a mid Chosŏn period to show the important nature of the transitions that took place at that time. The nature of the mid Chosŏn period was markedly different from the early and late Chosŏn in many ways. This work will cover the transitions in the family and lineage; other works show changes in politics, economics and other areas. The mid Chosŏn period is roughly the seventeenth century, from the time of the Japanese invasion in the late sixteenth century to the beginning of the eighteenth century, perhaps 1592 to 1700 or 1724, the rise of King Yŏngjo, marking the beginning of the late Chosŏn.[4]

## The Sources

Each section has its own set of sources to explore. For section one, inheritance, there are numerous inheritance documents (similar to wills in the West), some recently published in collections and some as single sheets in private and public holdings. There are three notable collections: one comprehensive collection published during the Japanese period; one published in 1982 features the documents of one lineage, the Puan Kim's; and one published in 1981 features the documents of one region, North Kyŏngsang province. The *Shillok*, the "veritable records" or the annals of the Yi dynasty, was used somewhat in section one but was particularly useful for sections two and three. Chapters six and nine also used, the collected writings of Chosŏn period scholar-officials (*munjip*).

Chapters seven and eight, the pre-transitional institutions of adoption, relied mostly on the *Shillok*. Chapter nine, the achievement of the ideal institution of agnatic adoption, relied on the *Kyehu tŭngnok*, the government's register of adoptions, and on private collection of writings as well as the *Shillok*. At times, genealogies were examined and included in the narrative. Two genealogies are particularly noteworthy, the two oldest extant genealogies. The earliest is the *Andong Kwŏn-ssi sebo* of 1476; the

---

[4]Fujiya Kawashima has been writing for some time about the Mid-Yi period; see "Lineage Elite and Bureaucracy in Early Yi to mid-Yi Dynasty Korea," "Historiographic Development in South Korea: State and Society from the Mid-Koryŏ to the Mid-Yi Dynasty," and "The Local Gentry Association in Mid-Yi Dynasty Korea: A Preliminary Study of the Ch'angyŏng Hyangan, 1600-1839."

second is the *Munhwa Yu-ssi sebo* (*MYS*) of 1565. Both have come to light in recent years and provide an interesting window on early Chosŏn society. The *Andong Kwŏn-ssi sebo*, for example, lists no cases of adoption at all. The *Munhwa Yu-ssi sebo* shows that by the sixteenth century only a few adoptions were recorded including a few cases of posthumous adoptions for some of the men who had been recorded in the fifteenth century, Andong Kwŏn genealogy with a notation that they were without heir. Indeed, comparisons of the *Kyehu tŭngnok* entries (which give dates of adoptions) with listings in genealogies (which give birth and death dates) show that close to half the adoptions made were posthumously arranged.

The fact that the *Shillok* contains so much primary data about the family and the lineage is noteworthy. Disputes over seemingly petty family matters frequently reached the king, particularly in the early Chosŏn period. The king often functioned as a judge of a family court and personally adjudicated numerous cases. The detailed accounts of family disputes are in and of themselves instructive at a number of levels. In addition to providing at least a summary of both sides of a particular argument, the rationale behind the king's judgment is usually given in the *Shillok*. One sees that the king was not completely independent; in numerous cases his decisions were challenged and at times reversed by the bureaucracy. The fact that so many seemingly petty matters reached the king is an evidence of the importance the highest levels of government placed on proper relationships in the family—a striking manifestation of the importance placed on Confucian values.

## Neo-Confucian Teachings

Many of the deliberations reveal the dramatic influence of neo-Confucian philosophy. In some cases, each side would argue that it was correct on the basis of divergent interpretations of Confucianism; but in other cases, the conflict was between native traditions (*kuksok*) and imported Chinese or Confucian traditions. Eventually, a particular orthodox Confucian view held sway and did so with such authority that the term "Confucianization" can be used to describe the transformation. Another way to look at the subject is to say that the Koreans "out Chinese the Chinese." In other words, the Koreans were more orthodox in their interpretation of Confucian precepts than were the Chinese.

It is easy to assume that Confucian influence was coterminous with Chinese influence, but although there is a degree of convergence between the two, the reader must be cautious not to assume that one equals the other. The inheritance issue is a good case in point. For at least the first two centuries of the Chosŏn period, and for as much as we know about the Koryŏ period (918-1392) as well, Koreans practiced equilateral inheritance. The Chinese did, too, but only for the sons whereas the Koreans included the daughters. In the later Chosŏn period, after considerable efforts to adopt Confucianism, the Koreans disinherited the daughters but did not continue the equal division of property among sons as did most Chinese. Rather, as was stipulated by the Confucian classics, the eldest son became the principal heir.

## Literature Summary

The first comprehensive study of the Korean family system was that by Kim Tu-hŏn.[5] The work was first published in 1948, but revised in 1969. In terms of detailed accounts of various aspects of family studies, it is as yet unsurpassed; however, in terms of analysis and theoretical interpretations, subsequent works made additions to this important basic work. For example, in terms of the two primary areas of interest here (inheritance and adoption), Kim's work on adoption is thorough and gives several examples. In regard to inheritance, his coverage is not as complete, and he does not see the dynamics of the mid Chosŏn period, the change between the early Chosŏn and late Chosŏn; but he does include a transcription of one of the most important inheritance documents available- —that of Yi I with his brothers and sisters inheriting property from their parents.[6]

Ch'oe Chae-sŏk, a sociologist, and Yi Kwang-gyu, an anthropologist, have both written books that treat the family in a comprehensive fashion, as well as several articles that touch on the subjects of inheritance and adoption.[7] They each have made comprehensive studies of inheritance documents. Both have also applied anthropological theory to Korea's historical family and lineage.

Several researchers have written on various aspects of the inheritance transformation; a few have written about adoption. The first comprehensive work on inheritance, citing numerous inheritance documents (*punjaegi*) was compiled by the Japanese director-general office in colonial Korea.[8]

---

[5]Kim, Tu-hŏn. *Han'guk kajok chedo yŏn'gu* [Research on the Korean family system] (Seoul: Seoul National University Press, 1969).

[6]*Ibid.*, p. 237.

[7]Ch'oe Chae-sŏk, *Han'guk kajok chedosa yŏn'gu* [Research on the Korean Family System] (Seoul: Ilchisa, 1983) and Yi, Kwang-gyu, *Han'guk kajok ŭi sajŏk yŏn'gu*, [Historical research on the Korean family] (Seoul: Ilchisa, 1977).

[8]*Richo no zaisan sozokuho* (RZS) [Yi dynasty property inheritance practices]. (Seoul: Chosen Shotokufu Chusuin, 1936).

9

In post-colonial times, the first article in Korean has not attracted much attention, and in spite of the fact that few subsequent scholars cited her work it precisely analyzed the situation without examining a single inheritance documents. That excellent work by Kim Il-mi published in 1969 analyzed the inheritance practices of the early Chosŏn times on the basis of the *Shillok* and the *Koryŏ-sa*. Her conclusions coincide with those of later scholars who used inheritance documents to show what actually took place. Kim concluded that the changes in the inheritance system were created by the acceptance of Neo-Confucian ideology and changes in the economic system.

Yi Su-gŏn and Kim Yong-man, based in the Taegu area, an area rich in documents held by aristocratic families, have relied on field work and the discovery of primary documents. Prof. Yi has provided a gold mine of primary sources in his *Kyŏngbuk chibang komunsŏ chipsŏn* (KCKC) [A collection of ancient documents from the North Kyŏngsang area].[9]

Kim Yong-man's first article in 1983, and a follow-up article in 1985, made milestone contributions to the field. In the first he argues that the previous studies did not deal with inheritance documents in their historical context; he points out that they surveyed the data in the documents but did not read the prefaces nor post-scripts.[10] He posits that there were two reasons for the changes that marked the seventeenth century: (1) the spread of Neo-Confucianism, and (2) fragmentation of property holdings.[11] In the later article, Kim develops his conclusions; with the changes in inheritance practices, there were economic impacts on the society, including: surplus capital used for ceremonies rather than for economic growth, an environment wherein the wealthy could better weather economic bad times and "confiscate" at unusually low prices the land of the poor who could neither manage their property nor pay their taxes, and overall there was less control of society leading to runaway slaves and fewer taxes collected.[12]

Subsequently Yi Su-gŏn, in articles in 1991 and 1992, accepts the views of Kim Yong-man, and adds a few additional conclusions: that there were even more economic and social ramifications of the changes in the

---

[9]Yi Su-gŏn, *Kyŏngbuk chibang komunsŏ chipsŏn* (KCKC) [A collection of ancient documents from the North Kyŏngsang area] (Kyŏngsan: Yŏngnam University Press, 1981).

[10]Kim Yong-man. "Chosŏn shidae kyunbun sangsokche-e kwanhan ilyŏn'gu," [A study on the equal inheritance system of the Chosŏn period] p. 2, footnote 3.

[11]*Ibid.*, pp. 25-34.

[12]Kim, Yong-man, "Chosŏn shidae chaeji sajok ŭi chaesan soyu hyŏngt'ae (I)," [The forms of property ownership of the landed aristocracy of the Chosŏn period], p. 89-159.

inheritance system.  He argues that the early Yi kings preferred the partible inheritance system because it kept possible rivals to the throne from amassing fortunes, and that later kings accepted the Confucian model of the patrilineage and were secure enough in their positions that they did not mind the growth of power in the hands of then numerous aristocrats.[13]  The result was however, that the economy was already ruined by the fragmentation of land-holding, what little surplus income that was available was spent on ceremonies which led to impoverishment of the nation.  At the same time, the lack of major dynamics in the society led to stability and the longevity of the dynasty.[14]

Yi Sun-gu addressed the subject of inheritance from the perspective of the social position of women and the affect upon them by the dissemination of Neo-Confucian dogma.[15]  Yi cites several examples of heirship by daughters and of non-agnatic adoption in the early Chosŏn and concludes that in the early period "succession" to a family line was not an issue.[16] There were many more cases of ancestor ceremonies by daughters than there were adoptions.  Whereas partial shares were allocated for children of *ch'ŏp*, thereby indicating that dividing of shares and discrimination of statuses was possible, yet daughters were guaranteed full shares and full rights with the sons.[17]

The spread of Neo-Confucian texts through Korea in the early period is also covered by Ko Yŏng-jin, who shows that the process was not without resistance; that it took time for the new doctrine to permeate through society.[18]

The finest treatment overall, and the only significant work in English is *The Confucian Transformation of Korea*, by Martina Deuchler.[19]  She is concerned with many of the questions that I am, but has taken a broader view of the issue by going back into Koryŏ institutions, by looking at

---

[13]Yi-Su-gŏn, "Chosŏnjŏn'gi ŭi sahoe pyŏndong kwa sangsokchedo" [Social change and the inheritance system of the early Chosŏn period] in *Han'guk ch'ingchok chedo yŏn'gu* [Studies on the Korean family system].p. 106 & p. 109.

[14]Yi Su-gŏn, "Chosŏnjŏn'gi ŭi sahoe pyŏndong kwa sangsokchedo" [Social change and inheritance in the early Chosŏn period], in *Yŏksa hakpo*, p. 64 & 76.

[15]Yi Sun-gu, "Chosŏn ch'ogi Chujahak ŭi pogŭp kwa yŏsŏng ŭi sahoejŏk chiwi" [The dissemination of the philosophy of Chu Hsi in early Chosŏn and the social position of women].

[16]*Ibid.*; see, for example, p. 70ff.

[17]*Ibid.*, p. 77.

[18]Ko Yŏng-jin "15/16 segi Chuja karye ŭi shihaeng kwa kŭ ŭiŭi" [The implementation of Chu Hsi's *karye* and its significance in the fifteenth and sixteenth century].

[19]The full title is *The Confucian Transformation of Korea: A Study of Society and Ideology* (Cambridge:  Harvard University Press, 1992).

more institutions, such as marriage, and also by looking specifically at the ideological underpinnings of social change.  I have tried to look more deeply at only two institutions (although I felt compelled to look briefly at concubinage and the *sŏja* [the child of a *yangban* father and a commoner or slave mother]), and to present detailed cases showing how options were considered as the institutions developed over time.

And although both her work and mine look at some of the same events and documents, her work concentrates on transition from late Koryŏ to the early Chosŏn period, and I have researched the mid Chosŏn, the pivotal seventeenth century.  Whereas I emphasize the transitional nature of the mid Chosŏn period, indeed, much of her work has helped me to understand how Korea became the way it was in an earlier period of transition, the founding of the Yi court, the state of Chosŏn.  Her work answers bigger questions; mine tries to provide a close-up view of what happened.  She presents more answers to ideological questions, while I have tried to deal with specific people making difficult decisions.  We have few disagreements, but there are some that I will highlight in the conclusion.  We both have studied anthropology and allow it to influence our approach.

Anthropological Theory

Much of what happened in the development of Korea's family system is illuminated by anthropological theory.  A British anthropologist who has written several articles on kinship, Jack Goody, has written that transmission to the next generation can be achieved, when an heir is not born into the household, by one of the following methods:  (1) concubinage, (2) adoption, and (3) "filiacentric union" (better known as either matrilocal or uxorilocal marriage).[20]  We will see that in Korea, at certain times, each of these options had currency over the others.  In another article dealing with the question of "heirship," he phrases it slightly differently:  one can increase options of obtaining an heir by either "adding wives" ([1] polygyny, [2] concubinage, or [3] divorce and remarriage); or by "adding sons" ([1] by "in-marrying sons-in-law" [also called the *epiklerate*, an ancient Greek practice] and [2] by adoption).[21]  Again each option is found in Korea, but as we will see, polygyny was disapproved in the early, founding years of the Chosŏn court; concubinage, since it produced an heir who was restricted in social status, thus was a problematic alternative; and divorce and remarriage

[20]Jack Goody, *The Oriental, the Ancient, and the Primitive* (Cambridge: Cambridge University Press, 1990), p. 43.

[21]Jack Goody, "Strategies of Heirship," *Comparative Studies in Society and History*, p. 7-8.

was allowed but seldom practiced. Confucian dogma provided for divorce in the event of sonlessness and some other reasons, but the sundering of a relationship based on the alliance of two families was not taken lightly. Adding wives was attempted, but was not the answer. Adding sons, however, perfectly describes the Korean choice. Therein, the first option, the marrying-in son-in-law, was preferred in the early Chosŏn period, but adoption became the best recourse by the time they moved through the seventeenth century transition.

Goody also concludes that where women are prevented from acting as heirs, then adoption may be used more frequently[22] — a perfect fit for Korea. He writes of the preference in some societies to "subtract children" or eliminate contestants to heirship, to reduce the number of candidates.[23] Indeed, in Korea, that end was achieved by eliminating daughters as heirs after the seventeenth century, and then to restrict the sons in the eighteenth century.

Goody makes what appears to be a rather chilling forecast of what we might find in Korean history when he states that "loss of men in war, may lead people to adopt new strategies and hence extend, perhaps permanently, the alternatives available to them."[24] The case of Korea, with the destructive Japanese invasion of 1592 followed by the Manchu invasions of 1627 and 1636, calls for evaluation in light of Goody's generalization. Did the devastating wars of the late sixteen and early seventeenth, by the "loss of men" precipitate a change in the inheritance system? Or was it a matter of war creating martyrs, who needed to be honored as heroes, for whom adoptions were necessary? In either case, Goody's observation looks for application in Korea.

Goody quotes two China specialists who have begun to re-examine the development and interpretation of the lineage system in China, James Watson[25] and Patricia Buckley Ebrey.[26] They are discovering that the heretofore accepted description of the Chinese lineage is based on studies of

---

[22]Ibid., p. 12.

[23]Ibid., p. 13.

[24]Ibid., p. 13.

[25]James Watson, "Anthropological Overview: The Development of Chinese Descent Groups," in Kinship Organization in Late Imperial China, 1000-1940, edited by Patricia Buckley Ebrey and James L. Watson, (University of California Press, 1986), p. 277ff.

[26]Patricia Buckley Ebrey, "The Early Stages in the Development of Descent Group Organization," in Kinship Organization in Late Imperial China, 1000-1940, p. 40, and also Evelyn S. Rawski, "The Ma Landlords of Yang-chia-kou in Late Ch'ing and Republican China," p. 270; both in Kinship Organization in Late Imperial China, 1000-1940, edited by Patricia Buckley Ebrey and James L. Watson, University of California Press, 1986.

southern China, primarily the work of Maurice Freedman,[27] and some others.[28] More recent studies show that northern China has lineages that do not fit the mold of southern China, particularly in regard to corporate holdings, which has been the primary criteria defining a Chinese lineage. And that criteria has been the largest difference between Chinese and Korean lineages; now we see there are more similarities than previously assumed, most notably, the importance of the ancestor ceremony,[29] which is the glue that holds the Korean lineage together as well.

Indeed, recent studies of China show numerous similarities with Korea, particularly when one looks at the varieties of practice over the history of Korea, and the varieties of practice over the wide terrain and long history of China. We find that smaller lineages in China handled stewardship for rituals on a rotational basis[30] in a way that sounds similar to the Korean practice called *yunhaeng*, taking turns holding the ceremonies. Pre-Neo-Confucianized China of the post-T'ang, early Sung period is described as having limited inheritance for daughters (this appears to be the only time there was any inheritance for daughters in China[31]), important affinal ties,[32] where graves were more important to individuals than to groups,[33] and where the family was more important than the lineage.[34] When Confucianization took hold there was an emphasis on the patrilineal line and a view that ties to affinal kin were potentially disruptive.[35]

Ebrey describes the Confucianization of the Sung period and contrasts the old order with the new, where the old order was centered on the family, and the new order centered on the lineage; in the old order, a non-agnatic

---

[27]Maurice Freedman, *Chinese Lineage and Society: Fukien and Kwangtung*. (London: Athlone Press, 1966).

[28]Hugh Baker, *Chinese Family and Kinship*, New York: Columbia University Press, 1979; Jack Potter, "Lang and Lineage in Traditional China," in *Family and Kinship in Chinese Society*, edited by Maurice Freedman, Stanford University Press, 1970; Emily Ahern, *The Cult of the Dead in a Chinese Village*, Stanford University Press, 1973; and others.

[29]Patricia Buckley Ebrey, "The Early Stages in the Development of Descent Group Organization," p. 55. and James Watson, "Anthropological Overview: The Development of Chinese Descent Groups," p. 280.

[30]Jack Goody, *The Oriental, the Ancient, and the Primitive*, p. 74, quoting Hugh Baker, *A Chinese Kinship Village: Sheung Shui* (Stanford: Stanford University Press, 1968).

[31]Kim Il-mi noted this largely ignored fact in her 1969 article, "Chosŏn chŏn'gi ŭi namyŏ kyunbun sangsokche e taehayŏ," p. 62.; twelve years later Patricia Ebrey makes note of this situation, "Women in the Kinship System of the Southern Song Upper Class," p. 116.

[32]Ebrey, *Ibid.*,p. 116ff.

[33]Patricia Buckley Ebrey, "The Early Stages in the Development of Descent Group Organization," p. 19 (here, actually speaking of pre-Sung times).

[34]Patricia Buckley Ebrey, "Conceptions of the Family in the Sung Dynasty," *Journal of Asian Studies*, p. 229.

[35]*Ibid.*

adoption was the order, but in the lineage system, an agnatic adoption of the proper generation was required.[36] She also mentions the non-agnatic form of adoption whereby a child is adopted before the age of three and is entered in the genealogy and in other ways treated like an agnatic adoption.[37] The Koreans had a similar practice called *suyang* adoption.

Comparisons of China and Korea are multilayered. At the first level, the two countries appear to be quite similar with an obvious and strong emphasis on a kind of Confucian orthodox patrilineality. But, at the next level, researchers on each side have found unorthodox practices that would make one look different from the other. When, however, one compares the unorthodox forms, we find similarity in the kinds of unorthodoxy that each practiced. One can hardly find an unorthodox form in one country that one cannot be found in the other at some point or place.[38]

<u>Cognatic Kinship</u>

The most important assistance provided to us by anthropologists is their explanation of kinship theory. The assistance is not given without its costs, however. The cost is the pain and effort needed to wade through the polemics of the anthropologists on the subject. A subject as universal to humankind as blood ties and relationships, a subject the anthropologists call "kinship," turns out to be extremely complicated. There are nearly as many types of kinship organizations as there are societies or cultures on the face of the globe. One of the most respected anthropologists in America, David Schneider, has written a monograph on the subject titled, *A Critique of the Study of Kinship*.[39] Therein he makes the surprising statements, "'kinship,' . . . is a non-subject since it does not exist in any culture known to man," and "'kinship' is an artifact of the anthropologists' analytic apparatus and has no concrete counterpart in the cultures of any of the societies we studied."[40] After saying there is no such thing as kinship he proceeds to write 208 pages about the subject.

---

[36]*Ibid.*, p. 233.

[37]*Ibid.*, p. 234.

[38]If that is the case, it raises one disturbing prospect—that of purchase and sales of children. Chinese literature is replete with such cases, but we do not find any in Korea. Are they out there but we just have not found them yet?

[39]David M. Schneider, *A Critique of the Study of Kinship*, (Ann Arbor: University of Michigan Press, 1984).

[40]*Ibid.*, p. vii.

15

David Johnson, an historian, in his critical response[41] to an article by
James Watson,[42] an anthropologist, noted that the problem in kinship
studies in China is that the anthropologist holds onto his terminology,
ignoring Chinese perceptions of their own kinship structure.
In spite of the limitations, ambiguities, and discord among theorists,
anthropology has provided us with a set of useful terms and constructs to
help us perceive the kinship system that most probably existed before the
Confucianization process.  Anthropology tells us that the system in Korea
after Confucianization was a classic patrilineal system; logic dictates that if
there is a patrilineal system, then there is a matrilineal system, and there is.
But the matrilineal system is not the only alternative to the patrilineal.
Many history texts assume in a simplistic fashion, based on theories of the
early anthropologist, Henry Morgan, and adopted by marxist historians, that
there was once an archaic matrilineal system.  In reality, where matrilineal
systems do exist, they are not simple systems; they are found in highly
complex social systems.  But there is more variety available than
matrilineality and patrilineality.

There is a kind of consensus among anthropologists that has been in
place for about twenty years now, that there are basically three classifica-
tions:  patrilineal, matrilineal, and cognatic.[43]  There are variations within
each system.  Categories of cognatic systems include bilateral systems,
double descent systems, ambilateral[44] systems and some others.  Bilaterality
is defined as equal affiliation with both parents' kindred.[45]  A double descent
system is fairly rare;[46] a person is a member of only one line of the father's
side and one line of the mother's side; for example, a child might belong to
his father's patrilineal group and his mother's father's patrilineal group.  In

---

[41]David Johnson, "Chinese Kinship Reconsidered," *The China Quarterly* , p. 364.

[42]James Watson, "Chinese Kinship Reconsidered:  Anthropological Perspectives  on Historical Research," *The China Quarterly*.

[43]One of those holding out is Ward Goodenough who in *Description and Comparison in Cultural Anthropology* (Chicago: Aldine, 1970) argues that the early classification of patrilineal, matrilineal and bilateral (or cognatic) is not adequate. He also refers to "stocks" in a cognatic system, and ambilineal ramages, and personal kindreds, and as well as double descent systems, p. 41-44.

[44]Raymond Firth, "A Note on Descent Groups in Polynesia," in *Readings in Kinship and Social Structure* edited by Nelson Graburn (New York: Harper and Row, 1971), p. 197. The term multilineal has also been suggested by William Davenport, in "Nonunilinear Descent and Descent Groups," also in *Readings in Kinship and Social Structure*, p. 207.

[45]Perhaps the best author on bilaterality is Robin Fox, *Kinship and Marriage*. (Harmondsworth, England: Penguin Books, 1967), p. 152.

[46]Deuchler makes a similar statement and rules out double descent in Korea, *The Confucian Transformation*, p. 81.

ambilaterality, a child chooses one parent's line or kindred for a primary affiliation.

The ambilateral descent group is the one that seems to best describe the early Chosŏn (and late Koryŏ) system. In it, one is a member of a flexible unit that shifts membership with personal needs or other social factors. One hallmark of the ambilateral system is that membership is often determined by marriage locale.[47] If a man moves into his wife's family home, he becomes a member of his wife's kindred.

Anthropologists use the term "descent group," but not lineage in reference to ambilateral kinship or the ambilateral kindred. It is a descent group, because membership is determined by birth; but it is not a lineage, in that the line, per se, does not continue in a consistent or unbroken fashion. Needs determine membership and affiliation with a group of kinsmen—a kindred, and those needs can vary from time to time and generation to generation. One hallmark of an ambilateral kindred is flexibility of membership.

Most often, when the term cognatic is used, the concept of bilaterality is assumed. Cognatic systems tend to be bilateral. But in the Korean case ambilateral might be a better term than cognatic for one other reason. Not only could early Chosŏn Koreans choose membership in either their father's kindred or their mother's kindred, they could choose membership in their wife's kindred. Paternal, maternal, or affinal—trilateral may be a more accurate term than bilateral.[48]

We do not know the exact structure of the early kinship system, but there are enough indicators to say that it was a cognatic system, although No Myŏng-ho has recently made quite convincing arguments that we ought to use the term kindred in describing the kinship group of the Koryŏ and early Chosŏn periods. Without arguing that it was a specific type, hereinafter, I will use that general term, cognatic, to describe the system prior to the seventeenth century, prior to the transition to what became a classic Confucian patrilineal system.

---

[47]Robin Fox states that membership in the group is available through both male and female ties, but one must choose, on the basis of residence; "only those who reside with the group are members of it." *Kinship and Marriage*, p. 152.

[48]Martina Deuchler and Ch'oe Sun-hŭi also refer to these three options; *The Confucian Transformation of Korea*, p. 80; and "Sangsan Kim-ssi punjaegi sogo" [A brief study of a Sangsan Kim-ssi inheritance document], T'aedong kojŏn yŏn'gu, p. 909; but neither suggest the use of a new term, such as trilateral.

## The Value of Using Case Studies

The transformation of the kinship system from its early form to that which is described in the case of Yi Ka-myŏng above, who was presented as a symbol of the patrilineal lineage system, was a remarkable event. Societies are constantly changing, but documentation of such a basic change of the entire kinship structure is rare. Most social change is found only in evidence that has often been lost in shadowy prehistory only to be explored in analysis of myth and linguistics. But Korean history provides numerous important cases in the available historical documents which allow us to trace the transformation in detail. Although such radical transformations are rarely documented, a similar transformation occurred in Japan in an earlier time frame than Korea's and for reasons that were somewhat different on the one hand, and somewhat the same on the other. In the final chapter, we will evaluate the forces that created the transformation, and compare the events in Korea with those in China and Japan.

The cases discussed herein are sometimes complicated and include a dizzying array of names and relationships. When helpful, I have included lineage diagrams to assist the reader in keeping track of who's who.

In using a case study approach, the reader can get close to those caught up in the controversies. I have described more cases, naming names, and translating their statements, than have others who have worked on this subject. At times, it is easy to be sympathetic to one side, but in other cases both sides draw us into their feelings. I have intended a close-up view, a personal view, of these events. The case study approach allows the participants to speak to us over the years, to appeal to us for support for their side of the argument. In a sense, for me, and I hope it seems so for the reader too, they have come alive after years of silence.

# 1

# Inheritance Laws and Practices

The Chosŏn dynasty Code (*Kyŏngguk taejŏn*) outlined the inheritance laws of the dynasty.[1] Although there can always be a huge gulf between the ideal (or the legal) and the actual in social practice, the early dynasty practice largely conformed to that outlined in the Code. The later dynasty practice did not.

The basic law of inheritance provided for partible inheritance, what we here will call equilateral inheritance—sons and daughters were all guaranteed equal shares of inheritance. Actual inheritance documents of the early dynasty clearly show that the society indeed practiced equilateral inheritance in the first half of the dynasty, well into the seventeenth century. This fact is surprising, if not shocking, to the vast majority of contemporary Koreans who tend to assume that the late dynasty practice (and, for the most part, the contemporary practice) in which inheritance is provided only for sons, with the lion's share going to the eldest son, primogeniture, originated in the earliest times.[2]

---

[1]There are several editions of the Code. The most frequently cited is the *Taejŏn hoet'ong* which was published in the late Chosŏn dynasty and included all the updates of the earlier editions. Citations here will be to the 1978 edition published by Kyŏngmunsa in Seoul. "Inheritance" does not have its own heading but particulars on inheritance are listed under the topic "private slaves" in the Hyŏngjo (Ministry of Punishments) section, p. 713, and under "lands and houses" in the Hojo (Ministry of Finance) section, p. 225. The listing under the former is much more detailed than the latter. In the slave section there are several notes which state, "It is the same for land and houses," and in the land and houses section there is one cross reference which states, "It is the same for slaves."

[2]For example, see *Chŏnju Yi-ssi Korim-gunp'a sŏnjo yumunjip* [Documents Left by the Ancestors of the Korim-gun Branch of the Chŏnju Yi Lineage] (Ch'ilsan'gunp'a chongch'in-hoe publication, 1975) wherein the authors register their surprise at finding a document of their ancestors which states that property is to be divided equally between seven sons and daughters, p. 2. They conclude that their ancestors were truly exceptional to propose such a radical approach to property division. In actuality, of course, it was common practice in those early days, and it is the surprised reaction of the recent commentators that is revealing.

Although recent laws have provided inheritance for daughters once again, a full

19

## The Law

The Chosŏn dynasty Code was patterned after that of Ming China. There were six sections, one for each of the six administrative divisions of government—the ministries of personnel, rites, taxation, military affairs, punishments, and public works. The first edition (although no longer extant) was published in the third year of the dynasty, 1394; the basic code was published in 1460 and revised several times before a finished product was released in 1485. There were revisions in 1746, 1785, and 1865.[3] The basic law governing inheritance was not changed, yet the practice came to diverge markedly from the law. The law provided for equal inheritance among siblings of equal status, irrespective of sex.[4] Children of concubines (*sŏja*) were to receive less than the children of the legitimate wife. Children of a commoner concubine (*yangch'ŏp*) were guaranteed one-seventh as much as a legitimate child, while the children of a base (usually a slave) concubine (*ch'ŏnch'ŏp*) were guaranteed a one-tenth-sized share.[5]

The Code had provisions for extra allocations to be given to certain categories of ritual heirs. For example, the eldest son was to be given "an extra one-fifth share," or twenty percent more than the other siblings. The Code gave an example to make the point clear: ". . . if the other siblings were each given five slaves, the ritual heir would be given six slaves."[6]

The property of the father and of the mother was treated as if it were owned separately. For example, the Code dealt with the problem of the property of a wife who had no children and whose husband gave his property to his heirs by a concubine. She should give a share one-seventh the size of a legitimate heir's share to each of her husband's *sŏja* children, and an extra share, three-sevenths the size of a legitimate heir's share, to the ritual heir

---

share for an unmarried daughter and a one-fourth share for a married daughter, an anthropologist, Clark Sorensen, conducting a village study in 1977 found laughter the uniform response to his questionnaire about how much property a daughter inherited. The idea was beyond the conception of all of the villagers, he reported. (Personal conversation with Sorensen, Seoul, 1977.)

[3]In addition, there were minor revisions at other times including 1492, and 1543. Decrees also had the force of law; a major collection was published in 1698 and titled *Sugyo chimnok* [Collected edicts].

[4]The law gave specific instructions to assure the equality of the division. For example, if after each sibling received an equal number of slaves, it said, and there were only a few slaves left over, the code said that they should start with the oldest sibling and give each one slave until they ran out. See the case of Yi Yulgok and his siblings below, page 25.

[5]*Taejŏn hoet'ong*, p. 713 (*Hyŏngjŏn*, p. 33a). Note that in this indicator of status the commoner is much closer to the slave than to the slave-holding *yangban* class. Some authors argue that there were virtually only two classes in traditional Korea (see Arthur Wolf and Robert Smith, "China, Korea, and Japan", in *Religion and Ritual in Korean Society*, ed. Laurel Kendall and Griffin Dix, (University of California Press, 1987).

[6]*Ibid.*

(*sŭngjung*) while the balance was to be returned to her extended family (*chok*), meaning her siblings or cousins.[7] If she had no living relatives, the Code went on to say, the property should be turned over to the government.[8] The usual term for children was "*chanyŏ*," literally "son and daughter." Although the term itself implies a degree of equality between siblings of opposite sexes and although inheritances were divided equally between sons and daughters, there was a slight bias in favor of the son written into the law. There was a preference to have a male heir perform the ancestor rituals as is indicated in the following excerpt from the Code:

If the legitimate wife has no children and the commoner concubine has no son but has only a daughter, then the ritual heir shall be the son of the slave concubine, and he shall be given a one-fifth share plus an extra two-fifths.[9]

Detailed inheritance provisions were outlined for a stepchild (*ŭija*) and adopted child (*yangja*). A stepchild was to be allocated a one-fifth size share of the parent's property (an additional share one-fifth the size of the equilaterally divided share given to each legitimate child) if the stepmother had no children, but a one-ninth size share if she did.[10] The matter of the adopted child was more complex. The generic term for an adopted child is "*yangja*," but another term, "*kyehuja*," is also found. The "*kyehuja*" was at times also called a "*yangja*," but more specifically *kyehuja* was used to mean the successor in an aristocratic family who was adopted (or "established" [*iphu*]) from among the nephews of the father's lineage, an agnate. (Here, nephew means not only the son of one's brother, but the son of one's close or distant cousins—it is a classificatory term.) *Kyehu* is the term for agnatic adoption. The term "*yangja*" when it was not used as a general term to include the *kyehuja*, was used to denote commoner adoptions, or the types of non-agnatic adoption practiced by commoners. In its technical usage *yangja* stood in contrast to the *kyehuja*, which denoted aristocratic usage of the preferred form of agnatic adoption.

---

[7]The term "*chok*" [-*jok*] is found in *ssijok*, lineage, and *kajok*, family; used alone it may have either meaning. The commentary defines *chok* in this context by stipulating that the property will go to an aunt/uncle or a niece/nephew if there are no siblings, or, if there are no aunts/uncles or nieces/nephews, then it will go to a first cousin. This shows that the concept of *chok* was wider than the family, but as a lineage was quite narrow.

[8]*Taejŏn hoet'ong*, p. 714.

[9]*Ibid.*

[10]*Ibid.*, p. 715.

In technical or legal terms, there were two categories of *yangja*, the *shiyangja* and the *suyangja* according to the Code.[11] Either could be a child who was unrelated to either of the adopting parents. The *shiyangja* was adopted when over the age of three. The *suyangja* was not only under the age of three but the child's surname could be legally changed to that of the parent.[12] The *shiyangja* or *suyangja* could be male or female. A *kyehuja* was always an agnate from the generation below that of the adopting father in his patrilineage.

The term "*sŭngjung*" used in the Code meant the ritual heir but was used elsewhere at times to mean an adopted heir and at times was used to denote a special case of adoption, such as using a grandson as an heir for the grandfather without having someone standing in the intervening generation. It was also used, although rarely, to refer to a *sŏja*, a son by a concubine, who became promoted to legitimate status and who served as a ritual heir.[13] The usual term for ritual heir who was also the lineage heir was "*chongja*" or "*chongson*."

The Code indicated that the procedure for establishing the division of property was for the children of a deceased parent to meet, usually after the mourning period, and record their decisions on how to divide the property. The record of that proceeding was called a *tongsaeng hwahoe mun'gi*, "a record of the harmoniously assembled siblings." The document was copied for each sibling and each copy was signed by each sibling. If one sibling

---

[11]China was the source of this practice. There, too, one could adopt a child under the age of three and give that child full rights of inheritance and succession. See Patricia Ebrey, "Conceptions of the Family in the Sung Dynasty," p. 234; But unlike Korea, China continued to practice non-agnatic adoption; whereas Korea, eventually accepted orthodox agnatic adoption as preferred, and left non-agnatic adoption, even of an infant under age three, for the lower classes.

[12]In the later dynasty adoptions of aristocrats were entered in the *Kyehu tŭngnok*; see chapters nine. The *Suyang shiyang tŭngnok* recorded the adoptions of slaves and commoners; see chapter nine, p. 197.

The *shi-* of *shiyangja* means to serve. The *su-* of *suyangja* means to receive. The implication of the differences in status is reflected in actual practice. The *suyangja* was received into the household as an infant, the name was changed, became an heir to property at least and often to the ceremonial responsibility, and in all ways treated as if born into the household. The *shiyangja* was at times brought in to take care of elderly parent(s) or, according to some reports, to be a farmhand or domestic worker. And since the *shiyangja* could not take the surname of the adopting parent(s), there was more of a sense of temporariness about the arrangement, more for the sake of fostering than for heirship.

[13]The heir of Yi Yulgok (1536-1584), the prominent Confucian scholar, was a *sŏja* who was promoted to lineage heir status and designated as *sŭngjung* in the *chokpo*. A copy of the relevant page of the Tŏksu Yi genealogy appears on color plates of *A New History of History*, Ki-baik Lee, translated by Edward W. Wagner (Cambridge: Harvard University Press, 1984). A more common term for a promoted *sŏja* is "*sŭngjŏk*," literally, "promoted to legitimacy." See chapter nine for reference to a late dynasty government register called the *Suyang sŭngjŏk ilgi*, page 258.

dissented the document was voided.[14] As long as the document contained the signatures of the siblings, it did not require government registration or official involvement. If, however, a distant relative or a non-relative was included among the heirs, then it had to be approved by the government to be legally binding.[15] The private document was also at times called a *paengmun*, literally, a white paper.[16] The *Shillok*, in recording an issue centering on the *paengmun*, illustrates an inherent ambiguity in the laws of inheritance as recorded in the Code. The problem was that principles for determining heirship, and the conveyance of property, were found in two sections of the Code. The former, heirship, was found in the section on ritual;[17] the latter, concerning property (slaves) was found in the section on punishments. In 1529, the Censorate raised the problem of contradictions in the Code. In the subsection of the Code titled "private slaves," it indicated that for close relatives, a private inheritance document (*paengmun*) is sufficient but for others a public document is necessary. Which is proper for the adoptive mother is not indicated, they said. They also said it is unclear whether a *suyangja* should be treated as an actual son or whether he receives a one-seventh sized share (like a *sŏja*). The Censorate urged that the high officials meet and resolve the contradiction. The king denied the request.[18] Four days later, the Censorate again asked that the high officials meet and clarify the issue. They said there had been numerous decrees, but they were as contradictory as were the provisions of the Code. They urged that a conference of high officials be called to resolve the issue. The king

---

[14]*Taejŏn Hoet'ong (Sok Taejŏn)*, p. 747 (*hyŏngjŏn*, 50a). Men would sign the document with a brush; Chosŏn period signatures were highly stylized and not unlike the signatures of Westerners today. The personal use of the *tojang*, the seal, was apparently uncommon in Korea before the Japanese period. Widows, however, would use a *tojang*, but unlike the contemporary practice of using vermillion ink, they would use black ink. The wording on the widow's *tojang* was formulaic; it would say: "Mme [surname], wife of [husband's full name]"; for example, "Hong Kil-tong *ch'ŏ* Kim-*ssi*" [Mme Kim, wife of Hong Kil-tong].

[15]*Ibid.*, p. 748 (50b).

[16]For more on the *paengmun* see Kim Yong-man. "Chosŏn shidae kyunbun sangsokche-e kwanhan ilyŏn'gu," p. 22, and Yi Su-gŏn. "*Chosŏnjŏn'gi ŭi sahoe pyŏndong kwa sangsokchedo*," p. 97, note 67.

[17]Therein was another contradiction (between interpretations of *pongsa* [what Deuchler calls ritual succession] and *iphu* [jural succession]) that was to take up the king's and court's time in the 1550's; see page 143 below and Deuchler's *The Confucian Transformation of Korea*, p. 142, 147, 148.

[18]Chungjong 24, 1529.11.ŭlmyo; 66:58a (17:172).

agreed,[19] but another reference to the subject does not appear in the *Shillok* in the months immediately thereafter. The legal interpretation of the Code was ambiguous throughout the dynasty, as will be discussed hereafter. One should never assume a kind of social activity on the basis of the written code alone. To interpret a passage from the Code as evidence of the way society actually functioned is a mistake.[20] In Korea, the inheritance practice coincided with the written law in the early dynasty, but, as will be demonstrated below, as the practice changed in the mid and late Chosŏn periods the law did not.

The Practice: The Chŏng Document

The basic principle of inheritance was equality between sexes but discrimination between statuses. Legitimate brothers and sisters of equal status would have equal claim to property and illegitimate (*sŏja*) brothers and sisters would have rights equal to one another, but less than that of the legitimate siblings. Was property actually divided equally between siblings, whether male or female? An examination of the inheritance documents that have survived from the early Chosŏn period show that, until the seventeenth century, indeed it was. A good example is the inheritance document of the Chŏng household, kept in the Central National Library.[21] The first section has been damaged and some of it is missing so we do not know the date, but based on the biographic data therein, we can put the date between early 1658 and early 1659.[22] There were ten children who divided the property, seven

---

[19]Chungjong 24, 1529.11 *kimi*; 66:63a (17:174).

[20]Quoting the law and assuming that such is reflected in social practice is a common error. Even in the meticulous work *The Confucian Transformation of Korea* the author writes of the Chinese prohibition against non-agnatic adoption (p. 214), yet several researchers on China write of the abundance of non-agnatic adoption, some of which were even included in the genealogies, in spite of the law against the practice. For example, see J. Watson, "Anthropological Overview: The Development of Chinese Descent Groups," p. 284; Ebrey, "Conceptions of the Family in the Sung Dynasty," p. 234; and Wolf, *Marriage and Adoption in China, 1845-1945*, chap 8.

[21]Central National Library catalog no. *han*-51 *ta*-197; for the Tongnae Chŏng Genealogy, see CNL catalog no. *han*-58 *ka*-24-60.

[22]Based on the offices held by some of the sons and sons-in-law, from outside sources, and on the genealogy (which states that the mother died on the ninth day, first month of 1656) and the statement that the division was made after the mourning at the death of their mother, we can conclude that the document created at the meeting of the "harmoniously assembled siblings" occurred after the first month 1658. The number five sibling, a daughter, married a member of the P'ungsan Hong lineage who passed the *munkwa* examination in 1650, was herein listed as a former clerk in the Ministry of War in the document. Later he served as a county maginstrate, and then died in 1661. Since he served as the magistrate after the document was written (say 1660) but before his death in 1661, the document had to have been written between 1658, and 1660. Most likely it was written at the point the mourning period was completed, the second month of 1658.

legitimate (four brothers and three sisters) and three *sŏja* (two sisters and one brother).[23] As outlined in the Code, each legitimate child, male and female, received an equal share of property, in this case 30 slaves and 64 *majigi* of land.[24] Each *sŏja*, whether male or female, received 4 slaves and 10 *majigi* of land. The amount each *sŏja* received was about one-seventh of that received by the legitimate children, clearly within the guidelines prescribed in the Code for the *sŏja* of a commoner concubine.

## The Documents of Yi Yulgok

Three surviving documents that touch the life of the great Korean scholar of Neo-Confucianism were typical of the sixteenth century. The documents include that of Yulgok and his six siblings (1566); that of his mother, Shin Saimdang, and her four sisters (ca. 1545); and that of his wife, the daughter of No Kyŏng-nin, and her two sisters and two *sŏja* brothers (ca. 1568). Yulgok's siblings' document is typical in many ways (and atypical in some ways), but those of his mother and wife were strikingly unusual in some ways.

The document of seven siblings including the most famous of them, the fifth child (third son) named Yi I, but better known in history as Yulgok, was dated the twentieth day of the fifth month of 1566. The property was divided equally with obviously scrupulous care to be sure that the division was as equal as it could possibly be. In Yulgok's case, the first three children, male and female, received sixteen slaves each; the remaining four children each received fifteen slaves each which format was precisely in line with the Code.[25]

---

[23]Only a few names are given in the document, but by searching the genealogy for the generation name given we found a family with ten children of the exact structure of the family in the document; they are the children of Chŏng Kwang-gyŏng (1584-1644). The wife, the mother of the legitimate children, was a Yŏhŭng Min (d. 1656).

The segment of the lineage they represent was important in Chosŏn period politics; Chŏng Kwang-gyŏng had served in the State Council as had several of his direct line ancestors. The amount of property dividing is indicative of such political prominence.

[24]A *majigi* is the unit of land most commonly found in inheritance documents. The characters can also be read *turakchi*, but since the term is an *idu* form (Chinese characters used to express pure Korean words) *majigi* is probably the proper pronunciation. The amount of land in modern measure is difficult to calculate because it varied according to the fertility of the soil. For an explanation of the complexities, see Edward W. Wagner, *The Literary Purges* (Cambridge: Harvard University Press, 1974), p. 175; James Palais, *Politics and Policy in Traditional Korea* (Cambridge: Harvard University Press, 1975), p. 62 & 312 note #22; Susan Shin, "Land Tenure and the Agrarian Economy in Yi Dynasty Korea: 1600-1800."

[25]In regard to the Code, see footnote #4, above; in regard to Yulgok's document, a transcription is available in Kim Tu-hŏn, *Han'guk kajok chedo yŏn'gu*, p. 246ff.

Inheritance documents, in addition to lists of property for each sibling, contain a foreword that often explains special circumstances and often contains admonitions to the posterity to be faithful in the ancestor ceremonies. There is also a provision for taking care of the grave and one that sets aside property to provide food for the ceremonies. In the early dynasty the ritual provision was generally brief, but with time, the amount of property set aside for ceremonies grew markedly.

In the document that provided for the equal division of property between Yulgok and his siblings (1566) the ritual provision contained three special admonitions that tell us of the times and the trends. They were:

- Among us siblings, we will select one to be the executor (*yusa*). All the ritual affairs will be decided by discussion between the lineage heir (*chongson*) and the executor; the ceremonies will be held at the home of the lineage heir unless for some reason they cannot be held there, in which case the ceremonies will be held at the home of the executor.

- Carrying out the ceremonies in rotation between the siblings (*yunhaeng*) is forbidden, but rather the ceremonies must be carried out at the lineage heir's house; the siblings should all contribute rice to assist with the expenses of the ceremonies each year. The sons and daughters of those being honored will each contribute ten measures or rice; grandsons and granddaughters, five measures; great-grandsons and great-granddaughters, two measures.

- The produce from the land set aside herein for the ceremonies, the payments of the slaves set aside for that purpose, and the grain donated by each of the descendants each year, shall all be overseen by the lineage heir and the executor and all shall be kept at either the lineage heir's or the executor's house for the purpose of carrying out the ceremonies.

The ritual provision (*pongsa cho*) outlined in the Yulgok document are unique; that was the reason they were written there. The first provision above is unusual in that the executor (*yusa*) plays a major role, one on par with the lineage heir. In other cases, the executor is not even mentioned; only the lineage heir is.

The concept of donations from each descendant is another item that is not seen in other such documents. The usual case is to assume the ritual provision itself provides sufficient produce to carry out the ceremonies.

Finally, and perhaps the most important conclusion to be drawn from the Yulgok document concerns the restriction on carrying out ceremonies in rotation. Such a restriction is found later in other documents, for example, the Puan Kim lineage makes the break with that tradition in 1669 (see chapter two). Similar references are found in other documents of the seventeenth century (see chapter three). In this regard, the Yulgok document is one of the earliest to show a separation between equilateral inheritance and rotation of ritual duties.

## Property Division Document of Shin Saimdang and her Sisters

The document of Yulgok's mother has also survived the centuries although it is not in quite as good condition—the front portion is partially destroyed but one can make out fragments of sentences that speak of "not having a son" and "having the ceremonies carried on by a *oeson*," (a grandson via a daughter, a grandson that does not carry the surname).[26] Undated but *circa* 1545, it lists the five daughters of the deceased Shin Myŏng-hwa and Mme Yi, his widow. The daughters are listed by the names of their husbands. The document clearly indicates that there was no male heir and that the daughters received the property of their father, mother, and their paternal grandmother. Each piece of property was labeled indicating from whence it came. Saimdang was the second daughter and received a share of the property equal to that of each of her sisters. The handling of the ritual provision revealed a male bias, however. The ceremonial property and property set aside for maintenance of the grave were each given to a specific grandson. The tending the grave was given to one grandson, probably a Kwŏn, a descendant of the eldest daughter. The responsibility for carrying out the ancestor ceremonies was given to a grandson listed in the document as Kyŏnyong,[27] but better known as Saimdang's son, Yulgok. It is interesting that he was chosen; he was the third son of the second daughter and was only nine years old in 1545. We can conclude his brilliance was already starting to show; he later passed the first level of civil service exam at age 13, and went on to take first place in all nine levels exams.

---

[26]The original document is held by the small museum on the grounds of the Ojuk-hŏn, the shrine near Kangnŭng where Saimdang gave birth to Yulgok. Recently, they have displayed a full-size copy rather than the original. A photocopy is also found in Kim Tong-uk, *Komunsŏ chipchin* (Seoul: Yonsei University Press, 1977), p. 62.

[27]Kyŏnyong means "to see a dragon"; Saimdang had a dream in which she saw a dragon when she was pregnant with Yulgok.

Inheritance of No Kyŏng-nin and his wife, Mme Kim

Yulgok was the featured heir in the document of his wife as well. We do not have the document, but the issue was included in entries in Yulgok's biography. Yulgok married the oldest daughter of No Kyŏng-nin and a Mme Kim (of Andong). Between them they had three daughters and no sons, but No did have two sons by a concubine. According to an entry in 1568 in the chronological entries of Yulgok's biography, Mme Kim asked her husband what they should do about the issue of a successor; to which No responded, "We have Suk-hŏn (a childhood name of Yulgok); he will handle it fairly." The entry goes on to say that after the death of his father-in-law, Yulgok addressed the question by asking his mother-in-law to divide the property equally between all five of No Kyŏng-nin's descendants, including her own three daughters and the two *sŏja* sons. This decision corresponds with the manner in which Yulgok handled his own successor; he promoted his *sŏja*, since he had no daughters or sons by the first wife, Mme No. The decision is somewhat remarkable because it ignores the Code's prescription which provides for smaller fractions, as seen above,[28] for *sŏja* descendants. Indeed, there were provision in the Code for a parent to give special added amounts of property on occasion. The occasion could be the passing of an exam, marriage, birth of a child, or anything else the property owner chose.

Wills Counter to the Legal Code

The majority of inheritance documents that predate the eighteenth century conform to the guidelines of the Code. There were exceptions, however, a few early in the dynasty, but more and more as time went by. In 1451, Pak P'aeng-nyŏn submitted a memorial stating that wills providing exceptional divisions of property were a problem:

> Recently our office has handled numerous cases of suits between legal wife and concubine, and between father and son. The source of these suits is fighting over property — slaves, land, houses, and other possessions. These are disputes between flesh and blood that cause our social customs to deteriorate. This is no small matter. The matter of inheritance for the children of legitimate wives and for the children of concubines has been set forth in the Code and yet when a

---

[28] See the reference to the Code above, page 19-23, and the example in the Chŏng family case, page 24.

of transitory affection instead of in accordance with the Code, then the division of inheritance becomes disorderly. When this happens and deeds to property are unclear, then it seems to me that in such cases, according to law, the government should act as proprietor and see to the allocation of inheritances.[29]

The king responded that he would not make a decision at the moment but that he wanted to think about it for a while, and after Pak P'aeng-nyŏn left, the king asked what others thought of Pak's statement that "the government should act as proprietor and see to the allocation of inheritances." Another censor, Yi Kye-jŏn, quoting a passage from the classics expressed the opposing argument:

"In all the realm, we should assume that there are no bad parents." Even if a parent desires to give an unequal distribution of slaves on the basis of "transitory emotion," how can we go against the parent's decision and have "the government act as proprietor and see to the allocation of inheritances?" The government office ought to examine these issues carefully to determine what is right and wrong in making judgments, and yet we should follow the parents' will.

At that point, the king accepted Yi Kye-jŏn's argument.[30] An exception to the provision of equal inheritance in the Code was allowed on the basis of a parent's will.

## The Yi Ch'u Case

In a similar case thirty-eight years later, however, the outcome was the opposite; equal inheritance took precedence over a conflicting specific allocation. Yi Ch'u brought suit to the government saying that his father's adoptive mother, Mme Kim, indicated in her will that all her property should go to him, her favorite grandson. But Ch'u's father had divided the property equally among his sons and daughters. Ch'u charged that his father had violated his adoptive mother's will. After considerable argument, the king decided that although the father had violated his adoptive mother's will, the greater offense was on the part of the son who fought against his father.

---

[29]Munjong 1, 1451.8.kabo; 9:20a (6:426).
[30]Ibid.

"Ch'u knows what it is to have land, but he does not know what it is to have a father."[31]

## Property Divided among Daughters

With very few exceptions, the rule of equilateral inheritance held sway through most of the first half of the dynasty. Even in situations where there were no sons in the household, the property was divided equally among the daughters. We have seen the examples of the inheritance documents of Shin Saimdang, the mother of Yulgok above (page 27).

Another document which records property given only to daughters is found in the Kyujanggak collection of the Seoul National University Library. Dated *circa* 1535, the preface stated that the author, the father, had hoped to have a son and waited as long as he could but was finally allocating the last portion of his property to his two daughters (he had given shares to the two daughters earlier). He charged them with the responsibility of having their posterity (*oeson*) carry out the ancestor ceremonies for him after he was gone.[32]

## Inheritance Documents

The above documents are typical of the documents that have survived the centuries. In recent years, more and more documents have come to light. The best collection from one lineage is that of the Puan Kim lineage that was given to the Museum of Chŏnbuk University in 1980 where they were photocopied and made available for research. An effort was made to publish the documents at the museum, but that effort reached fruition in

---

[31] Sŏngjong 20, 1489.12.*pyŏngshin*; 235:12a-13b (11:553-4) and *Richo no zaisan sozokuho* (hereafter *RZS*) [Yi dynasty patterns of property inheritance] (Seoul: Chosen Sotokufu Chusuin, 1936), p. 138. The possibility of the government taking the land for general reapportionment was discussed, but since the other children had cultivated the land for over forty years, on the basis of a statute of limitations it was decided to let them keep the property.

Ch'u had been in trouble with the court three years earlier over another property dispute. He had sued his father and uncles (sons of Hyoryŏngdaegun, a brother of King Sejong) for an alleged unequal distribution of inheritances. Although the court found the uncles guilty of dividing property too quickly after the death of their father, "in front of the coffin"; they also found Ch'u and his brothers guilty of a more-serious offense that of bringing suit against one's close kin. He was given 80 stripes. Sŏngjong 17, 1486.11.*kiyu*; 197:3b-4a (11:157) Ch'u was given 100 stripes for his second offense. Sŏngjong 21, 1490.2.*kapshin*; 237:1a (11:571).

[32] A photocopy is found in *Komunsŏ chipchŏn*, (Seoul: Seoul National University Library, 1972), p. 202.; see also Ch'oe Sŭng-hŭi, *Han'guk komunsŏ yŏn'gu*, p. 295. Also see p. 110 below.

1983 when the project was taken over by the Academy of Korean Studies.[33] And also a collection of 797 documents from the North Kyŏngsang Province area published in 1979 by Yŏngnam University contains a cache of inheritance documents and other materials from several prominent households in that area including the well-known aristocratic villages of Hahoe, Yangdong, and Naeap. Since it is becoming a source of status to have one's documents published, even more documents are coming to light. Although more documents are still to be studied, at this point the Puan Kim collection is unique in several regards. The length of time covered, the number of documents and the contents of one particular proclamation make the Puan Kim documents worthy of a closer look, in chapter two. The Kyŏngsang documents will provide validating comparisons in chapter three.

Conclusions

More important than the Code, because it was sometimes observed in the breach, are the early dynasty inheritance documents that show an equal division of property between sons and daughters.[34] They also indicate that each parent had inherited property from both of his or her parents. The property of the two parents was brought into the conjugal household and, usually just after the death of one or more parent, the property was divided and passed on to the next generation. There were special allocations of property for special reasons (examples of these will be given in chapter two) such as a marriage, a birth, or the passing of an examination. When there were only daughters in the household, the property was divided among them. A son was not adopted in, as was the case in the mid dynasty and after. Disputes arose, but the principle of equal inheritance was dominant in most settlements. At times an exception to the equilateral principle was, for various reasons, advocated by a parent; but in doing so, never did anyone argue for primogeniture, nor did they quote from a Confucian text about the role of the eldest son. Confucian concepts were not the basis for the unequal division. That approach became the rationale later. Property was set aside to provide for the ceremonies, and although the Code specifically stated that it should be one-fifth the size of the equilateral-sized share, only small amounts were set aside. As time passed the proportion of property set

---

[33]*Puan Kim-ssi Uban komunsŏ* [Ancient documents of the Uban Branch of the Puan Kim lineage] (hereafter PKK) (Sŏngnam City: *Han'guk chŏngshin munhwa yŏn'guwŏn* [Academy of Korean Studies], 1983).

[34]Kim Il-mi's 1969 article, "Chosŏn chŏn'gi ŭi namyŏ kyunbun sangsokche e taehayŏ," [Concerning equal inheritance between men and women in early Chosŏn] based mostly on the *Shillok*, however, even without citing a single inheritance document was an accurate description of the early Chosŏn period inheritance practices.

aside for ceremonies grew dramatically. Such allocation were very small in the earliest records, and grew to be the largest of shares in later periods.

In the late sixteenth century the picture just described began to change, and by the end of the seventeenth century, the picture was radically changed. In the next two chapters we will see numerous cases from various parts of the country that will illustrate the change. Chapter two will be a study of the collection of one lineage over time, the Puan Kims of the northern Chŏlla area; chapter three will examine documents from northern Kyŏngsang province and other areas to reveal that changes occurred throughout the country. The result was a disinheritance of daughters, first, and then a similar disinheritance of the sons other than the first son. The growing acceptance of Neo-Confucianism will be one of the primary causes of the change; scholars and officials who argued for the "lineage principle" (chongppŏp) were finally seeing wide-spread acceptance. It took well over two hundred years, but the lineage principle became the ideal, and Korean society was becoming a thoroughly orthodox Confucian society.

# 2

# The Puan Kim Cases

The Puan Kim documents include census registrations, letters, office warrants, and other documents including twenty-nine inheritance documents which cover the period from 1571 to 1799.[1] It is interesting that there are more documents from the seventeenth century than there are from the eighteenth century, and that there are none from the nineteenth century.

There were basically two types of inheritance documents: (1) general divisions wherein property was divided just prior to or just after the death of the property owner, and (2) special allocations given by a property owner to an individual, usually a relative. General allocations (or divisions) were titled "*tongsaeng hwahoe*" documents if the division took place after the parents had both died and the siblings divided the property. If one or both parents were alive the same purpose was achieved under the parents' direction, and the document was called a "*hŏyŏ mun'gi*." A special allocation was called a "*pyŏlgŭp mun'gi*, but often the term "*hŏyŏ mun'gi*" was also used for this purpose.[2] The dates of the special allocations

---

[1]When a document was written, either for a general allocation or for a special allocation, multiple copies were often made. Following is a list of the dates of the Puan Kim documents with the number of copies in parentheses and, in some cases, a comment about the occasion for which a special allocation was made: 1571 (1), 1581 (2), 1588 (1) Hong-wŏn passed the *sama* exam, 1607 (1), 1609 (2), 1669 (5), 1672 (2) Birth of a grandson, Su-jong, 1677 (2), 1678 (2), 1688 (2), 1735 (3) Marriage of Pang-gil, 1736 (3), 1778 (1), 1779 (1), & 1799 (1).

[2]The function is more important than the particular term chosen for the title of the document. Deuchler attempts a legalistic translation of the important terms. The *Tongsaeng hwahoe mun'gi* she calls "writ on the mutual consent of the siblings," *pyŏlgŭp mun'gi*, "special gift writ," and *hŏyŏ mun'gi*; "promissory writ". See Deuchler's *The Confucian Transformation of Korea*, pages 217 and 358, note #27 and #29. The futility of trying to pin exact translations on inexact usage is also seen when she also makes reference to *pun'gŭp mun'gi*, and *kŭmbu mun'gi* without providing a translation. In addition, the Puan Kim collection includes a category called *chŏnhu mun'gi*; see *Puan Kim-ssi uban komunsŏ* [Ancient documents of the Uban Branch of the Puan Kim lineage] p. 213. The function seems to be consistent in spite of the inconsistency in terminology. See for example, the number of documents in the KCKC collection that are classified as *pyŏlgŭp*, yet the document

correspond to the dates of special occasions, such as a marriage, a birth, recovery from an illness, or the passing of a state examination. The documents cover one Puan Kim lineage segment from the sixteenth to the twenty-fifth generation according to the lineage genealogy, *chokpo*.³

### Table 2.1
### The Generations of the Puan Kim Lineage
### in the Documents

The table below outlines the generation, name of the *chongja* (eldest son), his birth and death dates, and examination success, if any. The asterisk indicates dates which correspond to the dates of an inheritance document.

| Generation | Chongja | Born | Died | Exam |
|---|---|---|---|---|
| 16. | Sŏk-p'il | 1478? | ? | *munkwa* 1502 |
| 17. | Kae | 1508 | 1592 | |
| 18. | Kyŏng-sun | 1528 | 1595 | |
| 19. | Hong-wŏn | 1571 | 1645 | *sama* 1588* |
| 20. | Myŏng-yŏl | 1613 | 1677* | *munkwa* 1651 |
| 21. | Pŏn | 1639 | 1689* | |
| 22. | Su-jong | 1671* | 1736* | *chinsa* 1710 |
| 23. | Pang-gil | 1715 | 1742 | |
| 24. | Tŭng-mun | 1732 | 1767* | |
| 25. | Chŏng-ha | 1750 | 1798* | |

The Puan Kim lineage was a respectable *yangban* (aristocratic or elite) lineage throughout the Yi dynasty. While a small lineage in number, it produced several successful examination candidates and central government officials and was unquestionably considered part of the elite stratum of society by the local residents.⁴ As members of the aristocracy, they held a considerable amount of property, both land and slaves. The way the property was passed from one generation to the next over the critical

---

themselves use the term *hŏyŏ*. Regardless of which term the authors of a document chose, in function, there were two categories of document— *general divisions* between all siblings and *special allocations* usually to one heir. General divisions can be divided into two categories, those written by one or both parents while yet alive, and those written by the children after the death of both parents.

³The lineage genealogy was published first in 1584, and updated in 1785. The most recent edition was published in 1981.

⁴In the lineage as a whole there were 28 men who passed the *munkwa* exam, according to the Wagner-Song index. Most lived in Puan but there was a branch that lived in nearby Namwŏn. In the particular segment of the lineage with which we are concerned those who were successful in the exams are listed in Table 2.1. Two passed the *munkwa*, the highest civil service examination, and two passed the *sama* or *sokwa*, lesser exam. Actually, both passed the *chinsa* exam, one of two divisions of the *sama*. The *chinsa* is translated as the literary licentiate; the other division is the *saengwŏn*, classics licentiate. In the table above, the terms used in the documents were used, i.e., *sama* in one case and *chinsa* in the other.

transitional period of the mid dynasty is revealed in the inheritance documents.[5]

Pre-*Imjin* Documents

There are eleven inheritance documents that predate the Japanese invasion of 1592 (*imjin*). The first three were all dated in the year 1506, but were written on different days. The first was written on the ninth of an unknown month (the page was torn and the character is missing), the second on the twenty-ninth day of the sixth month, and the third on the fifth day of the tenth month.[6] Each is addressed to Kim Sŏk-p'il (Puan Kim, 16th generation) by his maternal uncle (*oe samch'on suk*), identified only by the surname Shin. In each document, one slave is given. It is unclear why it was done over the period of several months rather than all at once. Such a case does not appear later in the documents.

The next document is a special allocation document dated 1521 in which a father, whose identity is uncertain, stated that all his children but his last daughter had died and he therefore gave two slaves to her.[7]

The next two were dated 1564. One is a special allocation made by Kang Chu-bo to his niece's husband, Kim Kyŏng-sun, in which he stated that he had no heirs but had been living with the niece and her husband. In appreciation for their caring for him he gave six *majigi* of rice paddy.[8] The other one with the same date was written by Kang Chu-shin, an older brother of Chu-bo above, in which he stated he was getting old, and after a

---

[5]The Academy of Korean Studies (*Chŏngshin munhwa yŏn'guwŏn*) recently published the documents in modern printed characters, with a few examples reproduced photographically. *Puan Kim-ssi uban komunsŏ* (hereinafter PKK) [Ancient documents of the Uban branch of the Puan Kim lineage] Ancient Document Resources Compilation Series #83-3, (Sŏngnam City: Academy of Korean Studies, 1983). Before the Academy received the documents they were photocopied and numbered at the Museum of Chŏnbuk University. See Appendix I for the index number used at the Museum correlated to the Academy's number.

[6]These are numbered 1, 2, and 3 in the PKK publication, all on page 201. We know that the one numbered 1 is first because of an unusual condition concerning the dating system. Since the month is not recorded one could argue that it could be the twelfth month as easily as it could be the first. One can tell it predates the other two, however, because the date is given in the Chinese reign date, *Hung-ch'i* 19. The other two, dated in the sixth and tenth month of 1506, contain the Chinese reign date *Cheng-te* 1. Chronological tables show *Hung-ch'i* ended at 18. In rural Korea, they had not received word early in the year of the change of emperor, but by the sixth and tenth month they knew they should use the new calendar, but prior to that, at the time the other document was written, they were still using the old calendar.

[7]1521.7.23, PKK #13, p. 204. It is unclear who the author of this document was. The *chokpo* does not list anyone who held the offices indicated for the father in the document and who was succeeded only by a daughter.

[8]1564.10.24, PKK #14, p. 204.

conference with his kin he gave one slave and fourteen *majigi* of paddy land to Kim Kyŏng-sun.[9] The next document was a special allocation dated 1571, written by Kim Kae in the seventeenth generation of the lineage, and addressed to his last son, Kyŏng-su.[10] The boy was only eleven at the time. Kae mentioned that he had been seriously ill the previous spring and while his other sons had been away in distant villages, Kyŏng-su had stayed with him "like a suckling calf near its mother." He stated that Kyŏng-su had truly fulfilled the role of a son; the significance of the statement is only understood when one knows that the other sons he mentioned were legitimate sons, but Kyŏng-su was a *sŏja*. Property included three slaves from the father's side and two from the mother's side and a considerable amount of land. Presumably the perspective of the document was that of the son, so that the terms "father" and "mother" referred to the father and mother of Kyŏng-su, meaning Kae and his concubine. The document concluded by saying that the property was Kyŏng-su's and his heirs forever and should any of the "other descendants or your mother disregard the intent of the original landowner [Kae] and try to confiscate or sell the land, then on the basis of this document, report it to the government for a adjudication."[11]

General Allocations

The first general allocation was dated 1581; it was the document written by an in-law to the Kim's, Kang Chu-shin. Property was given to his "four children, legitimate and illegitimate, male and female."[12] The eldest daughter married Kim Kyŏng-sun, a legitimate son of Kae. Kang stated that he divided his property equally but that he wanted to give his *sŏja* an extra portion. On tabulating the amount given each, it is clear that the *sŏja* had less than his half siblings, but he was given more than would ordinarily be allowed a *sŏja* if the one-seventh or one-tenth rule were applied.[13]

There are two documents from 1588; one is similar to one seen above, the other is the first to mark a great occasion for the family. The

---

[9]1564.10.24, PKK #15, p. 204.

[10]1571.8.28, PKK #4, p. 201.

[11]*Ibid.* This document is somewhat unusual in that the amount of property given to a *sŏja* is generous, more than that prescribed for a *sŏja* by law, but not equivalent to the amount a legitimate heir would be given.

[12]1581.8.5, PKK #5, p. 202.

[13]An exchange of nine *majigi* of land for forty-five bolts of cloth is mentioned. At that rate, one *majigi* was worth five bolts.

one dated 1588, fourth month, twenty-fifth day, is similar in content to the 1571 document. Again Kae gave property, one slave, to Kyŏng-su, for taking care of him during his illness in Seoul.[14] The second was a special allocation from Kae to his grandson, Hong-wŏn, on the occasion of his passing the *sama* (lesser civil service) examination.[15] Kae said:

I am eighty-one years old and could die anytime. I had three sons who grew to adulthood, but the younger two have already died. The eldest, Kyŏng-sun, is a concern now because he is ailing. I have feared the extinction of our ceremonies for the ancestors. Now, happily, you have passed the *sama* exam, at the age of eighteen, which has brought great honor to our family.

He then gave nine slaves from his father's side, two from his mother's, and two from his wife's side.

Three years later, 1591, Hong-wŏn's father, Kyŏng-sun, the man who received property from his wife's father and uncle (Kang Chu-shin and his brother) in 1564, above, decided to give his bright young son a present for passing the exam.[16] He commented on how the boy had had no trouble studying from the beginning. However, the young man's scholarly career and his chances to take the higher civil service exam were apparently truncated by the tragedy that befell all of Korea the following year, the Hideyoshi invasion. Hong-wŏn became a war hero and survived to receive numerous honors and government positions after the war.[17]

---

[14]1588.4.25, PKK #6, p. 202.

[15]1588.3.25, PKK #16, p. 204.

[16]1591.10.5, PKK #17, p. 205.

[17]Among the memorabilia held by Hong-wŏn's descendants is the sword reputed to be his. He was the most prominent man of this particular segment of the lineage. He was named a merit subject (*kongshin*) and served an magistrate of several counties.

He was not without his problems, however. Later in life a woman he knew threatened to create trouble for him if he did not take her as a concubine; he refused and she, with help, reported to the government that Hong-wŏn was involved in an anti-royal conspiracy. The government initially believed her and had him banished. Four years later, at age 63, king Injo came to believe that Hong-wŏn was innocent and it was the concubine who swore falsely. He ordered the release from banishment and had the woman executed. (Injo 7, 1629.2.*imjin*; 20:3b-4a (34:314-315).

Yang Man-jŏng of Chŏnju, a retired teacher/principal and friend of Song June-ho told me of the incident. It is also written in Yang's *Hyŏn'gok hyangt'osa nonmunjip* [Collected essays about local history of Hyŏn'gok Yang Man-jŏng], p. 241.

Post-*Imjin* Documents

The first document written after the war, dated 1607, was a general allocation that provided one slave to each of three siblings, a son and two daughters. The younger daughter married Kim Hong-wŏn (19th generation).[18] The benefactor, Hong-wŏn's father-in-law, was a member of the Ch'ŏngdo Kim "lineage." The Puan Kim "lineage," if viewed as a patrilineal organization, thus again was bringing property into its organization from other "lineages."[19]

The second document recorded after the war, dated 1609, is the first recording of a general allocation created in the Puan Kim household.[20] It is the instrument that outlines the disposition of the property of Kim Kae (17th generation) when given to his children including Kyŏng-sun, the eldest son, and Kyŏng-su, the *sŏja* seen in documents above. The document also lists a sister who married a certain Kim Sŏk-ho and another *sŏja*, Kyŏng-sang, who had died leaving only a daughter. She was not given any property but provisions for her care were included.

The ritual provisions of the 1609 document are of interest. There were three aunts and two younger siblings who had died for whom property for ceremonies was set aside. For general ritual purposes (*sŭngjung cho*) twelve *majigi* of land and three slaves were set aside. For the ceremonies to the three aunts, three slaves, and for the ceremonies to the two siblings, two slaves were set aside (*panbujo*)[21].

Property was divided equally between the legitimate brother and sister; the son received eleven slaves and the daughter twelve. The *sŏja* received three slaves, which is somewhat more than the one-seventh or one-tenth outlined in the Code and coupled with the extra allocations given him in 1588 (one slave)[22] and 1571 (five slaves)[23] he had a total of nine slaves, in the documents that have survived; there could have been others. He also held a government position, at the junior eight level.

---

[18]1607.12.6, PKK #23, p. 207.

[19]This book below will argue that early dynasty lineages, if they can be called such, (perhaps kinship system would be preferable) should not be viewed as patrilineages in the way that they were in the late dynastic period.

[20]1609.1.13, PKK #24, p. 207.

[21]This provision is preserved and passed on in numerous subsequent inheritance documents thereafter. See 1669.7.8, PKK #35, p. 225; 1677.7.1. PKK #26, p. 209; 1688.3.7, PKK #29, p. 213; 1736.4.7, PKK #30 & #31, p. 217 & 218.

[22]1588.4.25, PKK #6, p. 202.

[23]1571.8.28, PKK #4, p. 201.

The next document, dated 1657, was addressed to Mme Yi, the wife of Myŏng-yŏl (20th generation), by the widow of Yi Shi-ch'un, a Mme Cho, who had adopted her (*shiyang*) as an infant.[24] Mme Cho stated that she regarded this daughter as her own as much as if she had given birth to her.[25] She praised the girl for her filial piety which had been manifest for over forty years, and particularly in the mourning rites which she had performed for her adopted father. Mme Cho said, "She has nurtured the living and memorialized the deceased." But, in somewhat apologetic tones, Mme Cho explained that her late husband was the ritual heir to a major lineage (*taejong pongsa chi in*) and the matter of his heirship had to be decided by submitting documents to the Ministry of Rites in Seoul. Therefore, Mme Cho explained to Mme Yi that her (Mme Yi's) natural brother, Chŏng, had been adopted to be her (Mme Cho's) heir and that after allocating the property to the adopted son, she had set aside ten slaves to be given to Mme Yi.[26] This document was written at a time when women were beginning to be excluded from participation in ritual and inheritance to property. In this case, as Mme Cho implied, if it were not for the fact that her husband was the heir to a primary lineage, Mme Yi may have inherited everything. If this situation had occurred a century later, the thought of giving any property at all to the daughter would not likely have been discussed.

## The Statement of 1669

The next significant year was 1669, and it was of the utmost significance for the Puan Kim lineage. There were four different documents written that year.[27] The first was written on the eighth day of the seventh month; the others were written on the eleventh day of the eleventh month. The one written in the seventh month was the last document in the

---

[24]For more on adoption of daughters see chapter seven.

[25]Although the document states in the heading that the Mme Yi to whom it is addressed is a *shiyang* daughter, which should mean she was over age three when she was adopted, yet the document itself says she was adopted as an infant before the age of three, which by legal definition means she was a *suyang* adoptee. For more on *suyang* and *shiyang* adoptions, see chapter nine.

[26]1657.10.2, PKK #8, p. 203. Mme Cho's document was witnessed and signed by two men, one named Hŏ and one named Ko, both relatives of her husband. It was common in the early period for documents to be signed by relatives who were not members of the patrilineage. By contrast, in the late Chosŏn period, the only relatives involved in lineage affairs, as a rule, were members of the surname group.

[27]There were five documents but two were identical to each other. The Academy of Korean Studies publication printed only one of the two and made no mention of the fact that there was another copy in the collection, but the Museum of Chŏnbuk University collection has all five copies including the two that are duplicates.

collection to show property brought into a Puan Kim household through marriage; those written in the eleventh month began to limit the property that the Puan Kim's would allow to leave the household via a daughter through marriage.

In the 1657 document above, Mme Yi, the *shiyang* daughter of Mme Cho, as the wife of Myŏng-yŏl, brought property into this Puan Kim household; in the first 1669 document, Myŏng-yŏl received property from his mother-in-law, Mme Yun. Apparently he had remarried or his father-in-law had.[28] The document provided Myŏng-yŏl with five slaves and some land in both paddy fields and dry fields.

The inheritance practices of the Puan Kim lineage radically changed with the documents written on the eleventh day of the eleventh month of 1669:[29]

> The law governing ancestor ceremonies by the lineage heir's household (*chongga*) is clearly recorded in the ritual texts of ancient China. Since this matter is so important and is so serious, more ceremonial property (*pongsa chŏnmin*) should be set aside so that the lineage heir's household may perform all the ceremonies; and the performance of ceremonies by the younger siblings (*chungja*) on a rotational basis (*yunhaeng*) will not be allowed.
>
> In our country the rule of the lineage heir's household (*chongga*) has been corrupted for a long time. All the aristocratic families have allowed [the ceremonies] to be performed by all the siblings on a rotational basis for so long that it is difficult to correct the situation. In the case of daughters, after they leave the household to marry, they become members of the other household. The principle of following the husband is important. That is why the standard of etiquette established by the sages stipulates that daughters wear mourning clothes for a shorter term after they have married. Both the affection and duty is less important for the daughter.
>
> These days, we frequently see aristocratic households allowing the household of the sons-in-law to perform the

[28]1669.7.8, PKK #35, p. 225. The *chokpo* indicates only that Myŏng-yŏl married Mme Yi, and does not indicate that there is either a Mme Cho, or a Mme Yun who would have been the mother-in-law to Myŏng-yŏl.

[29]1669.11.11, PKK #33, p. 225.

ancestral ceremonies on a rotational basis, and we often see that the sons-in-law or their children (*oeson*) are tempted to make excuses and omit the ceremonies. Even when they carry out the ceremonies, they use inferior offerings or they are not sincerely respectful to such a degree that it is better that they not perform the ceremonies at all. In our family we once brought up this matter with our now-deceased father and we brothers discussed the issue fully and have decided as a point of principle that the household of the son-in-law or *oeson* shall in no wise be allowed to perform the ceremonies in rotation (*yunhaeng*). This is a rule set for all succeeding generations.

There is no difference in the degree of affection between parent and child whether son or daughter; but daughters are different from sons in that there is no way for them to nurture their parents [since they leave the household when they marry] when the parents are alive, and they do not perform the ceremonies for the parents when they die. This being so, how can a daughter possibly expect a share of property equal to that of a son? Therefore, on the basis of both emotion and propriety, there is nothing unfair or wrong about giving a daughter a one-third share. How could a daughter or the *oeson* possibly dare to challenge this principle? Read this document and understand its intent, and then you will know this is a fair way to handle this matter. Who could ever say this differs from the commonly accepted rule and is therefore wrong?

If the primary line descendant (*chongjason*) is at any time so poor that he cannot perform the ceremony, then he can be forgiven, but if he disobeys and allows the ceremony to be carried out on a rotational basis (*yunhaeng*) then how dare we call him a our descendant.

Signed:    The former magistrate of P'yŏngsan, Myŏng-yŏl, and brothers, Yong-yŏl and Yu-yŏl.

On that same date, the property of Hong-wŏn and his wife was divided among their three sons,[30] and a special allocation was given to the grandsons, Pŏn and Mun (21st generation), sons of Hong-wŏn's eldest son,

---

[30]1669.11.11, PKK #25, p. 208.

Myŏng-yŏl.[31] In the documents written that day, Myŏng-yŏl and his brothers received property, but the *sŏja* brothers and the sisters received nothing.[32] Also on that day, the grandsons, Pŏn and Mun, were given a special allocation, but their three sisters received nothing,[33] in spite of the declaration that they should receive a one-third share.

Son preference was again evident three years later when the birth of a son in the next generation was celebrated. Su-jong (22nd generation) came along late in the life of his grandfather and was born to the second son, Mun, not the first son, Pŏn. The elderly grandfather, Myŏng-yŏl, was overjoyed and decided to give the baby a special allocation. In the document he wrote of the very tender regard he had for his grandson:

When I reached the age of sixty I still had no grandson so I have not had the enjoyment of holding a grandson on my knee, and not only that, I have always worried about the tragedy of seeing my family line come to an end. Then fortunately, my second son, Mun, has begotten a son and named him Su-jong. Even though he is now only one year old still I can see that his eyes sparkle, his face is fair, his looks refined and his future has great things in store. If my eldest son, Pŏn, never has a son, then this boy will be the one to perform the ceremonies. I have no way to express my great joy.

How happy will I be when I become old and frail and have nothing to do but pass the time holding a little one on my knee.

It is common practice to give special allocations when one has happiness. With such good fortune in having a grandson like this, how could I not give a special allocation?[34]

The document went on to itemize a gift of eight slaves and eight *majigi* of land.

Myŏng-yŏl lived for another seven years; and with his demise his children, led by his older son, Pŏn, held a siblings' conference to divide the

---

[31]1669.11.11, PKK #18, p. 205.

[32]1669.11.11; PKK #25. There were 15 slaves in the ceremonial section. The eldest brother, Myŏng-yŏl, received 25 slaves; the second brother, 36; and the third, 34 slaves.

[33]1669.11.11; PKK #18.

[34]1672.1.7; PKK #11 & #12, p. 203 & p. 204. This document was one of many that was recorded in duplicate but is the only one for which both copies were transcribed and published in PKK.

inheritance. The second son, Mun, had already died but was represented at the conference by his widow, Mme Yi. They quoted the injunction of their father saying they would give the daughters only a one-third share of property, and yet, the daughters were each given two-thirds as many slaves and one-half as much land as the sons. The property was divided as follows:[35]

Table 2.2
The Puan Kim Twentieth Generation Property Division

| Category | Slaves | Land (in majigi) |
|---|---|---|
| Ceremonies (pongsa) | 5 | 15 |
| Pŏn | 13 | 76 |
| Mun's widow | 12 | 75 |
| Yun I-hong's wife | 8 | 33 |
| Yi Chi-wan's wife | 8 | 33 |
| Song Mong-dŭk's wife | 8 | 33 |

In the preface, the document said:

Now the mourning period is over it is time to divide the property. . . . Our father had indicated when he was alive that a certain piece of property or a certain slave was to go to a particular son or daughter, but since daughters are not to participate in the chesa observance, they are to be given only a one-third share. . . .

Property passed on from the ancestors as lineage property (sŭngjung chŏnmin), property for the rituals for the collateral lines (panbu chewi), and special allocations (pyŏltŭk chŏnmin) will not be listed. The property allocated to our illegitimate sister is recorded elsewhere and will not be mentioned here.[36]

On the heels of writing this document there may have been some discussion about the legitimacy of the deceased father's decision, which had been announced eight years earlier, because a year later another document was written which strongly reiterated it. Property that had not yet been divided was the subject of the document titled "A special allocation of the Uban

---

[35]1677.7.1. PKK #26, p. 209. The three sisters married Yun I-hong, Yi Chi-wan and Song Mong-dŭk. Song was recorded in the chokpo as Song Pyŏng-nyŏn.
[36]Ibid.

property."[37] The proclamation that the daughters would not receive ritual land was reiterated in the statement, "This property is that which the ancestors said should not be given to daughters. The property is passed down through the generations only for the sake of the sons."[38] In contrast to the reaffirmation of the policy of not bequeathing property to daughters, the document reiterated the principle of equal inheritance for the sons.

## The 1688 Document

Ten years later, 1688, the lineage produced its longest and most detailed inheritance document of the collection.[39] It was unusually long for two reasons. First, the preface contained a long explanation of an unusual adoption. Therein, Pŏn explained that he had adopted Su-jong, the son of his deceased younger brother, Mun, but then Pŏn's wife had died. Pŏn remarried and had had two sons by 1688. He wrote that he would keep Su-jong as his heir and would send one of his own sons to be adopted, posthumously, to his brother. And second, there was a large amount of property. This generation marks the apex of wealth for this lineage segment. Su-jong passed the *chinsa* exam, his father had held office, his grandfather passed the *munkwa* exam (in 1651), and his great-grandfather, Hong-wŏn, passed the *sama* (*chinsa*) exam, was a war hero, and held important offices. Each had acquired more property to add to the estate. The largest acquisition was apparently that mentioned above, the Uban property, added by Hong-wŏn. After Su-jong's time no other descendant passed an exam or held major office.[40] The size of each subsequent inheritance document together with the family fortune grew smaller with each generation.

Unlike the 1677 siblings' conference when daughters were given two-thirds of a share, in spite of the edict that they be given one-third, the 1688 decision was more strict. Pŏn wrote:

---

[37]The so-called Uban property had been purchased by Hong-wŏn in 1636. He bought the site which had two houses and a sizable tract of land from Yu Sŏng-min for 100 bolts of cloth. Subsequently, the lineage descendants built up the village (and continue to live there today). 1636.3.17, PKK #16, p. 177.

[38]1678.7.1, PKK #27, p. 210.

[39]1688.3.7, PKK #29, p. 213. For the adoption aspects of this document, see chapter eight, p. 155.

[40]The lineage genealogy claims that Kim Sang-hyŏn passed the *saengwŏn* exam, but he does not appear in the comprehensive file of *sama* exam passers compiled by Professors Wagner and Song.

Our ancestors left us instructions stating that our family is different from other families, since married daughters are not allowed to participate in the *chesa* ceremonies on a rotational basis, they should be given only a one-third share of property. As long as I am alive, and I handle the inheritance in this manner, who would dare to raise a dispute? Who of my sons or daughters, could read this and not be moved?

As was earnestly taught by our late father, the property received by me and my brother as special allocations (*pyŏltŭk chŏnmin*) will not be passed on to the daughters; only sons will be inheritors of that property. That property already given to you as special allocations (*pyŏlgŭp*) with documentation need not be discussed here.

Now since Su-jong has already been designated the lineage heir (*chongja*), he has every reason to inherit my property. This is also true for Su-ch'ang who has already been adopted out to my deceased younger brother. He should inherit all the property of his adopted father. However, since it is for me to administer, only the property set aside for the ancestral ceremonies (*sŭngjung chŏnmin*) will I record for the lineage heir (*chongja*), Su-jong; the remaining property given to me as special allocations (*pyŏltŭk chŏnmin*) will be given completely to Su-ch'ang and his brother. By the same token, the special allocations given to my deceased younger brother will be in the total and sole control of Su-jong with the exception of ten *majigi* of land and several slaves that ought to be set aside for the *chesa* of my deceased younger brother [and therefore given to Su-ch'ang].

Although our manner of handling the inheritance is different from what is done in other households, still, I have already decided that it should be carried out this way. The lineage property (*sŭngjung chŏnmin*), although it is not much, should not be touched, and it, together with the property for the rituals for the collateral ancestors (*panbu chŏnmin*), should be passed on to the lineage heir's household (*chongga*) for one hundred generations.[41]

There followed a detailed list of property Pŏn gave his children both natural and adopted. The eldest (and adopted) son, Su-jong, was given the

---

[41] 1688.3.7, PKK #29, p. 213.

lineage property (*sŭngjung chŏnmin*) consisting of 31 slaves and land, and the 12 slaves and land for the rituals to the collateral ancestors (*panbu chŏnmin*). The other sons, Su-ch'ang and his unnamed brother, received a total of 48 slaves and land.[42] A daughter (who married Song Ha-p'il) was given 10 slaves and land; and a *sŏja*, Su-dong, was given 4 slaves and land. It is difficult to say whether the daughter received a one-third share because her brothers did not get equal amounts. But it appears that they made the effort to apply the one-third rule for the daughter and the one-seventh rule for the *sŏja*. She received one-third as much as the eldest son, which was about one-half as much as the two younger brothers.

In addition to the property left to his children, Pŏn left property to his concubines. The woman labeled as the first concubine, Mrs. Yun, received four slaves and land; the woman labeled as the second concubine, Mrs. Chu, received two slaves and land.[43] An interesting note was added to Mrs. Chu's allocation: "In the end, if she has no children, this property will revert to the holding of the legitimate son." Pŏn's *sŏja*, Su-dong, was born before Su-jong, but it is not explicitly stated who his mother was. She was most likely Mrs. Yun or she may have even been another concubine who had already died.

### The Documents of Kim Su-jong

As mentioned above, the time when Su-jong was the lineage heir may have been the apex for the lineage in terms of the wealth of the line (an apex in prestige would have been achieved when Hong-wŏn was alive). As an indication of the continued expansion of the estate of Su-jong, there is an interesting document preserved in the collection. It is a bill of sale, dated 1704, for two slaves sold to Su-jong by a certain Kim Shi-man for 25 *yang* of cash.[44]

---

[42]There were eleven pieces of property purchased by Pŏn and given to Su-ch'ang. They included that purchased from one male slave, one female slave and three others who, judging from their names, appear to be slaves. The remainder of his allocation included pieces of property from six other people, including two parcels of which one was purchased from a man and the other from his wife.

[43]A concubine is distinguished from a legitimate wife by a different appellation. A wife gets the label -*ssi*, e.g. Kim-*ssi*. A concubine is given the term -*jori*, e.g. Kim-*jori*, a term also used to indicate commoner status, whereas -*ssi* indicated *yangban* status. Herein, -*ssi* is translated "Mme", whereas for -*jori*, "Mrs." will be used. There is an alternate pronunciation of the pure Korean *chori*,, the Sino-Korean pronunciation, *sosa*; but it was most likely pronounced *chori* more often.

[44]1704.2.15, PKK #8, p. 162. For the price of slaves see Ch'oe Sun-hŭi, "Sangsan Kim-ssi punjaegi sogo," p. 916.

Another indication of wealth is that Su-jong was the author of the only special allocation document written by a Puan Kim to a daughter-in-law. It was written shortly after the marriage of his only son to a Mme O, in 1735. He stated:

> After you completed the wedding ceremony [at our home] with my son who was born to me late in life, and while you were at your natal home waiting for the *shinhaeng* date [when the bride and groom return to the groom's house after spending a year or more—often until the birth of the first child], you got the word that my wife had suddenly taken ill and died. You did not hesitate but left immediately and "traveled with the stars on your back" to take care of the funeral ceremonies. Since then, midst the bitterness of my loneliness as an aged widower you have made every effort to take care of me and also in carrying out the various ancestor ceremonies with a kind of devotion that has been ideal. Your personality is gentle and tranquil and the way you handle the slaves has been exemplary. There cannot be a greater blessing for our family. I strongly feel I should express my feelings in the form of some gifts. . . . I am giving you eight slaves . . . [and several pieces of land].[45]

Fifteen days later, he wrote a document for his son, Pang-gil, in which he said:

> You were born after I was fifty years old. There was nothing like my joy on that occasion. The heirs of our household are few and we had waited and worried. After you were born, naturally, we loved you whole-heartedly. What is more your countenance is impressive and you show excellent literary potential assuring us of your success in the future. It is beyond imagination how I as an old father have been so happy. In such a circumstance, it is customary to make special allocations which I should have done long ago, but for various reasons, I had not done so. Then, unexpectedly, two years ago your mother died before I could give you this special allocation. Midst the bitterness of my loneliness, you and your wife have made every effort to take care of me and also to

---

[45]1735.10.15, PKK #20, p. 206.

48

carry out the various ancestor ceremonies with perfection. In the twilight of my life, my joy could not be more full. There cannot be more than this. So I am now giving you some property as a special allocation.[46]

The reference to the marriage ceremony is of interest. It may look, at first, as if the couple were in permanent residence at the bride's home, uxorilocal marriage, but that practice was mostly abolished by this time; but rather, they were practicing the custom of visiting the bride's house for a period of time, usually more than a year and often until the birth of the first child, before taking up permanent residence in the patrilocal home.[47]

Table 2.3
The 1736 Puan Kim Inheritance Document

| Category | Slaves | Land (in *majigi*) |
| --- | --- | --- |
| Ceremonies (*chewi cho*) | 24 | 75 |
| Pŏng-gil | 11 | 65 |
| Yi Pyŏng-ch'u's wife | 3 | 25 |
| Yu Myŏng's wife | 3 | 28 |
| Pak Hyŏn-wŏn's wife | 3 | 25 |
| Pak Sa-ch'ŏn's wife | 3 | 28 |
| *Sŏja*, Tüg-i and brother(s) | 3 | 35 |
| *Sŏja* daughter | 0 | 20 |

A year later, on the seventh day of the fourth month of 1736, four days before Su-jong died, he presided over the division of his property. Pang-gil, the son who came along late in his life, was apparently born after four daughters. The term used for the property set aside for the rituals was "ceremonial property" (*chewi*). Each was given shares as shown in table 2.3.[48]

In this case, the amount of property given the daughters was close to the one-third share advocated by their great-grandfather. The daughters were falling even farther behind, though, since the son controlled his own full

---

[46]1735.11.1, PKK #19, p. 206.

[47]The term for visiting the bride's home was *shinhaeng*. For more on the early Korean marriage practices see Martina Deuchler's "Neo-Confucianism: The impulse for social action in early Yi Korea," *Journal of Korean Studies*, 2(1980): 71-111, and also *The Confucian Transformation of Korea*, pp 251-256.

[48]1736.4.7, PKK #30 & #31, p. 217 & 218; There are three copies in the Museum of Chŏnbuk University, #28, #26 & #73. Although this document has been preserved in triplicate, there are slight variations from document to document. PKK #30 (The Museum of Chŏnbuk University #28) lists 24 slaves in the section on ceremonies, but omits mention of the *sŏja* daughter. PKK #31 is the same as both The Museum of Chŏnbuk University #26 and #73; they list only 19 slaves in the section on ceremonies.

share and the ceremonial property as well. By that measure, the daughters each received one-twelfth as many slaves and one-fifth as much land.

### The Adoptions of Tŭng-mun and Chŏng-ha

The primary heir, Pang-gil, died childless at the age of twenty-seven, six years after his father's death. His widow, Mme O, requested that a nephew, the son of Pang-bo, a first cousin (*sach'on*) of Pang-gil, be adopted.[49] The boy was eleven and was named Hyŏn-dŭk at the time of the adoption but was later known as Tŭng-mun. There is no inheritance document in the collection that shows the passing of the property from Pang-gil to Tŭng-mun. Since he was the only person in that generation there was apparently no need to document the obvious; the adoption took care of the inheritance.

Tŭng-mun had four daughters but died in 1767 at the age of thirty-five without a son to serve as his heir. A year later, his widow, Mme Na, arranged to adopt the son of another widow, Mme Min.[50] The deceased husbands were twentieth-*ch'on* cousins, e.g., they were related through a common ancestor who lived ten generations earlier. The son was eighteen years old and named Tar-hyŏn at the time of the adoption but was later listed as Chŏng-yŏl in the inheritance document and finally recorded as Chŏng-ha in the *chokpo*. Although the long distance adoption apparently caused some contention among lineage members, the adoption survived and Chŏng-ha became the primary heir of the twenty-fifth generation.[51] The inheritance document for that generation was not composed until eleven years after the adoption and twelve years after Tŭng-mun had died. It stated:

> The lineage property (*sŭngjung chŏnmin*) passed down from the ancestors, the property for the collateral line ancestors (*panbu chewijo*), together with special allocations of property (*pyŏltŭk chŏnmin*) of the former generations and the Uban property (*Uban chŏnmin*), without reference to whether it is a large or small amount, is all to be transmitted to the lineage heir (*chongson*). And there is to be no discussion of dividing it among others; the ancestors were clear in their directives on this point. Our father often said that the property that he acquired could be divided among the sons and daughters, but

---

[49]1743.7.1, PKK #9, p. 203.

[50]1768.7.15, PKK #10, p. 203.

[51]Undated but *circa* 1768, PKK #1, p. 139. See chapter nine for the details on the adoption and the dispute.

that which was inherited from the ancestors must not be considered for distribution [to the children] since this is what was clearly directed by those ancestors. Now that the eldest sister and the second sister are married, we cannot but hold a conference [of harmony for dividing the property—*hwahoe*], and thus we have all met, and in accordance with the family customs that have been handed down, we have discussed the division of the property. Among the property that our father has acquired, excluding the Uban property and the ritual provision (*chewi cho*), there is some that he acquired from external sources, and that will be divided equally (*p'yŏnggyun*) among the five siblings. As for the Uban property, according to the directions of the ancestors, only the sons shall inherit it from generation to generation for a hundred generations to come without change.[52]

The siblings in this case were the adopted son and four daughters, two of whom were married and two were single. The son received 56 slaves and claim on 17 escaped slaves and 451 *majigi* of land. Each daughter received either 10 or 11 *majigi* of land, but no slaves. No longer were the daughters given a one-third share. Rather, and strangely, the document revived the principle of equal inheritance but limited it to the property newly acquired by the parents' generation. All the inherited land was decreed to be the property of the son, albeit an adopted son. Compared to the amount of property the son received, what each daughter received was closer to one-third of one percent, specifically, three percent-sized share of land and no slaves. The transition was all but complete.

Chŏng-ha died in 1798 and his property was divided the following year by his four sons. No daughters were listed in either the document or the *chokpo*.[53] Since this is the last inheritance document to be found in the collection, we do not see the property rights of daughters actually dwindle to zero, but it is a safe assumption that that was indeed the case.

Conclusions

The Puan Kim documents are typical of the aristocratic documents of the Chosŏn dynasty in many regards. The fact that there are none dated in

---

[52]1779.2.16, PKK #28, p. 211.

[53]1799.5.3, PKK #34, p. 224. The *chokpo* did not list any daughters and only recorded three sons. When a son died young, if he was not the eldest son, he would often be dropped from the *chokpo*. *Puan Kim-ssi taebo*, 1981 ed., 2:81-95.

the eighteenth century probably indicates that the rights of the eldest son had become so well established that he, as heir, would control the division of property if any were to take place, and there was no need to write it into a document.

The Puan Kim documents, although the best collection from a single lineage yet to be published in Korea, were not the only collection that has recently been published. The Academy of Korean Studies has subsequently published the collections of several other lineages.[54] The best publication that covers multiple lineages is the collection by Yi Su-gŏn and published by Yŏngnam University. Therein, several of the aristocratic houses of North Kyŏngsang have provided copies of their collections of documents. The results are similar to those found in the North Chŏlla area of Puan. The Puan Kim documents are unique in many regards, but as for the social phenomena that were unfolding around the country, such is revealed in other places as well as Puan. The documents covered in the next chapter show that although the Puan Kim's provide a unique account of what happened, still the same things were happening in other parts of the country.

---

[54]*Kwangsan Kim-ssi Och'ŏn komunsŏ* (Old Documents of the Yean Branch of the Kwangsan Kim Lineage) is the only one, out of six or seven, published since the Puan Kim documents were published with significant numbers of inheritance documents. See also Ch'oe Sŭng-hŭi, *Han'guk komunsŏ yŏn'gu* [Study of Old Documents of Korea]; *Chŏnbuk chibang ŭi komunsŏ (1)*, [Old Documents from North Chŏlla Province, Part 1]; and Pak Yong-suk, *Chosŏn hugi sahoesa yŏn'gu* [Studies on Late Chosŏn Social History].

# 3

# Loss Of Inheritance For Daughters

The documents from the North Kyŏngsang area come from the homes of several prominent lineage groups and in many ways are similar to those in the Puan Kim collection. The documents reveal typical aristocratic values and practices of the Chosŏn period in many regards. Table 3.1 compares the Puan Kim documents with those from the North Kyŏngsang (Kyŏngbuk) area[1] and with a collection from around the country found in the Kyujanggak (Chosŏn period government archive) kept at the Seoul National University Library.[2] There is no discernable variation based on region; but

### Table 3.1
#### Changes by Century in Numbers of Inheritance Documents in the Kyŏngbuk, Puan Kim, and Kyujanggak Collections

| Category | Century/15th | 16th | 17th | 18th | 19th |
|---|---|---|---|---|---|
| Kyŏngbuk Documents (totals) | 13 | 87 | **97** | 22 | 2 |
|    Sibling Agreements (*hwahoe*) | (4) | (18) | **(23)** | (3) | (0) |
|    Wills (*hŏyŏ*) | (8) | (26) | **(21)** | (6) | (2) |
|    Special Allocations (*pyŏlgŭp*) | (1) | (43) | **(53)** | (13) | (0) |
| Puan Kim Documents | 0 | 11 | **13** | 6 | 0 |
| Kyujanggak (SNU) Documents | 0 | 3 | **27** | 11 | 2 |

---

[1]Yi Su-gŏn, *Kyŏngbuk chibang komunsŏ chipsŏng* (KCKC) [A collection of old documents from the North Kyŏngsang area] (Kyŏngsan: Yŏngnam University Press, 1981), pp. 100-115.

In the table, I have translated *hŏyŏ mun'gi* as "will," *hwahoe mun'gi* as "sibling agreement" and *pyŏlgŭp mun'gi*, as "special allocation." The sibling agreement and the will are general division documents; the difference between them is that the sibling agreement takes place after the parents have died; the will (like the special allocation) is made by either father or mother (or both) while alive. For more details see page 31, footnote 2.

[2]These documents have been analyzed by Yi Kwang-gyu, *Han'guk kajok ŭi sajŏk yŏn'gu*, p. 360.

53

54

rather we can draw conclusions similar to those we drew from the examination of the Puan Kim documents: the inheritance system was markedly changed by the turn of the eighteenth century. The near-absence of this type of document in the nineteenth century is most striking. The system had so changed that it was not even necessary to write down who inherited what. The eldest son, who was usually the principle heir, appears to have assumed such authority that he did not need a document to back up his claim of control over the inherited property. Those who lost the most in all these changes were the daughters.

The Kyŏngbuk Collection
Some of the particular issues that we saw in the Puan documents are also seen in the Kyŏngbuk documents. The 1669 Puan Kim document that announced the one-third inheritance rule for the daughters was unique in that it was a separate document devoted to that stipulation. In the Kyŏngbuk collection one can also see statements which announce a reduction in inheritance rights for the daughters. These statements, however, are located in the preface portion of inheritance documents; the separate declaration of the Puan Kim lineage elders is thus the only one of its kind that has come to light at this date.

Among the 797 documents in the collection, the first 221 pertain to inheritance. The remainder are mostly simple sales agreements. Of these numerous documents, several show the decline in inheritance ratios for daughters, as seen above, but few make revealing statements about how the transformation took place.

Table 3.2
Adopt a Son, Marry in a Son-in-Law

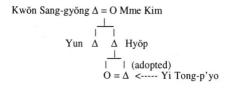

In 1660, the widow of Kwŏn Sang-gyŏng, Mme Kim, wrote two documents, one addressed to her son, Kwŏn Yun, the other to her adopted grandson, Yi Tong-p'yo. Tong-p'yo had been adopted by Yun's younger brother, Hyŏp, who had only a daughter.

Tong-p'yo was adopted as a son but was later married to the daughter, his sister by adoption.[3] Mme Kim, the grandmother, wrote that the ceremonies for the parents' generation could be conducted on a rotational basis but that the daughter's descendants were not to participate in the ceremonies for the ancestors. The older son alone had that privilege.[4]

In the next generation, the property of Kwŏn Yun and his wife was divided by his widow, Mme Pak. Since the previous generation had set the precedent and reduced the share of property given to the daughter, the amount of property given to each of the five daughters was about one-tenth of that given to each of the two sons.[5]

Reasons for Disinheriting Daughters

In the Puan Kim documents, we saw one rationale for decreasing the amount of property to be given to a daughter: daughters only mourned for one year, whereas sons mourned for three; therefore, daughters were given one-third as much property. Among the Kyŏngbuk documents, there are two documents that give explanations (unlike Mme Kim's directive, above) for initiating an unequal division of property between sons and daughters. One is dated 1615, the other 1688. The one dated 1615 is a testament written by Kwŏn Nae who argued that daughters' children do not bear the same name and are not as faithful in carrying out the ceremonies for their maternal grandparents; and that dividing the property among so many daughters as well as sons weakens the economic position of the lineal grandsons who would certainly keep the incense burning at the graves of their lineal ancestors even if they were extremely poor.[6]

The one dated 1688 revealed another rationale for reducing the inheritance given to a daughter. The author of the document, Mme Chŏng, the widow of Yi Kae, wrote that her five sons and one daughter were to

---

[3]This is perhaps the only case of *teril sawi* (son-in-law adoption) to be found in historical documents. But the practice was common in Taiwan (for example, see Arthur Wolf and Chieh-shan Huang, *Marriage and Adoption in China, 1845-1945*) and in Japan (for example, see Robert J. Smith, *Ancestor Worship in Contemporary Japan*.) Unlike the situation in China and Japan, it is considered an embarrassment or a substandard status. When this author interviewed lineage leaders and others involved in adoptions, I found several people who knew of those who were *teril sawi*, but when I tried to personally interview them, none would agree to meet with me. The practice was rare a generation ago and is probably even more difficult to find today. On the other hand, there is some speculation that some of the very wealthy may pass their companies on to sons-in-law as is commonly done in Japan.

[4]*KCKC*, #195 & #196, both 1660.7.1, pp. 462-463.

[5]*KCKC*, #55, 1695.1.7, p. 255.

[6]*KCKC*, 1615, p. 795. Deuchler refers to this case and has a translation of part of the testament, *The Confucian Transformation*, p. 227.

divide her property equally, except that "the daughter will be given a little less since she lives in another county." She was given as many slaves (seven) but sixty percent as much land as her brothers (thirty compared to fifty *majigi*). The basis for cutting her share of property was not just that she lived farther away but that she would not be able to attend the ceremonies. In fact, it said that she would be disallowed participation in the ceremony for the ancestors, but she could take her turn in the ceremony for her parents.[7] The tendency toward patrilocal marriage as the dynasty entered its third century became linked to the decision to disinherit daughters. With daughters moving out, it became increasingly difficult for them to claim rights in their natal homes.

In the three cases above that make statements about reducing shares of property for daughters, there are four different reasons for reducing the size of a share given to a daughter: (1) the classics say she only mourns for one year, not three; (2) daughter's children have a different surname and therefore tend to be less attentive to the ceremonies for the maternal line; (3) giving property to all the daughters weakens the economic position of the sons and lessens their ability to perform proper ceremonies; and (4) daughters marry out and live too far away to attend to the ceremonies. Common to each rationale, however, is the element of the ancestor rituals. These are four different facets of the single concern for carrying out the ceremonies.

### Lesser Shares of Inheritance for Second Sons (*Ch'aja*)

For daughters to lose their inheritance rights was an early stage in the transformation; the next step was the limitation of ceremonies held in rotation by the sons. The ceremonies were left in the hands of the eldest son, a son who came to be called the *chongson*, the lineage heir. A good case is seen in document number 56 in the Kyŏngbuk collection. Yi Kye-jin left instructions for his two sons, wherein he directed them not to carry out the ceremonies in rotation. He said:

> The inherited and purchased property will be divided equally, but the ceremony for my parents will not be conducted on a rotational basis. The ceremony for me and my wife, however, you may perform taking turns as you wish.[8]

---

[7]*KCKC*, #52, 1688.2.x, p. 247.

[8]*KCKC*, #56, 1709.3.x, p. 257. There was apparently conflict between the father and the second son over one particular female slave. The father had stated that she, in particular, should not be given to the second son. When the father stated, therefore, that the second son could perform ceremonies for him if he wants to, it implied that the second son was still angry with the father and may indeed have chosen not to perform the ceremonies.

The father wrote of equal division, and at first glance, it looks like the two sons are given equal amounts, but on reading the document there is a reference to inherited slaves set aside for the ceremonies, which were given to the first son which greatly tipped the scales away from equality, and away from the second son. It is interesting that the father insisted that the ceremonies for his father and mother be carried out by the eldest son, yet the ceremonies for himself and his wife he allowed to be carried out in rotation between the two sons. Societal norms were changing in such a way that for the formal ceremonies, outside the house and involving other descendants of the ancestors, they conformed to the new order; but still for their own ceremonies, at home and less formal, they still allowed the old order of rotation between siblings.

## The Kwŏn Family Dispute

There is an interesting case from the Kyŏngsang area in the late seventeenth century that shows how hard the old system of equilateral inheritance died. In 1682 a large family led by Kwŏn Mok met to divide the inheritance. The eight siblings, three sons and five daughters, indicated in the preface that the sons, and particularly the eldest son, were to be given larger shares of property. Five years later they met again and reversed the earlier decision, returning the inheritance document to a near-equilateral basis.[9] In 1682, they stated:

> Our father indicated that if this small amount of property were divided equally among the eight siblings, the share for each would be insubstantial, and the sons who perform the ceremonies on a rotational basis would not be able to properly carry them out. . . . Therefore, the property should go completely to the three sons. The sons-in-law will not be given any.[10]

The foreword did state, however, that one son-in-law, who came from an exceptionally poor family, and one orphaned grandson, the son of a daughter who with her husband died young, ought to be given some property. The orphaned boy had been raised by his maternal grandmother, the mother of the eight siblings in question here, who had written in her will that the boy should get extra property.

---

[9]*KCKC*, #103, 1682, p. 401; & #104, 1687, p. 405.

[10]*Ibid.*, 1682. Although the document states that sons-in-law will not be given any property, the document went on to allocate property for the daughters.

The foreword went on to emphasize the specific responsibilities and privileges that were to be given the primary lineage heir. The portion in brackets below was deleted when the document was reissued in 1687.

> From this time forth the share of property to be used for maintaining the ancestor ceremonies will not be divided among the descendants even if there are a hundred slaves born to those slaves now assigned to the ritual land. The other descendants will not make stratagems to take over any of those slaves for themselves. Although several generations pass, [the ritual property may not be divided and the lineage heir may not parcel out the property to the other descendants either, but the property shall remain intact and the lineage heirs shall be in charge forever. As to the parents' ceremonies, even after several generations], the labor of these slaves and the produce of those fields should be dedicated for use "in the ceremonies forever without falling into disrepair" as is stated in the ritual classics. If there is ever insincerity on the part of the primary heir in carrying out the ceremonies, then the lineage elders and the other descendants can discuss leveling a penalty on him.[11]

During the five years between the issuing of the first document and the second, the substantially disinherited daughters, their husbands, and children, must have marshalled their forces. In 1687, the time was right for reconvening the siblings' conference and realigning the division of property. In 1682, the three sons were each given 21 slaves and about 200 *majigi* of land. The five daughters were given 13 slaves and no land. (As mentioned above, exceptions were provided for two of the daughters' families. One was given 14 slaves and the other 89 *majigi* of land.) In 1687, the property was completely reallocated. Each son was given 17 slaves and each daughter 15; each son was given about 90 *majigi* of land and each daughter around 70. The sons were still receiving more than the daughters, but compared with the earlier division of property, the sons' holdings were drastically reduced, while the daughters' holdings were greatly enhanced.

In the new document, there was still a provision for the eldest son to carry out the ceremonies as the lineage heir:

> Even after several generations the offspring of the slaves assigned to the ancestral ceremonies should not be divided and

---

[11] *Ibid.*, 1682 & 1687.

given to the descendants; only the lineage heir (*chongjason*) should control those slaves. They should never be given to any of the other descendants.[12]

The amount of property set aside for the ceremonies, however, was reduced from 49 *majigi* of land in 1682 to 35 in 1687. More than that, the wording of the article outlining the privileges and responsibilities of the lineage heir was weaker in the later document, as is shown in the excerpts above. The special provisions for the two daughters' families was also readjusted. In the earlier document, the grandson by the eldest daughter was given 14 slaves because his parents, the daughter and son-in-law of the household in question, had died young leaving the boy to be reared by his paternal grandmother. The husband of the second daughter, Yi Ch'ŏn-gi, was noted to be especially poor and was therefore given 89 *majigi* in the first document. In the second, the orphaned boy was given 77 *majigi* whereas the other daughters' families received around 70. The poor son-in-law received 69 *majigi*, no more than the other daughters/sons-in-law households and considerably less than the 89 he had been allocated five years earlier. Had he been pulled into an alliance with the outnumbered sons?

It appears the three outnumbered sons had enticed two of the five daughters' heirs to agree to the 1682 division and ran it over the three other daughters by a five to three majority. In the aftermath, the unfairness of the procedure yielded to a reconsideration.

Whatever the manuverings behind the scenes were, the overall picture is clear. This household had attempted to conform to the new order, the son-dominated order, but the old order, the equilateral order, prevailed. Unfortunately, we do not have a long chain of documents for the Kwŏn household, like that of the Puan Kim lineage, so we do not know when they completed the transition; but there is no doubt that they, too, eventually conformed. Their documents do show us that the transformation was not without its opposition or struggles.[13]

<u>The Ma-Chin Dispute</u>

One final case shows an even greater conflict in the transition from the old order to the new. The dispute arose over the property for the

---

[12]*Ibid.*, 1687.

[13]Yi Su-gŏn also makes this point; his conclusion was that there were more in-law disputes in the transition period. "Chosŏnjŏn'gi ŭi sahoe pyŏndong kwa sangsokchedo" [Social change and the inheritance system of the early Chosŏn period], 1992, p. 113.

60

ceremonies dedicated to the memory of Ma Ch'ŏn-mok, a merit subject (*kongshin*), who helped keep T'aejong secure on the throne in 1400. On one side of the dispute were three Chin brothers whose mother was a Ma, a primary line descendant of Ma Ch'ŏn-mok. On the other side was Ma Sŏk-ki, a descendant through a collateral line. The case was brought to court first in 1680 by Ma Sŏk-ki but was not settled until 1751, when Ma Chung-myŏng, a grandson of Ma Sŏk-ki, won the suit.[14]

Table 3.3
The Ma Lineage Diagram

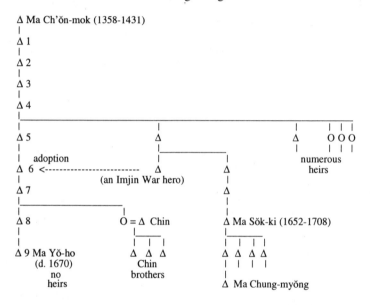

At issue was the inherited property left by Ma Ch'ŏn-mok who was given a large fief as a merit subject. For four generations, the property was passed through only sons, but in the fifth generation there were six siblings, three sons and three daughters. The eldest son did not have an heir, but adopted the elder son of his younger brother. In the subsequent generation

[14]Seoul National University Library, Kyujanggak collection catalog no. 11981. This document is preserved as a long scroll that was written by the magistrate at the time of the final adjudication in 1751. It recounts the history of the suit in addition to giving the final verdict in favor of the Ma plaintiffs.

there was only one son, who in turn had a son and a daughter. That son had one son, Ma Yŏ-ho, who was without an heir; that daughter married a man named Chin and had three sons. Thus, the property of the primary heir's line fell into the hands of the three Chin brothers. Mme Ma's cousin (eighth-*ch'on* by adoption, sixth-*ch'on* by birth), Ma Sŏk-ki, petitioned in 1680 for the property to be turned over to the Ma line.[15]

The dispute was finally resolved in 1751 after years of suits, counter-suits, and appeals. Initially, the decision favored the Ma line, but on appeal the Chin brothers won reversals. The Ma line continued to press their suit and eventually, Ma Chung-myŏng, the grandson of Ma Sŏk-ki, the first plaintiff, won the final judgment. The wording of the final judgment was highly biased in favor of the winning side. It quoted the statement of the Ma petitioner who said, "the property of a prominent ancestor should not fall into the hands of an almost insignificant *oeson*."

For the Ma lineage, the transformation was complete. The wording of the final judgment was so strong that one wonders how an alternate position could have even been considered. The critical factor, of course, was time. In the early period, everyone parceled out property on an equal basis. Gradually, through the late sixteenth and seventeenth centuries, the perception of what was proper changed. By the eighteenth century, the memory of the old order had faded to such an extent that in many cases, such as the Ma case above, the idea of giving inheritance to daughters was unthinkable.

Summary

The mid Chosŏn period saw a remarkable transformation in inheri-tance practices. The most visible aspect of the change was the disinheri-tance of daughters while the role of the eldest son was expanded. There were really two things happening: one was the exclusion of daughters, the other, the diminishing role of the other sons. In China, the common rule of inheritance was equality among the sons while the daughters were excluded. But Korea did not go in that direction. The same intellectual force was in operation in China as in Korea, yet the results were different.

The driving intellectual force was the influence of Neo-Confucianism which stressed the importance of the eldest son, and beyond that, ancestor worship and the organization of the patrilineage.[16] Yet the *Chiali* and other

---

[15]For more details see my article, "Women Without Sons: A Measure of Social Change in Yi Dynasty Korea," in *Korean Women: View from the Inner Room*, eds. Laurel Kendall & Mark Peterson (New Haven: East Rock Press, 1983), pp. 39-42.

[16]Deuchler, *The Confucian Transformation*, chapters two and three.

Neo-Confucian texts by Chu Hsi, and commentaries by Korean authors, provided a place for women to participate in the ceremonies. The Chinese took equilateral inheritance and Neo-Confucian ideology and ended up in quite a different place than did the Koreans. Chinese practice in many areas allows women to perform the ancestor ceremonies whereas men take care of the household gods—exactly opposite the situation in Korea.[17]

Arthur Wolf asks why, and proposes the answer based on the conclusions that the organization of the lineage in Korea performed a different function from that in China. In China the lineage controlled property, (in Africa it performed a political function), but in Korea the lineage provided status.[18] He concludes,

> . . . ancestor worship entered Korean society at the national level and with the explicit backing of the royal court, it acquired great prestige and was defined as an aspect of the public domain rather than of the private. The result was that the rites were assigned exclusively to men, in part because men were associated with high status and in part because they appeared to belong to the world of affairs. What mattered most was not the care and feeding of the dead, the focus of the domestic rites in both China and Japan, but emulation of one's social superiors.

There is another question that will be addressed in the final chapter, the question of why the transition occurred when it did. The ideology was available centuries earlier, and there were anti-transition forces active before during and after the transition who conceivably could have succumbed earlier, or who could have forestalled the onset of lineal thinking for some time longer. Those who were opposed to adopting Confucian/Chinese thinking argued for maintaining "national practice" (*kuksok*). They eventually, in the seventeenth century, lost the battle. But this issue will be addressed below.

Many inheritance-related documents make no mention of the transition, but some do. Some address the practice of *yunhaeng*, conducting

---

17P. Alfred Fabre, "Avril au Pays des Aieux," *Catholic Church in China: Collectanea Commissionis Synodalis*, vol. 8 (1935), p. 121, as quoted in Wolf and Smith, "China, Korea, and Japan" in *Religion and Ritual in Korean Society*, ed. Kendall and Dix.

18Arthur Wolf and Robert Smith, "China, Korea, and Japan" in *Religion and Ritual in Korean Society*, ed. Kendall and Dix, p. 192. See also Mutsuhiko Shima, "In Quest of Social Recognition: A Retrospective View on the Development of Korean Lineage Organization," p. 122-123. Deuchler makes the same point, *The Confucian Transformation of Korea*, p. 12.

the ceremonies on a rotational basis, and call for its abolition. Some address ritual concerns in terms of making changes. For example, the 1669

## TABLE 3.4

### Decline of Inheritance for Daughters

The graph shows the percentage of inheritance given to daughters compared to that of the sons. The Puan Kim documents are on one line, the Kyŏngbuk documents together with others from various sources are on the second line. It was not an even decline; some families disinherited daughters earlier than did others, as the graph shows.

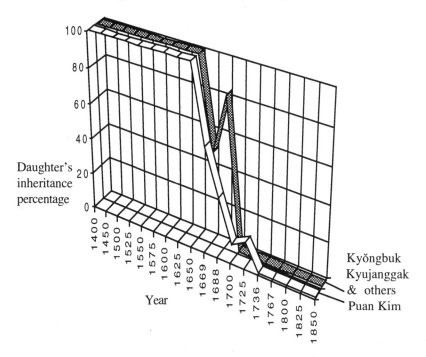

and 1688 documents of the Puan Kim household that declares that "unlike other households" they are no longer going to allow the participation of the daughter's line in the ceremonies. And therefore, the daughter need be given only one-third as much property as the sons; then in subsequent generations of the Puan Kim lineage it is interpreted to mean daughters' lines can have one-third of all the newly acquired property, not that of the inherited property. And there are the examples from Kyŏngsang province where those in senior generations stated that daughters' children have different names, the property is being too fragmented, and that daughters marry out of the area— all of which show that daughters do not participate in the ancestor ceremonies faithfully. Therefore they should be given lesser shares of inheritance.

With the exclusion of daughters from nearly all inheritance and ritual matters by the last century of the dynasty, greater emphasis was placed on the son, and in the absence of a son, an adopted son. Often, however, the heirship of the household was not clear because of multiple marriages which provided rivals or alternate choices in naming an heir. With the transition to a system where only one heir was essential, from a system wherein all were equal, we can expect greater competition for the singular position that provided both ritual (and thereby social) status as well as wealth. In the following chapters we will see examples of options that were considered and we will see that some options led to numerous arguments, but one option, that which developed into a kind of consensus, eventually came to be the preferred choice—agnatic adoption.

# 4

# From Multiple Marriage To Monogamy

The transition in the practice of inheritance, as seen in section one, was interrelated with other changes in Chosŏn society. Eventually, as will be seen in section three, that which was lost by daughters was gained by sons, particularly eldest sons and adopted sons. But before examining that subject, we must look at other related questions. As daughters lost their claims to heir status, what happened to their status in other areas, such as their status as wives and mothers? What of the women who were secondary wives (ch'ŏp)? And what role did the children of secondary wives, the sŏja, play in the inheritance transition? Most importantly, in considering the status of women, was an additional marriage a feasible solution to the problem of not having an heir?

## The Aphorisms and the Stereotypes

The stereotype of the woman of traditional Korea is described by a number of Confucian-inspired aphorisms. There are the samjong, the three obediences; yŏllyŏ, the faithful widow; and ch'ilgŏ chi ak; the seven grounds for divorce. Once a woman is married, she becomes the ch'ulga oein, "the one who left the house and became a outsider" (or "a married daughter is the same as a stranger"). The overall perception is namjon, yŏbi: men are exalted but women are lowly.

The samjong denotes the three men to whom a woman is obedient: first, her father, then, her husband, and third, her son. The yŏllyŏ was most often a young widow who refused to remarry but rather stayed with her aging in-laws and cared for them. Another typical category of yŏllyŏ was one who showed extreme devotion in caring for an ailing husband or parent-in-law. The ultimate in this category was the woman who would excise a part of her flesh, usually from her thigh or buttocks, to prepare a medicine for the ailing. If word of these cases of extreme devotion reached the king, and if he authorized it, a monument was erected for the woman. Looking somewhat like grave markers, monuments—inscribed stone stele—were only erected for reasons of hyo (filial piety), ch'ung (loyalty),

65

and *yŏl* (devotion and faithfulness of women). In each case one had to have the royal imprimatur before the monument could be built.

## Mme Hyŏn and the Tiger

An interesting case from the late Chosŏn period recorded in the *Shillok*, the case of Mme Hyŏn and the tiger, dramatically shows the process of becoming recognized as a *yŏllyŏ*. The Ministry of Rites recommended to the king that a monument be erected for Mme Hyŏn, saying:

> In Anbyŏn county [northern Korea], the scholar Yi Chong-hyŏn and his daughter-in-law, Mme Hyŏn, were walking across a field when suddenly a ferocious tiger jumped out and grabbed the father-in-law. His life was in great peril; Mme Hyŏn began tugging at her father-in-law with her left hand and hitting the tiger with her right hand. She cried in a loud voice, "Take me, not him!", and continued unceasingly. This went on for what seemed like half a day. Finally, the tiger gave up, let the man go, and left. Mme Hyŏn carried Yi on her back to their home and nursed him back to health.[1]

After consideration, the king issued the decree that a monument be built.[2]

## Marriage

The "seven grounds for divorce" (*ch'ilgŏ chi ak*), was more than a mere aphorism. We can find cases of divorce based on each of them.[3] The seven grounds were disobedient of the parents-in-law, childlessness, adultery, theft, jealousy, chronic illness and talkativeness. A dispute involving divorce for reasons of childlessness that came before King Sejong (r. 1418-1450) in 1425 is illustrative.

Ch'oe Chu accused his son-in-law, Yi Mi, of bigamy. Yi's response was that his wife, Mme Ch'oe, was fortyfive years old and had no children, and therefore he had no choice but to divorce her. He then married the daughter of Kang Pi-ho. Ch'oe Chu brought the matter to the Censorate, accusing Yi Mi of criminality. The Censorate acquitted Yi but at the same time they reinstated Mme Ch'oe in the household on the basis of the

---

[1]Chŏngjo 13, 1789.7.*musul*; 27:46b (46:46).

[2]*Ibid.*, 27:47a (46:47).

[3]Yi T'ae-yŏng, *Han'guk ihon chedo yŏn'gu* [Research on divorce in Korea] (Seoul: Yŏsŏng munje yŏn'guwŏn [The Women's Research Center], 1957).

*sambugŏ*, the three principles of assurance against divorce, i.e., she had mourned for Yi Mi's parents.

Yi, however, said that Mme Ch'oe, in her embarrassment over the issue, left the household on her own. Yi provided housing at a farm of his and saw that she had food to eat and slaves to work for her. After several months, her father, Ch'oe Chu, again petitioned the Censorate, saying that Yi had sent Mme Ch'oe away and had taken Mme Kang back.

The Censorate questioned Yi, who responded: "She lives in my farm house, eats my food, and works my slaves. One cannot say that I sent her away." Yi argued that the primary role of a wife is to provide an heir for the ancestors; a wife who does not have a child offends the ancestors, he said. From the ancestor's point of view, he asked, could they possibly consider not having an heir unimportant? Taking a second wife, he argued, was the lesser of two evils.

Yi argued that of the seven grounds for divorce some are minor and some are serious. Divorce for reasons of jealousy, chronic illness and talkativeness are three minor reasons that can be overridden by the *sambugŏ* rule. Divorce, however, for disobedience to the parents-in-law, childlessness, adultery and thievery are four serious criteria. He went on to argue that although law must conform to morality, law must also conform to emotion, especially in regard to the issue of childlessness. Of the offenses of the children of men, none is greater than being unfilial, Yi said [quoting Mencius], and nothing is more unfilial than being childless.

Yi's defense was based on his argument that disobedience, childlessness, adultery, and thievery—four serious grounds for divorce—could not be overridden by the *sambugŏ* assurances. The Censorate did not accept Yi's argument and judged that he had not obeyed the order to reinstate Mme Ch'oe. They recommended 90 stripes. Sejong concurred.[4]

The underlying principle in the above case is monogamy. Although Koryŏ dynasty Koreans could have more than one wife, in the early Chosŏn dynasty, in 1413, a law was promulgated limiting a man to one legal wife; he could have concubines but only one legitimate wife.[5] The charge of bigamy was a serious one.

---

[4]Sejong 7, 1425.11.*shinhae*; 30:14a (2:701). Two days later Yu Sa-gün asked that Yi Mi be given an even heavier penalty. Sejong responded that 90 stripes was enough; Sejong 7, 1425.11.*kyech'uk*; 30:15a (2:701). For an explanation of the function of the Censorate, see E. W. Wagner, *The Literati Purges*, p. 15.

[5]Martina Deuchler, "The Tradition: Women during the Yi Dynasty", *Virtues in Conflict: Tradition and the Korean Women Today*, ed. Sandra Mattielli (Seoul: Royal Asiatic Society/Samwha Publishing Co., 1977), pp. 15-17.

## The Case of Sŏng Chin, the Marriage Requirement

Not only could a man have only one wife, he was expected to have a wife. An amusing illustration from 1465 shows one opinion on the subject.[6]

Third Censor, Cho Min, said, "In our law, an unmarried man cannot serve in the Censorate. And yet Sŏng Chin, who is unmarried, was appointed."

King Sejo (r. 1455-1468) said, "When did such a law originate? Would you imply that a man should not take the exams until he is married?"

Cho answered that he did not know when the law was decreed but that the intent of the law was to see that the ancestors of the candidate and his wife were free from misconduct. "How can one be sure that his wife's ancestors are free of misconduct if he is not married yet?" he asked.

King Sejo closed the discussion by stating that such problems can be handled as they arise.

The king was often involved in settling family disputes. The throne, in its capacity as judge, functioned as the court of final appeal (although the criticisms of the Censorate would at times cause the king to reverse a decision). Among the issues pertaining to family and lineage that reached the ears of the king were numerous disputes about marriage, especially in the earlier centuries of the dynasty. At the outset of the dynasty, with its ruling against multiple marriage in 1413, there were numerous cases that served as tests of the court's resolve to enforce the decree. These cases also reveal the status of women and the changes in their status in the same time frame that their rights to inheritance changed.

In the following cases the central question became the status of the women in the marriage. Although a man could have only one wife, he could have a formal relationship with additional women, women who would be classed as secondary wives or concubines (ch'ŏp). There were two categories of ch'ŏp, a commoner woman and a slave woman.[7] Taking a ch'ŏp was not a great problem (although there are stories of conflict between

---

[6]Sejo 11, 1465.3.shinyu; 35:21b (7:676).

[7]For a comparison with the situation in China, see Patricia Ebrey "Concubines in Sung China," *Journal of Family History* 11:1-24 (1986). Therein she argues that concubines should not be considered wives or even secondary wives (p. 2) and that they were more like a servants (p. 12). She also argues that footbinding and other oppression of women, made wives more like concubines than vice versa (p. 20). In Korea, treatment of a commoner concubine was perhaps better than in China, but the slave concubine may indeed have been like the Chinese concubine.

the wife and the *ch'ŏp*); the problem was centered on the offspring of such unions. Called *sŏja*, they were lost between the *yangban* status of their fathers and the commoner or slave status of their mothers. But that subject will be presented in chapter five after an examination of the problems of marriage here.

## Bigamy: The Case of Ko T'ae-p'il

The outline of the Ko case was presented in the *Shillok*.[8] The Censorate charged that Ko T'ae-p'il falsely claimed that his first wife was dead when he submitted his documents for an appointment to office. "Now," they said, "we find that his first wife is alive. This should be investigated by the police and he should be charged with bigamy." The Censorate's complaint said:

Ko, the son of General Ko Tŭk-chong, is from Cheju Island and originally married the daughter of Ko Chun, a fellow villager. But he was ashamed of his wife when he achieved success. He, therefore, falsely claimed she had died and married the daughter of Kim Am, an aristocrat. Since his first wife did not die, he should be charged with perjury and dismissed.[9]

Ko was not sentenced for nearly a year, at which time, 1452, the *Shillok* stated: "The former official, Ko T'ae-p'il, was sentenced to 90 stripes, his second wife was expelled, and his first wife restored to the household."[10] A few months later it was proposed that Ko T'ae-p'il's office warrants be permanently revoked.[11] Ko weathered the storm, however, and later rose to hold high office including director of the National Academy (Sŏnggyun'gwan), ambassador to China, and governor of Chŏlla province. Practicing bigamy in the mid-fifteenth century was not a major obstacle to progress in Ko's official career. In the early phase of the transition one

---

[8]Munjong 1, 1451.7.*chŏngmi*; 8:32b (6:410).

[9]*Ibid.* The reason that Ko was ashamed of his wife may have been that she had the same surname, and was from the same village, and was therefore probably a close relative. Close cousin marriage was practiced in the Koryŏ and early Chosŏn period but came to be viewed as incestuous in later generations; perhaps at that time, Seoul residents had already come to look down on close kin marriage, but those living on distant Cheju Island had not yet.

[10]Munjong 2, 1452.3.*imsul*; 12:42b (6:480). The *munkwa pangmok* (examination roster) of 1451 lists Ko and gives Kim Am as his father-in-law.

[11]Tanjong 0, 1452.10.*shinmyo*; 4:2a (6:547).

could survive, but in later cases the question of proper marriage became more important.

## The Case of Kim Hyŏng

A censor, Min Chong-sun, submitted a memorial wherein he stated that the distinction between wife and concubine should be strictly observed. Whereas two wives were permissible in the Koryŏ period, the Chosŏn Code prohibited a man from having two legitimate wives, he said. Then Kim leveled a specific criticism at Kim Hyŏng saying that he had married the daughter of Min Yŏ-ik, had no children, and then married the daughter of To I-gong by whom he had two sons. Since he lived with both women at the same time, the censor argued, the two children were *sŏja*.

Kim Hyŏng's brothers and brothers-in-law were all interrogated; they all said Mme To was a *ch'ŏp*. As further evidence, Mme To lived with Mme Ha, the mother of Kim Hyŏng, but Mme Min lived in the patrilineal household. King Sejo directed that the matter be examined again at a later date.[12]

The Censorate, represented again by Min Chong-sun, raised the issue of Kim Hyŏng's multiple marriage a second time thirty days later. The attack was stronger. As one indication, now in reference to the second wife he no longer used the honorific, "-*ssi*," madam, but rather used a derogatory expression, the term "*yŏ*," woman, "*To-yŏ*," the woman To. He charged that Kim did not prepare a marriage document at the time of the second marriage but that he produced one later with a falsified date affixed. Although Mme To claimed to be of aristocratic status, the charge was that, since Kim had lived with both women at the same time, Mme To was a *ch'ŏp* and that her children were *sŏja*. Admittedly, Kim was only trying to attain legitimate status for his children, but the Censorate argued that the Code clearly stated that ceremonies can be performed by a *sŏja* in the absence of a legitimate heir; therefore, there was no need for Kim to promote the *sŏja* to legitimate status. The Censorate concluded with a fervent plea to the king that he rule in favor of a strict distinction between the legitimate and the illegitimate. The verdict, however, is not recorded.[13]

---

[12]Sejo 11, 1465.1.*chŏngch'uk*; 35:8a (7:670) and *Mansŏng taedong po* [The grand genealogy of the myriad lineages] hereinafter *MTP* A:178b,4d.

[13]Sejo 11, 1465.2.*chŏngmi*; 35:17b (7:674). One can speculate that Sejo agreed with the Censorate and that the brief indication of agreement was left out inadvertently by the *Shillok* compilers. However, as with the first hearing thirty days earlier, it is also possible that Sejo either postponed a decision indefinitely or rejected the Censorate's request.

## The Case of Hwang Hyo-wŏn

The late fifteenth century was marked with controversy over legitimacy of wives and children. Perhaps the most famous, certainly the most drawn-out, case of the period was the that of Hwang Hyo-wŏn (1414-1481).[14]

Hwang was a powerful figure at court. He had twice been a *kongshin* (enrolled as a "merit subject"); he had helped put Sejo on the throne and was on the merit list proclaimed in the second year of King Sŏngjong's reign (r. 1469-1494). He was sixty-one when the problem began at court. Sŏngjong was eighteen.

In the third month of 1475, the Ministry of Rites charged Hwang with bigamy, "taking a wife while having a wife." He was married to a Mme Shin but had married a Mme Im whom he claimed was also a legitimate wife, not a concubine. Sŏngjong stood by Hwang and the case was dismissed, for a time.[15]

In the fifth month of 1476, Hwang was accused of keeping three wives, not just two. Not only was the Censorate dissatisfied with the resolution of the Mme Shin-Mme Im controversy, but Hwang had begun to regard the children of a certain Mme Yi, who had been assumed to be a *ch'ŏp*, as legitimate heirs. Hwang was particularly anxious to see the two sons by Mme Yi succeed in social and political matters. She was the daughter of Yi Yu-gi, a man who had clearly been a member of the aristocratic class but who had been purged by Sejo when he usurped the throne in 1455.[16] Mme Yi was given to Hwang as a servant, but he assigned her to work in the home of his mother, Mme O. Mme O was good to the young girl, apparently regarding her as a member of the aristocratic class rather than forcing her to do menial work. As time went by, she attracted Hwang's attention. The argument against her centered on her status as the daughter of a traitor. The counter-argument was that she

---

[14]The standard biographical dictionary mentions Hwang Hyo-wŏn's marital problems and states, "He changed wife and concubine so frequently that to the end of his life he was embroiled in suits at court." It also says he was known for his greed and was called "*hwagaong*," ("rich old man"). *Han'guk inmyŏng taesajŏn* (hereinafter *HIT*) [Biographical dictionary of Korea] (Seoul: Shin'gu munhwasa, 1976), p. 1071.

[15]Sŏngjong 6, 1475.3.*kabin*; 53:3a (9:207).

[16]The *Shillok* records the awarding of Yi Yu-gi's daughter, "Chagŭnjori" (which means little girl, and may not have been her name) to Hwang Hyo-wŏn as part of the justice meted out to the "traitor" at the time of the Sejo takeover, Sejo 2, 1456,9. *kapsul*; 5:9a (7:151). Yi's wife and two other daughters were given to Chŏng Ch'ang-son, Sejo 2, 1456,9.*kapsul*; 5:8b (7:150). Yi's land, along with that of others accused of plotting to restore Tanjong to the throne, was confiscated and given to Sejo loyalists. A *shillok* entry for the following year indicates Yi's property was divided up and given to Yun Am, Yang Chŏng, and Cho Sŏng-mun, Sejo 3, 1457,3.*pyŏngsul*; 7:17a-b (7:188).

was an aristocratic woman entitled to legitimate wife status, in spite of her father's record.[17]

The arguments raged for days. Occasionally new information or a new approach was used, but generally the Censorate repeated the basic charge and Sŏngjong would either refute it or ignore it. In the fifth month, the case was aired seventeen times on fifteen different days. At one time Hwang was accused of seven specific crimes. The fact that the Koryŏ dynasty had allowed multiple marriage was mentioned, but it was stressed that the Yi court had laws against it. Initially, Sŏngjong insisted that Mme Yi was of aristocratic status because she was a descendant of Yi Saek[18] (a prominent scholar-official at the founding of the Chosŏn period), but later he relented and agreed that she should be deemed a *ch'ŏp*.[19]

In the sixth month, the case was brought up fourteen more times on eight different days.[20] On the first day of the month, Ch'oe Han-jŏng, who proved to be Hwang's most persistent critic, quoted a poem from the *Shih Ching* which said:

> The marabon is on the dam
> The crane is in the forest.

The poem implies that the queen and the concubine have traded places. The marabon, a scavenger, cannot become a crane; a concubine cannot become a wife; the illegitimate cannot become legitimate.[21] On the second day of the month, the *Shillok* records the issue as having been raised four different times.[22] In the seventh month, the issue was brought before the king twenty-seven times on fifteen different days. On several occasions, a censor indicated he wanted to raise the issue of Hwang Hyo-wŏn's marriages, whereupon Sŏngjong dismissed the subject out of hand.[23]

---

[17] The first of these arguments to appear in the *Shillok* was on Sŏngjong 7, 1476.5.*kapchin*; 67:2b (9:337). The events of the fifth month are found in 67:2b-21a (9:337-347).

[18] Sŏngjong 7, 1476.5.*kisa*; 67:19b (9:346).

[19] Sŏngjong 7, 1476.5.*kyŏngo*; 67:20b-21a (9:346-347).

[20] The record of the sixth month is found in Sŏngjong 7, 1476.6, beginning with *imshin*; it occupies all of volume 68 (9:347-354).

[21] Sŏngjong 7, 1476.6.*imshin*; 68:1b (9:347). The quotation from the *Shih Ching*, the Chinese classic of poetry, II.viii.v.6, is found in the Legge translation on page 417.

[22] Sŏngjong 7, 1476.6.*kyeyu*; 68:2b (9:348).

[23] The events of the seventh month are found in Sŏngjong 7, 1476.7; throughout volume 69 (9:355-367).

Finally, in the eighth month Sǒngjong was forced to agree that Hwang was not without error and gave him a token punishment.[24] Two days later, the Censorate complained that the punishment was too light.[25]

The case was mentioned once in the ninth month[26] and three times in the twelfth month.[27] Each of the last three occurrences was a detailed presentation of the basic argument all over again. Sǒngjong rejected each presentation and the matter was put to rest for four years.

Whether the Censorate had dropped the Hwang case over those four years or whether the *Shillok* was silent on the matter is difficult to determine, but in the fourth and sixth months of 1480 the case reappeared.[28] In the next year the Censorate warmed up with one mention in the first month and one in the fifth[29] but then unloaded in the seventh, eighth, and ninth months.[30] They dragged out all the old arguments that had consumed so much court time in previous years. The complaints tended to focus on the status of the third wife, Mme Yi, but did mention the other two as well. One new argument was interesting. Hwang had argued that the third wife, Mme Yi, although the daughter of a traitor, was, nonetheless, from a prominent family and therefore qualified to be a legitimate wife. But the Censorate found that her sister had married as a concubine, and they argued that two sisters in the same family should have the same status.[31] On another occasion one censor, Kang Cha-p'yǒng, dramatically stated that if this matter went unchecked the Chosǒn state would retrogress to the standards of the Koryǒ period when a man could have four wives.[32]

The newfound enthusiasm of the Censorate to pursue the case again in the fall of 1481 may have arisen because they perceived weakness in the opposition; Hwang died in the middle of the ninth month.[33]

---

[24]Sǒngjong 7, 1476.8.*ǔlmi*; 70:18a (9:377).

[25]Sǒngjong 7, 1476.8.*chǒngyu*; 70:22a (9:379).

[26]Sǒngjong 7, 1476.9.*shinch'uk*; 71:1a (9:380).

[27]Each occurrence was about a week apart. Sǒngjong 7, 1476.12.*kyǒngo, ǔlhae*, and *imo*; 74:1a, 3b, and 6b (9:397-399).

[28]Sǒngjong 11, 1480.4.*kyeyu*; 116:7a (10:120) and 1480.6.*shinyu*; 118:8b (10:138).

[29]Sǒngjong 12, 1481.1.*kyǒngjin*; 125:5a (10:184) and 1481.5.*musul*; 129:17a (10:218).

[30]These are found between Sǒngjong 12, 1481.7.*imjin*; 131:7a (10:243) and the ninth month, 1481.9.*chǒngch'uk*; 133:8a (10:255).

[31]Sǒngjong 12, 1481.9.*ǔlhae*; 133:2b (10:254).

[32]Sǒngjong 12, 1481.9.*pyǒngja*; 133:3b (10:255).

[33]Sǒngjong 12, 1481.9.*kyǒngin*; 133:8a (10:257).

The issue of Hwang Hyo-wŏn having more than one wife was laid to rest with him when he died. But the status of his heirs was not. Hwang's wives and children remained under scrutiny, it appears. It was not until three years had passed, in the tenth month of 1484, that Mme Yi again appears in the pages of the *Shillok*. She was accused of sleeping at a Buddhist temple, which good aristocratic women ought not do. The Censorate urged the king to send investigators to find out if it was true. Sŏngjong refused, saying Buddhist temples were sanctuaries.[34] The Censorate pursued the matter again two months later. On five separate occasions over a six-day period they insisted that she be arrested and interrogated.[35] They said: "An aristocratic woman goes about covered. Is she remaining covered in the presence of the monks?" Sŏngjong absolutely refused to yield and the matter was dropped.[36] But the posterity of Hwang Hyo-wŏn was yet to be free from scandal.

The daughter of Hwang and Mme Yi married Pak Yŏng-mun. The legitimacy of their son, Yang, was called into question when he was nominated for a post in 1507. The Censorate said he should not serve, but King Chungjong (r. 1506-1544) argued that he was certainly legitimate and should serve.[37] The issue was raised twice more and each time Chungjong stood by Pak.[38]

Six years later, however, Pak Yŏng-mun, along with Shin Yun-mu, was accused of plotting to overthrow the throne. The plot was discovered through the report of an eavesdropping slave, and Pak was found guilty and executed. Pak's two sons, Hwang's grandsons, were also executed. Pak's wife, the granddaughter of a traitor and the daughter of a woman once enslaved and then married to the man most notorious in all the Chosŏn period for his marriages, was herself enslaved.[39] Hwang's daughter was thus

---

[34]Sŏngjong 15, 1484.10.*chŏngmyo*; 171:8b (10:631).

[35]The five days are in Sŏngjong 15, 1484, twelfth month; *kyŏngshin*; 173:6a (10:650); *imsul*; 173:8a (10:651); *kapcha*; 173:10b (10:652); *ŭlch'uk*; 173:13b (10:654); and *pyŏngin*; 173:14a (10:654).

[36]Sŏngjong 15, 1484.12.*ŭlch'uk*; 173:13b (10:654).

[37]Chungjong 2, 1507.i1.*kyŏngsul*; 2:15a (14:116). The fact that she, with tainted status, could marry a man from an apparently prominent and untainted family shows that the prejudice did not prevent her from entering into a marriage with an aristocrat. It only became an issue when the man entered the political sphere.

[38]Chungjong 2, 1507.i1.*kapsul*; 2:27b (14:122) and 1507.2.*ŭlhae*; 2:28b (14:123).

[39]Chungjong 8, 1513.10.*pyŏngjin*; 19:11a (14:683). See also Wagner, *The Literati Purges*, p. 200, note 48. Also see page 80 for the details of the conspiracy. The other children of Hwang Hyo-wŏn fared much better. Many of his descendants held important government positions both military and civilian, and some passed examinations. See the *Sangju Hwang-ssi chokpo* (1969 edition).

sentenced to the status from which her mother had been rescued by her father.

## The Case of Hong Yun-sŏng

Hong Yun-sŏng (1425-1475) was a contemporary of Hwang Hyo-wŏn and, like Hwang, was the center of controversy at court over the issue of multiple marriage. Hong Yun-sŏng had a wife, Mme Nam, who had no sons;[40] he divorced her and married a Mme Kim. The problem was that there were witnesses who said that Mme Nam had not left the household but that she and Mme Kim lived together in the household at the same time. Furthermore, Mme Nam had performed the mourning rituals for Hong's father after Mme Kim came into the household. The conclusion was, therefore, that Mme Kim was a concubine, not a legitimate wife.

Han Myŏng-hoe and others testified that although the timing was not precise, it was clear that Mme Nam lived separately and that Mme Kim should be regarded as a legitimate second wife.[41]

It was alleged that Hong's marriage to Mme Kim was fraught with problems. Not only was there the question of the status of Mme Nam, but in the initial contacts with the Kim family, representations were made which suggested Hong was interested in a marriage mate for his son, not for himself.[42]

The argument had initially centered on whether there had been a ceremony at the time of Mme Kim's marriage, but later, when the issue was again brought before the king, the argument shifted. It was argued that whether there was a ceremony for Mme Kim or not, Mme Nam had not been divorced in actuality because she continued to reside in Hong's household. Therefore, Mme Kim was a concubine.[43] The queen mother, a relative of Mme Kim, entered the argument on Mme Kim's behalf.[44] After three more attempts, the Censorate gave up. Like the Hwang Hyo-wŏn

---

[40]Hong did have a daughter who married Shim Tam; Sŏngjong 7, 1476.4.*muin*; 66:3a (9:331). Hong passed the *munkwa* exam in 1450.

[41]Sŏngjong 7, 1476.7.*kiyu*; 69:4a (9:357).

[42]Sŏngjong 7, 1476.4.*chŏngch'uk*; 66:1b (9:330) and three times on the subsequent two days; *muin*; 66:3a (9:331); *kyŏngjin*; 66:4b (9:331); and 66:5a (9:332).

[43]Sŏngjong 7, 1476.8.*pyŏngch'uk*; 70:4b (9:370).

[44]Sŏngjong 7, 1476.8.*imo*; 70:10a (9:373), see also 70:11a. A year later, the *Shillok* records an anecdote about Hong Yun-sŏng included in a biographical entry for Hŏ Hyŏng-son. At a banquet in honor of Hŏ, who was preparing to leave on an embassy for Beijing, Hong offered him a glass of wine. Hŏ refused it. Hong said angrily, "Why don't you accept my wine?" Hŏ responded, "You have been a corrupt man all your life," at which Hŏ attempted to strike Hong. Hong ran off. Sŏngjong 8, 1477.*imja;* 75:16b (9:411).

case, the descendants of the additional wife, with the compliance of the king, escaped being labelled as *sŏja*.

### The Dispute Between Hŏ Hyŏng and Hŏ Hon

When there was a dispute over which of two wives was legitimate, generally the first wife was considered the primary, or legitimate, wife. The case of Hŏ Hyŏng is one where the opposite interpretation resulted (although in this case social status of the wives was also important).

Mme Nam, the wife of the deceased Minister of Public Works, Hŏ Yŏng, submitted a petition stating that her son, Hyŏng, had called her husband "father" and that Hŏ Yŏng took Hyŏng's mother (herself) as a legitimate wife. She submitted the documents of her marriage with her petition. She said the reason she was submitting a petition was that Hŏ Hon had been saying that she, Mme Nam, was a concubine and that his (Hon's) mother, Mme Ha, was the legitimate wife. But Hyŏng's mother, Mme Nam, was certainly the legitimate wife, she argued, because she was married to Hŏ Yŏng for three years before he took Hon's mother, Mme Ha, to wife.

The opposing argument was that Mme Nam had said nothing for over ten years since the death of Hŏ Yŏng. His heirs had already divided the inheritance and the document was registered in the Konyang county office. The government investigators found that the household documents had been destroyed in a fire, but the inheritance documents of Konyang county (South Kyŏngsang Province) were intact and made reference to "the *sŏja*, Hwa-sang." Hwa-sang was the childhood name of Hyŏng. In addition, the census registers of Yangch'ŏn county over a period of several years listed Mme Nam as Hyŏng's mother with the appellation "*chori*," commoner woman.[45]

The Censorate concluded: "The status of Mrs. Nam [Nam-*chori*] and Mme Ha [Ha-*ssi*] is clear. It is recommended that Mme Ha be considered the wife and Mrs. Nam the concubine." The king concurred.[46]

### The Pong Hoe Case

In a case that surfaced two years later, the debate on the legitimacy of a man named Pong Hoe, similar arguments emerged. He was the son of the first wife, who was the daughter of a petty government functionary

---

[45]The term *chori* is given in *idu*; although the prunnunciation of the characters is *sosa* in Sino-Korean pronunciation, the pure Korean version is *chori*.

[46]Sŏngjong 10, 1479.8.*musul*; 107:8a-b (10:43).

(*hyangni*). Hoe's father later married a *yangban* woman, Mme Yi. His father designated Hoe as a *sŏja* in his will.

The king, however, said that Hoe had served as a magistrate and in the old days men could have two wives, and just because a father loves a second wife and forces his son to sign a document does not make the son a *sŏja*. The Chief State Councilor concurred and said that loving one wife and hating the other is not the basis for designating a legitimate son as a *sŏja*. The king ruled that although the document stated Hoe was a *sŏja*, by emotion and logic, he was clearly legitimate.[47]

Eleven days later, Yi In-sŏk charged that Pong was the son of a concubine and that there was little to be said in his defense since he was specifically listed as such in his father's will. The king again argued that the marriage took place at a time when a man could have two wives simultaneously and, furthermore, Hoe held important office in his own right. Clearly, he was not to be regarded as a concubine's son.[48]

The following day, Kim Sŏk submitted a petition concerning the case to which the king reiterated his earlier judgment and added that Hoe had also held important government office, a position that a *sŏja* could not hold.[49]

The next day, Chŏng Kwal repeated the argument that Pong Hoe was referred to as a *sŏja* in a document written by his father and signed by Hoe himself. The king said that still Hoe had held an important post that a *sŏja* could not hold. Chŏng Kwal argued that since Hoe's own signature indicated that he was a *sŏja* his holding important office was a criminal offense. Chŏng concluded that although Pong Hoe's case did not harm the government, still it confused the moral order. The king disagreed and said he would have nothing to do with any further discussion of the matter.[50]

## The Ha Pok-saeng Case

The following year a case similar to Pong Hoe's was settled quickly. Kim Il-lyŏng petitioned the court saying his maternal grandfather, Ha Pok-saeng, was the son of Ha Ku who had married two wives before the decree of 1413 that prohibited multiple marriage. Although Ha Pok-saeng was the son of a second wife, since the marriage predated the decree, Kim argued, his grandfather should not be considered as a *sŏja*. (And if his

---

[47]Sŏngjong 12, 1481.2.*kyech'uk*; 126:5a (10:194).

[48]Sŏngjong 12, 1481.2.*kapcha*; 126:7a (10:195).

[49]Sŏngjong 12, 1481.2.*ŭlch'uk*; 126:7b (10:195).

[50]Sŏngjong 12, 1481.2.*pyŏngin*; 126:7b (10:195).

grandfather was not a *sŏja*, then he would not be viewed as a *sŏja*.) The king agreed.[51]

## Multiple Marriage and Heirship

Multiple marriage for the sake of begetting an heir was a path filled with pitfalls. The decree in 1413 that prohibited multiple marriage was accepted throughout society and enforced. Those few in the following decades that challenged the law failed. The Chosŏn period settled on monogamy as the legal and social norm, and yet when a man did not have a son, an additional marriage was still an alternative that he could pursue. An additional marriage with a yangban woman was not possible after 1413, but an informal marriage with a commoner or slave was. The problem then was the status of the heir; classified as a *sŏja*, by statute he was limited in opportunities to take exams and serve in government offices, which in turn made him less than a satisfactory heir. These issues will be taken up in chapter five.

Divorcing the childless wife was an option, but was seen as too severe an option for most aristocrats. In addition, if one defines marriage in traditional Korea as an alliance between lineages, divorce was not a simple matter of sending away an individual; it was the severance of a multifaceted alliance. It was not easily done.

As for the wife, there were changes in her status at various levels. On the one hand, she was losing her rights to inheritance and to participate in the rituals. But her standing in the household was protected by the law of 1413 which prohibited a wife of equal status from entering the household. Another woman could enter the household but she would clearly be of secondary, either commoner or slave, status. Underlying these changes were changes in marriage patterns. As in the Koryŏ period, uxorilocal marriage was still practiced well into the seventeenth century, but clearly the preference for patrilocal marriage was on the rise.

The status of the woman, as wife and mother, was being pushed in opposing directions. On the one hand, she was being disinherited in her natal home, was no longer bringing in a resident husband, but was moving

---

[51]Sŏngjong 13, 1482.5.*muin*; 141:5b (10:332). See *MTP* B:244a,4d for the Ha lineage, that of the wife of Ha Pok-saeng. See *MTP* A:154a,1a for the Kim lineage. Since Kim married the daughter of Ko Tŭk-chong, a *munkwa* passer (*MTP* B:241,4c), he apparently did not suffer from the *sŏja* stigma.

Notice that these two cases, Pong and Ha, the marriages had apparently taken place prior to 1413, the year of the proscription against multiple marriage, and the arguments were unfolding in 1481 and 1482, when the children of the marriage must have been over seventy years old.

out to the husband's home (and called "the stranger who moved out" [*ch'ulga oein*]). On the other hand, her position as the wife and mother in the home was reinforced by the rule of monogamy. She, and only she, was the wife and the one in charge of the domestic scene. Later, in chapter nine, we will see her authority in deciding adoptions was held inviolable, for example. Her husband could take in other partners (*ch'ŏp*), but a *ch'ŏp* could never become a legitimate wife. Divorce was rare; therefore, only if the first wife died could a man take a second wife. The wife was often referred to by the name of her home village (e.g. *Hahoe t'aek*)—a constant reminder of the noble lineage from whence she came. This claim of independent status which was tied to her natal home and lineage is probably the reason that Korean women today do not take their husband's name when they marry. It is not, as is easy to assume, that they are not allowed membership in the husband's lineage, but rather a recognition of the status of her natal home and lineage. Of course, as time went by, the value of the wife's lineage may have decreased as the emphasis on patrilineality grew and the role of males in society became ever more dominant. But in the beginning, and at its root, the independence of the wife's last name was a symbol of her prominence.

# 5

# *Sŏja*

The child of a man by his wife is a legitimate heir, a *chŏkcha*. The child of a man of aristocratic status by a woman other than his legitimate wife, e.g. his *ch'ŏp* (commoner concubine or his slave), is a *sŏja*.[1] Throughout the dynasty there were some *sŏja* who became heirs to property and ceremonies, but in the majority of cases, the *sŏja* were not considered adequate heirs. More and more, as the dynasty wore on, the man who had only a *sŏja* adopted a nephew to be his heir, although there were some even at the end of the dynasty who maintained a *sŏja* as an heir.

The story of the *sŏja* in the Chosŏn period begins with T'aejong (r. 1400-1418), the third king, who staged a preemptive coup in which the designated crown prince, his half-brother, was killed. The crown prince, Pang-sŏk, was the son of T'aejo (r. 1392-1398) by his second wife. Although one could argue the point of calling the son of a king a *sŏja*, to do so certainly helped T'aejong justify what he did. However, several of subsequent kings were born to palace women, not to queens, yet they did not seem to be impaired in their function as king.

T'aejong decreed that *sŏja* and their descendants would not be allowed to serve in high offices. The order was a response to the petition of Sŏ Sŏn. Allegedly, Sŏ disliked Chŏng To-jŏn, the chief advisor to T'aejo and

---

[1]The term "*sŏja*" is often translated as "illegitimate child," but the connotation in English, and in a Western cultural context, is somewhat different from that in Korean. Although several terms are available in Korean, each with a slightly different nuance, "*sŏja*" is the most general and most used. Herein, rather than using a translated term, because of the unique cultural usage of the term, *sŏja* will be used. The term is comprised of two characters, the first meaning "common," the second meaning "son." The term *sŏja* in a general sense applies only to a male member of the aristocratic class who has a son by a woman of the commoner class or of the slave class or by a woman who is herself of *sŏja* status. More specifically, *sŏja* means a son by a commoner concubine, whereas the term "*ŏlcha*" means a son by a slave woman. The term "*sŏŏl*" is used as a collective term to mean both *sŏja* and *ŏlcha*. Another term frequently encountered is "*ch'ŏpcha*," concubine's son. For the sake of simplicity, I will use the term "*sŏja*" throughout.

supporter of Crown Prince Pang-sŏk, and even after Chŏng's death was intent on vengeance against him. One of the sources of the story is the *Kyusa*, a compilation of various documents published in 1859 covering the period from the founding of the dynasty up to the time of publication.[2]

Arguing that *sŏja* were treated unjustly, the *Kyusa*'s accounts are somewhat biased at times. According to the *Kyusa*, Sŏ argued that, "To-jŏn was a *sŏja*. No *sŏja* descendant should hold high government office."[3] Also according to the *Kyusa*, Sŏ Sŏn returned home on that fateful day and was removing his robes when his wife asked, "What happened at court today?" Sŏ answered, "I petitioned the king that *sŏja* not be employed in officialdom." Her face lost its color. She said, "But you have no heirs." The account concluded with the ominous sentence, "And in the end, she was correct," implying that Sŏ got his just desserts for initiating prejudicial legislation against the *sŏja* of the Yi dynasty. The *Kyusa* version of the story is contradicted by other sources; the *Shillok* and the *MTP* indicate that Sŏ did have a child.[4] Other accounts in the *Kyusa* might be exaggerated as well.

Of course, the basis for T'aejong's acceptance of the proposal to impose restrictions on *sŏja* is much more complicated than one man's animosity for another. T'aejong's own interests were served. How could the discrediting of *sŏja* have appealed to the third king of the dynasty? One answer was offered by Cho Hŏn, a sixteenth century figure who eventually became one of the eighteen sages enshrined in the national Confucian

---

[2]Originally published in two volumes in 1859, the most accessible edition today is a photographic edition by Ewha University Press (Seoul: 1968). The *Kyusa* was patterned after earlier works and indeed may actually be a copy of a document submitted to the king—there were many times when *sŏja* petitioned the throne for redress. One such work, the *Soju yo o*, has recently be reprinted with the *Kyusa* and two other works in a volume titled *Chosŏn sŏŏl kwan'gye charyo chip* (A collection of resources concerning *sŏja* [*sŏŏl*] of the Chosŏn period). Whereas the *Soju yo o* was handcopied, the *Kyusa* was printed, indicating it had a wider circulation. For more on the *Kyusa*, see Yi Ki-baek, "Shipku segi han'guksahak üi sae yangsang," *Han U-gŭn paksa chŏngnyŏn kinyŏm sahak nonch'ong*, Chishik sanŏpsa, 1981; and Chŏng Yun-ju, "*Kyusa* (1859) üi p'yŏnch'an kwa kanhaengdonggi," *Yŏksa hakpo*, 137:33, 1993.3.

The term "*kyu*" means sunflower and "*sa*" means history. The sunflower was used symbolically to represent the *sŏja* because of a poem written by King Sŏnjo:
Sunflowers always face the sun;
Not just the large ones, but those that are all around.
The king's subjects desire to be loyal to him-
Is this only for the legitimate? (*Kyusa*, 1:6b)

[3]*Kyusa*, 1:3a-3b. The source cited by the *Kyusa* for this episode was a *yasa*, an unofficial history written by a private individual. The *Shillok* also covers the episode saying the legislation was sponsored by Sŏ Sŏn, and five other unnamed individuals. It makes no mention of Chŏng To-jŏn. T'aejong 15, 1415.6.*kyŏngin*; 29:47b-48a (2:72).

[4]Sejong 15, 1433.4.*kyemyo*; 60:5a (3:465), lines 3-8 contain Sŏ Sŏn's obituary.

shrine. His interpretation of the early Chosŏn events was that the founders of the dynasty sought ways of limiting access to power and thus concentrating power in the hands of a few who would pass power on to their descendants. By imposing restrictions on *sŏja* and sons of remarried women, Cho argued, the early Yi aristocracy sought to concentrate power in the hands of a relatively small elite class. He said:

> Since the mid Koryŏ period, the powerful have been in charge of the country. They feared the rising of people in the countryside; they themselves blocked the road of the *sŏja* and narrowed the pathway to government service. In our dynasty, those who control the country, in order to set up a plan so that only their descendants can serve, and without concern for the potentially great man in future generations, have also blocked the road for the descendants of twice-married women.[5]

Whatever the motivation or reasons for enacting the legislation,[6] the important fact is that for the remainder of the dynasty, the *sŏja* suffered the effects of the legislation. They did not suffer in complete silence, however. There were several occasions when one or a few or several *sŏja* made their complaints known.[7]

With limitations on the political status of *sŏja* in place, it was not long before their status within the family and the lineage came into question. The issue surfaced on the pages of the *Shillok* in the sixteenth

---

[5]*Kyusa* 1:3b, quoting Cho Hŏn's collected writings, *Chungbong chip*.

[6]One of the more important articles on this subject was written by Yi Sang-baek in 1934, "Sŏŏl ch'adae ŭi yŏnwŏn e taehan il munje" [One problem concerning the origins of discrimination against illegitimates], *Chindan hakpo*, 1:26-55 (Nov. 1934). His essay begins, "With respect to the origins of this legislation [law barring illegitimates from public office], unique in the annals of human history, there are a variety of assessments and suppositions, but there is general agreement on the fact that Sŏ Sŏn was the first to advocate this, in 1415. The view that the impetus of Sŏ Sŏn's advocacy of the bar-from-office law lay in his personal antagonism toward Chŏng To-jŏn appears to be a potent one." He alludes to the fact that there are other views but deals only with this "one problem" in this article.

[7]The *Kyusa* records many of these complaints. The following is a table compiled from the pages of the *Kyusa* of petitions submitted to the throne. Note that many of them were given to a new king in the first year of his reign.

| Date | Number of Petitioners | Reign Period |
|---|---|---|
| 1568 | 1,600 | Sŏnjo 1 |
| 1695 | 988 from Kyŏngsang | Sukchong 21 |
| " | 1,000 from Chŏlla | " |
| 1724 | 5,000 | Yŏngjo 1 |
| 1801.1.10 | ? | Sunjo 1 |
| 1823.11.12 | 9,996 | Sunjo 23 |
| 1848 | 9,000 | Hŏnjong 14 |
| 1851 | 1,200 (?) | Ch'ŏlchong 1 |

year of Sejong's reign, 1434. Sejong ordered a meeting of the high officials to discuss the issue of *sŏja* born of commoner mothers serving as heirs (*sŭngjung*, a term used in this case to mean one who is a substitute or replacement in the lineage ceremonies). Representing one side of the question was Chief State Councilor Hwang Hŭi who stated: "If the mother of a *sŏja* is not of artisan or merchant background, and if she is chaste and is not a wanton woman, then the *sŏja* son can become a ritual heir (*chongja*)."[8]

On the other side of the question, Ch'oe Sa-ŭi, et. al., submitted a memorial saying:

> According to the customs of our country, the division between the legitimate and the illegitimate is strict. Among our leading families, I have never seen a case where the *sŏja* performs the ceremonies. According to our country's custom when the eldest legitimate son dies and he has not a legitimate son, to therefore abandon one's full [meaning born of the same mother] younger brother's son and instead to install the offspring of a concubine as the principal officiant at the lineage rituals, is not in accord with our country's practices.[9]

Kwŏn To of the Ministry of Rites then gave a lengthy presentation on the status of *sŏja* and the advantages and disadvantages of adoption rather than the use of the *sŏja* as an heir. His was certainly one of the first substantial arguments for the disinheriting of a *sŏja* and the adopting of a lineage nephew to be found in the records of the new dynasty. Among other things, he said:

> Among those who have no other heir but a *sŏja* and who transmit their heritage to the *sŏja*, few are able to preserve their family standing because "it is a shallow stream that flows from a meager spring."[10]

In response to the criticism that in adopting a son from among the sons of one's younger brother one emphasizes the collateral line and slights the main line, Kwŏn argued:

---

[8]Sejong 16, 1434.4.*kyehae*; 64:10b (3:557).
[9]*Ibid.*
[10]Sejong 16, 1434.4.*kyehae*; 64:11a (3:558).

But this is not so. In the classics of ritual it states, "If a lineal descendant (*chongson*) does not have an heir he can make a collateral son his successor." The term "make a successor" (*wijija* [adopt]) means to make the adopted son the same as one's own son. The adopted son serves the shrine of his adopted father [meaning he mourns three years] and only mourns one year for his natural parents. The ancient texts are clear on this point; there is no room for doubt. But in our dynasty we do not carry out the regulations of ritual succession and there are those who do not understand the prescribed procedures of ritual inheritance (*iphu* [adoption]).[11]

Kwŏn went on to argue that social customs do not change overnight, and therefore:

I would recommend, on the basis of an examination of the ritual precedence and current mores, that only a legitimate descendant be adopted, and that he serve as the ritual heir (*sŭngjung*). . . . And then the lineages (*chongjok*) will be peaceful and human morality will be fortified.[12]

## The Mojiri Case

In spite of the growing prejudice against *sŏja* in the early Chosŏn period, there were still certain prerogatives open to them, and certain of the early Chosŏn *sŏja* were successful. One notable case involved a man named Mojiri[13] who, although born to a slave mother, had his rights as the son of a *yangban* protected when adjudicated by King Munjong (r. 1450-1452).

The Censorate reported that a certain man named Mojiri claimed to be the *sŏja* of Hŏ An-sŏk. In Mojiri's claim set before the Censorate, he had charged that Hŏ's legitimate wife, Mme Yi, had conspired with her adopted daughter[14] and repudiated Mojiri saying that he was not Hŏ's *sŏja*. The Censorate requested that Mme Yi be brought in for questioning but Munjong responded that a man's wife could be interrogated on a charge like

---

[11]*Ibid.*

[12]Sejong 16, 1434.4.*kyehae*; 64:11b (3:558).

[13]Mojiri, in Chinese character transcription, was probably meant to be *mŏjiri*, pure Korean pejorative for dimwitted or stupid. It was common for slaves to bear non-flattering names, and his bearing such a name did not help him to portray himself as a *sŏja* of an aristocrat.

[14]Notice the presence of an adopted daughter. For more on adopted daughters, see chapter seven.

that of adultery, but she could not be interrogated on charges brought by her husband's *sŏja*.[15]

The next year the issue surfaced again. This time Pak P'aeng-nyŏn testified that Hŏ An-sŏk sent Mojiri to school when Hŏ was the magistrate of Kŭmsan. That was said to be solid evidence that Mojiri was his son. Hwang-bo In stated that he was suspicious of Mme Yi's claims because they seemed to be inspired by the greed of her adopted daughter, Mme Kwŏn. Munjong indicated that Mojiri's charges had given him sufficient suspicion to warrant sending the whole matter to the State Tribunal (*ŭigŭmbu*) for investigation.[16]

Three days later the background of the case was explained in a little more detail. Ch'ung-gae, the mother of Mojiri, was a slave of Hŏ An-sŏk's wife, Mme Yi. Ch'ung-gae had once been married to Kim Sŭng-jae, the slave of Yi Paek-cha, the younger brother of Mme Yi (Hŏ's wife). Some said Mojiri was Hŏ's son; some said he was Kim's son. Those who said he was Hŏ's son pointed out that Hŏ sent him to school, and when guests visited he would point to Mojiri and identify him as his son. Those who said he was Kim's son pointed out that Mojiri used the surname Kim and was recorded in public documents as Kim. He had also contended with Kim Sŭng-jae's second wife over Kim's property and had received a settlement of a portion of that property. It was suggested that the State Tribunal investigate the matter.[17]

Two months later the State Council discussed the issue with the king. There were those who discerned that there was criminal activity involved in the Mojiri case and urged the king to arrest and interrogate Mme Yi and Mme Kwŏn and others. The king refused to arrest the women but allowed that an investigation by the State Tribunal should proceed.[18]

Seventeen days later the State Tribunal reported that they had concluded their investigation and judged Mojiri to be the *sŏja* of Hŏ An-sŏk.[19] Two days later they submitted their recommendations for punishments of those who had committed perjury, including many of Mme Yi's relatives who received property that should have gone, and in the end did go, to Mojiri. Two officials who had conspired in the scheme were also punished. The women were regarded as more or less innocent pawns and

---

[15]Munjong 0, 1450.12.*shinmi*; 5:1a (6:323)

[16]Munjong 1, 1451.9.*kihae*; 9:23b (6:428).

[17]Munjong 1, 1451.9.*imin*; 9:29b (6:431).

[18]Munjong 1, 1451.11.*kabo*; 10:16a (6:449).

[19]Munjong 1, 1451.11.*shinhae*; 10:24b (6:453).

escaped serious punishment.[20] Mojiri's rights as a *sŏja* were protected and, in spite of an attempt by full-blooded aristocrat relatives and the collusion of officials, the low-born man received a substantial inheritance.[21]

## A Dispute Between a Man's Sŏja and a Female Cousin

In 1481, another *sŏja* won a major victory; this time in a dispute with a woman who was of legitimate status. The *sŏja* was Kim Hyŏn; his cousin, Mme Kim, was the wife of Yun U. The dispute over the property reached the throne. When the case first emerged, Sŏngjong's response was:

> Although Hyŏn is a *sŏja*, he is the lineage heir (*sŭngjungja*). Mme Kim acquired one house but intends to take the house that has the ancestral hall. Her accusations that Hyŏn ridiculed her and her itemized list of his crimes of unfiliality are deceitful. The property should belong to Hyŏn.[22]

### Table 5.1
### Kim Hyŏn Versus Mme Kim

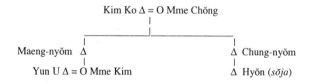

More details were recorded three years later. Mme Chŏng, wife of Kim Ko, had over 800 slaves and had given them all to her two sons, Maeng-nyŏm and Chung-nyŏm. Hyŏn was the *sŏja* of Chung-nyŏm; Mme Kim, the wife of Yun U, was the daughter of Maeng-nyŏm. Chung-nyŏm

---

[20]Munjong 1, 1451.11.*kyech'uk*; 10:26a (6:454). Mme Yi appears to have avoided all punishment, but Mme Kwŏn, her adopted daughter, had to pay a fine. The nephew of Mme Yi, Yi Hŭng-jik, and his father, Yi Paek-cha, Mme Yi's brother, were given 100 stripes and 90 stripes, respectively. The two government officials who conspired with them were both given 80 stripes and two years hard labor.

[21]Mojiri went on to amass a fortune as a tax broker and took the respectable name Hŏ Kye-ji. His greed went to excess, however, and he was indicted by the Censorate in 1469. See Ch'oe Yŏng-ho, "Civil Examinations and the Social Structure in Early Yi Dynasty Korea: 1392-1600" (Ph.D. dissertation, University of Chicago, 1971), pp. 160-162. (Therein he cites Yejong 1, 1469.7.*kyemyo*; 6:44a [8:405].)

[22]Sŏngjong 12, 1481.6.*imsul*; 130:17a (10:231) and *MTP* A:165a,3b.

apportioned his slaves among his legitimate daughter(s) and his concubine's son, Hyŏn. After Chung-nyŏm died, since Mme Chŏng disliked Hyŏn, she destroyed an earlier document and reapportioned the property cutting Hyŏn out. After Mme Chŏng died, Hyŏn brought suit charging the revised document was incorrect and won the case heard by the king.[23]

After recording the story, the *Shillok* historians added the following note:

> The high officials at court all judged that the reapportionment document of the legitimate grandmother, Mme Chŏng, should have been followed. The king alone stood by the precedent that once an heir had died there could not be a redistribution of the property he had inherited. He forcefully opposed the unanimous opinion of the court. Some say that Kim Hyŏn bribed the king's wet nurse.[24]

The *Shillok* compilers' note gives the impression that by 1484 it had already become unusual for a *sŏja* to perform the ancestral ceremonies. The tide was clearly against the *sŏja*, and although Kim Hyŏn won a battle, his comrades were losing the war.

### A Dispute Between a *Sŏja* and His Uncle

On other fronts, there were numerous examples of *sŏja* losing ground to uncles, cousins, and nephews. For example, there was a dispute over inheritance between a *sŏja* and his uncle in 1473. Cho Pang-nim had no legitimate heir; he made his *sŏja*, Pok-hae, his heir. But Pang-nim's younger half-brother, Pu-rim, said that according to the Code, he, as a second son, should succeed to the heirship of the ancestor ceremonies. He confiscated the property set aside for the ceremonies held by Pok-hae. When the dispute reached the court, the officials were divided in their support of the two positions. Those against the *sŏja* were led by Chŏng In-ji, at the time a seventy-year-old man and veteran of many court battles. Sŏngjong, who was seventeen, judged that Chŏng's argument was correct. Pu-rim, not the *sŏja*, Pok-hae, was made the heir.[25]

The losses suffered by the *sŏja* became more frequent as the dynasty grew older, but the downward spiral was not without its moments of reprieve. The Cho case above preceded the Kim Hyŏn case by eleven years. The Yi kings tended to be more sympathetic to *sŏja* than the officials

---

[23]Sŏngjong 15, 1484.1.*imjin*; 162:1b (10:556) and *RZS* p. 84.

[24]Sŏngjong 15, 1484.6.*chŏngsa*; 167:1b (10:597) and *RZS* p. 84.

[25]Sŏngjong 4, 1473.10.*kimi*; 35:1a-3a (9:63) and *RZS*, p. 224.

of the bureaucracy but there were times when even the kings ruled against *sŏja*. While each case had its own particular set of variables, the two cases above are interesting in that they reveal the same king responding in opposite ways over issues concerning *sŏja*. In the Cho case the court was divided; the boy king, Sŏngjong, followed the lead of one of the most powerful men of the dynasty, Chŏng In-ji, who had been a close adviser to the boy's great-grandfather, Sejong, and each of the intervening kings, Munjong, Tanjong, Sejo, and Yejong as well. Could the seventeen-year-old who had been on the throne for only three years have disagreed with the powerful old man? Eleven years later Sŏngjong disagreed with the entire court, an action that was unusual enough to cause a historian to insert a note basically repeating court gossip about a bribe from a royal wet nurse. It is possible that Sŏngjong had not been influenced by a bribe but had, with the years, developed the wherewithal to stand on his own.

## Sejo's Defense of the Hŏ Brothers

Although the decree restricting *sŏja* access to government positions was issued in the early fifteenth century, the mid fifteenth century saw the kings trying to employ *sŏja* and override objections from the bureaucracy. The kings, perhaps in a desire to be fair to all the people, an ideal easily found in Mencius and other Confucian texts, took the *sŏja*'s part in two related areas—appointments to office and permission to take examinations.

One of the first of the reform cases surfaced in the fourth year of Sejo's reign, 1459. Chŏng Nan-jong submitted a memorial stating:

> In our dynasty the examination is for those from outstanding lineages who are personally talented, but it is not for those with questionable ancestry nor for those who are illegitimate. The father of Hŏ An-yu and Hŏ An-hye married the illegitimate daughter of Cho Chun.
>
> Therefore, they should not have been given special permission. Please revoke that permission and thereby emphasize the importance of the examination system.

Sejo's answer was a strong rebuff.

> When Heaven gives life to people, there is basically no distinction between the noble and the base. How can this be a basis for deciding who can take the exams?[26]

---

[26]*Kyusa* 1:4a, (Sejo 4, 1459). His position was in agreement with Chinese practice where they did not check one's genealogy at the exam site.

He went on to say that this matter was in the hands of Heaven and that he could not interfere. Sejo, like his grandson, Sŏngjong, and many of the Yi kings, often advocated official appointments for the *sŏja*.

## Ch'oe Chŏk and the Military Exam (*mukwa*)

Sejo and Sŏngjong were both involved in the case of another famous *sŏja*, a colorful military figure who was not only the son of a *kisaeng* concubine, but his father was an immigrant from Manchuria (Jurchen). Sejo had placed Ch'oe Chŏk "on the road of military service" but the issue became the center of a court controversy in the fifth year of Sŏngjong's reign, 1474. A censor, Yi Sŏ-jang, objected to the appointment of Ch'oe as a general officer. On two successive days the issue was raised but rejected by Sŏngjong.[27] On the third day the censors Yi Sung-mun and Pok Sŭng-jŏng argued the case again. Sŏngjong turned to those around him for their views. A senior official, Hong Yun-sŏng (whose own story is found on page 79), related the following story:

> One time Sejo went to the Sŏnggyun'gwan to monitor an exam. On the way back to the palace he turned to me and said, "I intend to give Ch'oe Chŏk permission to take the exam. Do you think I should?" I replied, "We should examine the family background of all who sit for the exams. Ch'oe Chŏk is the son of the immigrant, Ch'oe Po-ro, by a *kisaeng* and should not take the exam." Later, at the Kyŏngbok Palace he called me several times and said, "The Northern Barbarians are strong; employing men of talent is my duty. Ch'oe Chŏk's military skills are beyond the ordinary. What do you think of letting him take the exam and appointing him?" Since he seemed bound to do it, I could no longer object and Chŏk was allowed to take the exam.
>
> At the exam, when they reached the textual explication part, Sejo said to me, "Chŏk is basically uneducated; if I let him take it he most certainly will not pass." Then selecting a simple text, Sejo had Chŏk select his own passage for explication; but even at that, he could not read even one character. Sejo then asked, "In battle, those who desert are beheaded. Why?" Chŏk answered, "That is because of the concern that the deserter will startle the other troops." Sejo

---

[27]Sŏngjong 5, 1474.8.*kyŏngja*; 46:9a and *shinch'uk*; 46:10b (9:139).

said, "You pass!", and on the spot he was certified as having passed the military exam and was started on his road to government service.[28]

The Censorate (OCG) insisted that an ignorant man ought not be given high government office. They asked that Sŏngjong think carefully about keeping him in the position. Sŏngjong said he would think about it and later that day directed the Ministry of Military Affairs to transfer Ch'oe Chŏk (but the specifics of post and rank were not mentioned).[29]

The Yi kings are correctly portrayed in the *Kyusa* as sympathetic to the *sŏja* in spite of the fact that they or the government issued discriminatory decrees from time to time. One such case involved King Sŏngjong. In the sixteenth year of his reign, a revision of the dynastic Code was issued. Therein, restrictions on political advancement of *sŏja* were made part of the Code. The *Kyusa* blamed the officials Kang Hŭi-maeng and An Wi for the legislation that not only blocked the path to high offices but limited the access to the examinations and lower offices as well.[30] In typical fashion the *Kyusa* does not blame the king, but rather makes an excuse for him: "Sŏngjong was saddened and intended to correct the law, but died before he could carry it out."[31]

## Yu Cha-gwang, an Infamous *Sŏja*

The revised Code was a setback to upwardly mobile *sŏja* but probably not as big a setback as the villainous reputation of one man who lived at that time—Yu Cha-gwang. Yu, a *sŏja*, placed first in the *munkwa* exam of 1468, and in spite of some objections from the Censorate, he rose in power both before and after the revision of the Code in 1485. He was involved in several bureaucratic fights. In 1468 he was named a first class merit subject for his role in exposing an alleged plot by Nam I and others, but then he was charged with misconduct and banished in 1478. Restored to power in

---

[28]Sŏngjong 5, 1474.8.*imin*; 46:10b-11a (9:139-140). Part of the story, the part favorable to the *sŏja* position, is found in the *Kyusa*, 1:4a.

[29]Sŏngjong 5, 1474.8.*imin*; 46:11a (9:140). The concluding portion, Ch'oe Chŏk's dismissal, is excluded from the *Kyusa* account. On the pro-*sŏja* side of the ledger, Ch'oe did go on to receive high government appointments; he was of 2-A rank when he retired. Although the *Shillok* and the *Kyusa* disparage his abilities, the standard biographical dictionary (*Han'guk inmyŏng taesajŏn* [*HIT*] p. 959) states that he took first place in a special military exam in 1466 and that he was a renowned archer.

[30]*Kyusa*, 1:4a (Sŏngjong 16, 1485). The *Kyusa* states that a severe drought that killed many people in the subsequent summer was a result of the promulgation of these unjust laws.

[31]*Ibid.* Sŏngjong lived for nine years after the promulgation of the revised Code.

1481, he was the principal force, or villain, behind the purge of 1498. He came under Censorate attack again in 1501 but helped Chungjong obtain the throne in 1506 and was named a merit subject again.[32] In the end, Yu, the only *sŏja* to be a merit subject twice and, more importantly, one of the few *sŏja* to serve in high government office, came to be considered one of the worst villains in the history of the dynasty. That he was a *sŏja* and that he was such a villain were subsequently assumed to be interconnected facts. For generations afterward, wherever the subject of concessions for *sŏja* was discussed, those opposed would cite Yu Cha-gwang as an example of why *sŏja* should be kept out of exams and/or office.[33] "Thereafter, whenever people mentioned the name Yu Cha-gwang, it was as an excuse for strengthening the discrimination against *sŏja*."[34]

The fifteenth century closed with laws restricting the status and activity of *sŏja* settled solidly in place. At the beginning of the fifteenth century, laws limiting both numbers of wives and status of *sŏja* were enacted. But like many laws affecting social practices, there were those who challenged the law and those who tried to ignore it. But by the end of the first century of the dynasty it was clear that both new laws were going to remain in force. As we saw in chapter four, multiple marriage gave way to monogamy, and yet men had wives who were not wives — they were lesser wives (*ch'ŏp*), and their offspring were called *sŏja*, some of whom escaped the restrictions on their status, but most did not. They were, in the words of the romantic hero, Hong Kil-tong, unable to call their father "father", and in other ways they were pushed to the margins of, or even out of, the aristocracy.

---

[32]For details on Yu Cha-gwang and his involvement in the political purges of the period, see E. W. Wagner, *The Literati Purges*, particularly pp. 10, 29, 41-44, 51-53, 74, 78, and 178.

[33]*Kyusa*, 1:5a. In this case, the account found in the *Kyusa* was probably not exaggerated. Yu Cha-gwang is consistently described as a villain throughout the historical record.

[34]*Kyusa*, 1:5b.

# 6

# In Support of *Sŏja*

By the mid-sixteenth century, the memory of past evils attributed to *sŏja* had faded sufficiently enough to allow another attempt to liberalize the restrictions on *sŏja*, an attempt which met with limited success and then was undone by an incident that again reinforced the negative perceptions of *sŏja*. The Yi kings of the late Chosŏn period were sympathetic to *sŏja*, some of them were actually born of palace women not of full-fledged queens, but liberalizations were minimal. The *sŏja* petitioned for change, were given some hope, but little changed. Real change would have shaken the society to its core; the society was based on a division between the elite and the commoner/slave. The Korean interpretation of Confucian dogma underscored their approach to society, and proposals for even minor changes were viewed as threatening or treasonous by most of the elite. Thus, a king could be in favor of a change in policy but the aristocracy would block implementation. And so it was for the *sŏja*.[1]

## The Hŏt'ong Movement

In 1553, King Myŏngjong (r. 1545-1567) allowed those *sŏja* who were descendants of commoner concubines to take the examination by granting them special *hŏt'ong*, "allowed to sit", status.[2] The impetus for

---

[1]For the best overview of the subject in English see Martina Deuchler's "Heaven does not Discriminate," Journal of Korean Studies, 6:121-163.

[2]Myŏngjong 8, 1553.10.*muja*; 15:42a-43a (20:166) & *kabo*; 15:43b-44a (20:167); and *Han'guk yŏsŏng-sa* [The history of Korean women] v. 3, p. 43. There were cases of special permission granted to *sŏja* so that they could sit for the exams prior to this time. The case of Ch'oe Chŏk, who received permission from Sejo to take the military exam, above (p.90), is a good example. Above (p. 91), we noted that Yu Cha-gwang took highest honors in the exam. Another case of special permission to take an exam occurred in 1469 when a *sŏja*, Hwang Chin, the son of former Chief State Councilor Hwang Su-shin, petitioned the king saying he wanted to join the Eagle Brigade, but he could not take the exam because he was a *sŏja*. Two members of the Royal Secretariat, Kwŏn Kam and Chŏng Hyo-sang, spoke out in favor of Hwang's joining the brigade but objected to allowing the *sŏja* to take the exam. The king

the movement was a petition from an unknown number of *sŏja* led by Chŏng Tae-un and Han Sŏk.[3]

The following day, Myŏngjong asked for opinions and received a variety of them.[4] The debate raged nearly every day for a month but ended in a less-than-consensus decision to allow sons of commoner concubines to take the exam.[5] About half of the higher officials at court were for the reform and about half were against. The balance was tipped by the king's uncle, Yun Wŏn-hyŏng, a man who favored allowing *sŏja* to take exams.

Yun Wŏn-hyŏng's support of the *sŏja* position was eventually another impediment for *sŏja* because Yun became known as another of the villains of the dynasty. He was the brother of Myŏngjong's mother and together they controlled the boy king. Yun's eventual downfall was due not only to his abuse of power (he held practically every major office in the country at one time) but due to his abuse of a social convention. His case is infamous. His concubine, Nanjŏng, the daughter of a *kisaeng*, allegedly poisoned Yun's first wife. Yun, undoubtedly through Nanjŏng's insistence, had proposed to his sister, Myŏngjong's mother and regent, that Nanjŏng be promoted to legitimate status. It was done; she was given high and noble titles which enraged the rest of the bureaucracy. The day the queen mother died, the bureaucracy turned on Yun by demanding that Myŏngjong issue an arrest warrant for Yun. Fearing the worst, Yun and his once-concubine-made-noble wife tried to flee but were caught and killed on the road at the edge of the city. In the discussion on whether *sŏja* should be allowed to sit for exams, the *Shillok* commented that the reason the law was passed was because of Yun Wŏn-hyŏng's personal interest in seeing his own children by his concubine succeed.[6] Again *sŏja* gained an ally who tried to help them while alive, but who after his death was cited as another example of the evil associated with *sŏja*.

The following year, 1554, the Censorate stated:

> *Sŏja* were allowed to take exams in the Koryŏ and early Chosŏn periods. For a while they were not allowed, but recently they have again been given permission. But we must

---

disagreed, directing that *sŏja* could indeed take the qualifying test for the Eagle Brigade. Yejong 1, 1469.8.*shinmi*; 7:11a (8:412).

[3]Myŏngjong 8, 1553.9.*imin*; 15:35a (20:163).

[4]Myŏngjong 8, 1553.9.*kyeyu*; 15:35b (20:163).

[5]Beginning with the fourth day of the tenth month, Myŏngjong 8, 1553.10.*kyŏngjin*; 15:36b (20:163), and continuing into the eleventh month, the debate can be found in the entries nearly every day.

[6]Myŏngjong 8, 1553.11.*imo*; 15:40b (20:165).

strictly preserve the distinctions and prohibitions. Our predecessors generally did not allow them (*sŏja*) to be called scholars . . . [but rather they were labeled in the rosters as *sŏja* or *hŏt'ong* in lieu of scholarly titles].[7]

The Censorate went on to argue that the preservation of the status distinctions was essential and, even though a *sŏja* passed an exam, he should be labeled as a *sŏja* in all the test application and certification documents. Myŏngjong accepted the proposal.[8] Although the *hŏt'ong* policy was adopted, implementation of the policy was done in such a way that it continued the prejudicial treatment of *sŏja*. The fact that the successful *sŏja* were labeled as such on the documents certainly affected their being selected for positions and promotions.

Another provision of the new decree was that "the census registers of the mother and the grandmother should be verified" to insure that the candidate was indeed born of a commoner, not base, concubine.[9] The test case soon emerged when Chŏng Tŏng-myŏng was about to take the military exam. The question arose as to whether the examination of the grandmother's census register also meant examining the grandmother's mother's register (in order to determine whether the grandmother was a commoner or a slave). Shim Yŏn-wŏn, Sang Chin and Yun Kae argued that the grandmother's mother's register should be examined. Yun Wŏn-hyŏng argued that it need not be since the grandmother's status was obvious to members of society. Myŏngjong concurred with his uncle, Yun Wŏn-hyŏng.[10]

In the years immediately following the liberalizations of 1553 only two men can be identified in the comprehensive examination rosters as *sŏja*. They were Kang Mun-u and An Kyŏng-bin, and both passed in 1558.[11]

---

[7]Myŏngjong 9, 1554.8.*kyesa*; 17:32b (20:229).

[8]*Ibid.*

[9]Myŏngjong 11, 1556.2.*kyesa*; 20:10b (20:321).

[10]*Ibid.* The *Shillok* authors added a note here saying that since Yun Wŏn-hyŏng had made his concubine his wife he desired to see the *hŏt'ong* policy implemented.

[11]See the Wagner-Song *Munkwa* index #3216 and #3241. The Wagner-Song index is a comprehensive list of all those who passed the high civil service examination drawn from the original *pangmok* for each exam as well as earlier attempts at compiling a comprehensive listing of those who passed. The most consistent in giving indications of *sŏja* and other non-*yangban* statuses was the *Munkwa pangmok* compiled in the eighteenth century. The edition that is reliable overall was the *Kukcho munkwa pangmok*, compiled by Yun Kŭp in the mid eighteenth century.

For more information see Song June-ho, "The Government Examination Rosters of the Yi Dynasty," in *Studies in Asian Genealogy*, edited by Spencer J. Palmer (Provo, Utah: Brigham Young University Press, 1972).

There were others who tried to take the exams and were either disallowed or failed.[12] In support of *sŏja* at that point Chief State Councilor Sang Chin quoted a phrase from the classics that was often used by the *sŏja* in their petitions for employment: "Employ the worthy without regard to origin."[13] He argued that China did so, but unfortunately Korea did not. In spite of the decree that was to open the door to government service for *sŏja*, the prejudice against *sŏja* was too strong to be changed by one king's decree.

Obviously frustrated at what must have appeared to be a promise broken and while perceiving an ally in the king but intransigence in the bureaucracy, some 1,600 *sŏja* submitted a petition directly to the newly crowned King Sŏnjo in 1568.[14] Sŏnjo (r. 1567-1608) was fifteen years old. His response was favorable but somewhat ineffective; there were only three more *sŏja* who passed the exams during his long reign.[15] It was at this time that he issued his oft-quoted poem wherein he said all sunflowers, large and small, face the sun, so will all subjects, including *sŏja*, be loyal to the king.[16]

## Yulgok's Attempts to Aid *Sŏja*

The most prominent man in King Sŏnjo's court was Yi I, the famous sage better known as Yulgok. He is not only regarded as one of the finest Neo-Confucian philosophers of the period but his visionary warnings that the nation needed to prepare for possible invasions from the north (although the first invasion came from Japan) went unheeded and subsequent generations thus hailed him as one who would have saved the country if only the bureaucracy had listened. Thus, the *sŏja* used the statements by Yulgok in a similar fashion; if only the bureaucracy would have listened to Yulgok and employ *sŏja*, the nation would have benefitted. Yulgok was certainly the most prominent and most loyal friend that Chosŏn period *sŏja* had.

---

The comprehensive *pangmok* indicated that the two men above were both "*sŏ*," in other cases the label "*hŏtong*" is used. Kang Mun-u also appears in the *Kyusa*, 1:6b.

[12]See the account of the petition of Pak Han-mu and others in Myŏngjong 13, 1558.9.*kyŏngo*; 24:58a (20:483).

[13]*Ibid.*

[14]See chapter 5, footnote #7.

[15]Wagner-Song *Munkwa* index: #3959 (1586) Hŏ Ching, #4147 (1592) Yi Cha-hae, & #4256 (1597) Yang Kyŏng-u.

[16]See chapter 5, footnote #2.

His specific proposal was that a *sŏja* be allowed to serve if he made a payment in rice (*napsok*) for the support of the army.[17] One reason Yulgok was interested in improving the situation for *sŏja* may have been that he had no children of legitimate status, but did have two sons and a daughter who were of *sŏja* status.[18] The older son was promoted to lineage heir (*sŭngjung*) status which gave him nearly all the prerogatives of a legitimate son, at least as far as the lineage was concerned. There were certainly those who continued to treat him as a *sŏja*; as one piece of evidence, his lineage to this day is considered less than untainted.[19]

One of Yulgok's closest friends was also of *sŏja* status, Song Ik-p'il. It is important to note that Song was not himself the son of a concubine, but rather his father was. The point to note is that the status was inherited and once labeled as *sŏja*, the posterity of that person would be so labeled forever. The term "*sŏp'a*", an illegitimate lineage segment, denotes a set of related people who have become labeled as *sŏja* even though it was a predecessor, father, grandfather or even a remote ancestor who was the actual *sŏja*.

Yulgok argued that if a man had a son, implying a *sŏja*, then he certainly ought not adopt.[20] At a time when concern for the lineage, the rituals, and heir status was growing, and many Koreans were beginning to see adoption as the solution to the dilemma of having no heir or an heir whose status was tainted, Yulgok and his support of *sŏja* stands out. The

---

[17]*Kyusa*, 1:7a. See also *Yulgok chŏnsŏ* 7:49b-50a & 34:30b-31b; *Munhŏn pigo* 187:1b-2a; Sŏnjo 16,1583.4.*ŭlchuk* & 5.*imo*; 17:12b-13b (21:389-390); & Ch'oe Yŏng-ho, "The Civil Examinations and the Social Structure in Early Yi Dynasty Korea: 1392-1600," (Ph.D. dissertation, University of Chicago, 1971), p. 178.

[18]The fact that Yulgok's son was a *sŏja* is implied, but not explicit in the Tŏksu Yi genealogy (*Tŏksu Yi-ssi sebo*, 1930, H-Y #K2290.5/4421a; 2:27b). Yulgok's wife was a Mme No, but his secondary wife, a Mrs. Yi (of the Kyŏngju Yi lineage) was the mother of Yulgok's sons. Mme No is listed in the Tŏksu Yi genealogy, but Mrs. Yi is not. We know Mrs. Yi's name because Yulgok's daughter, by her, married Kim Chip, a man who, like Yulgok, was inducted into the National Confucian Shrine. She, as an illegitimate daughter, was a secondary wife and is listed as such in the Kwangsan Kim genealogy (*Kwangsan Kim-ssi chokpo*, H-Y #K2290.5/8192.5; 2:124b) and her maternal grandfather is given as Kyŏngju Yi Yŏk, a military official. He is identified as the father-in-law of Yi I in the Kyŏngju Yi genealogy (both the 1931 sub-lineage genealogy [*Kyŏngju Yi-ssi Kuktanggong p'abo*, H-Y #K2290.5/4403.7; 1:15a] and the 1934-35 lineage genealogy [*Kyŏngju Yi-ssi sagan sebo*, H-Y #K2290.5/4403.5; 2:33a] list Yi I as a son-in-law). The 1931 edition explicitly labels the daughter who married Yi I as a *ch'ŏp* (secondary wife).

[19]I met Yulgok's primary line descendant in Seoul in 1974. When I discussed the meeting with others who knew the history of the lineage, they spoke in whispers of the problems the lineage had suffered over the years because of the taint of illegitimacy.

[20]*Yulgok chŏnsŏ* [The collected writings of Yulgok] (Seoul: Minjok munhwa ch'ujinhoe, 1968) pp. 154 & 624. This is a bilingual edition that gives a *han'gŭl* translation as well as the original Chinese.

inherent problems for *sŏja* in traditional Korea were becoming so ingrained, however, that even the arguments of a luminary like Yulgok did not make much difference.[21] And neither did the arguments of a number of other prominent officials over the remaining years of the dynasty.

## Other Sages Advocate Employing *Sŏja*

Several colleagues of Yulgok were also advocates of the *sŏja* cause. Cho Hŏn and Sŏng Hon, who were also later enshrined in the National Confucian Shrine at the Sŏnggyun'gwan, submitted memorials to the throne. Cho compared the situation in Korea to that in China, arguing that the Chinese did not take social status into account, and gave two examples of men from mean backgrounds who were employed in the Chinese Civil Service, Hsün Chieh-gao and Cheng Hsün. He said:

> I have examined the situation in China, and their method of employing people is very magnanimous. If only someone has ability, he is put to work and they do not discuss his family background.[22]

Sŏng Hon took up Yulgok's advocacy of employing *sŏja* in military fields after the Japanese invasion had begun. He wrote that even in times of peace the government ought to employ *sŏja*, how much more should we not hesitate to employ *sŏja* in times of war. This is a practice that should not exist anywhere under heaven. Since this should be corrected even in normal times, how much more should we correct the matter at this time of war? Therefore, we can not wait even one day in employing *sŏja*.[23]

Yi Hang-bok and Yu Sŏng-yong, two other high officials of the period who although not enshrined in the Confucian Academy were famous and respected and served in the highest offices in the government, also advocated employment of *sŏja* in this same, end of the sixteenth and early seventeenth century, time frame.[24]

---

[21]See the laudatory entries about Yulgok in the *Kyusa*, 1:7a-7b.

[22]*Kyusa*, 1:8a, quoting Cho Hŏn's *munjip*, *Chungbong chip*. The *Kyusa* version is faithful but not complete. See *Chungbong chip*, v.4, *so*, memorials, section. Actually, the memorial was not a *so*, a copy of an actually submitted memorial, but was a *wi*, a proposed memorial that was drafted but never submitted. In the *Kyusa* version he goes on to mention two Korean *sŏja* who were capable but who only served as private teachers, Yi Chung-ho (1512-1554) and Kim Kŭn-gong (b.?-d.?). The *Kyusa* did not include the portion in the *munjip* that said they both died of starvation, which would have actually helped the *Kyusa* argument that Korean *sŏja* were mistreated.

[23]*Kyusa*, 1:8a, quoting Sŏng Hon's *munjip*, *Ugyejip*, v. 3, p. 40b, 1592, 7th month.

[24]See *Kyusa*, 1:9a for excerpts of the writings of both men.

But just at the time when some progress was being made, when some powerful people were lending their support and the warfare of the time led to some openings for service, the *sŏja* encountered another setback. In 1613, seven *sŏja*, all frustrated sons of prominent men, met on the banks of the Han River in Yŏju and made a declaration complaining that *sŏja* were discriminated against. Later they built a pavilion called the Muryunjŏng, the pavilion of those without moral relationships, meaning they were excluded from the basic Confucian moral relationship—the father-son relationship. They were implicated in the murder of a silver merchant, charged with treason involving an alleged plot against the throne, and executed.[25] The incident served to deepen the prejudice against *sŏja*.

A few years later, however, the dust from the "seven *sŏja* incident" had settled sufficiently to allow the situation of *sŏja* to be considered again. In the reign of King Injo (r. 1623-1649) several *sŏja* were allowed to take the high civil service exam and passed. There were twenty-four who were clearly labeled as either *sŏja* or *hŏt'ong* in the rosters covering Injo's reign. There were two in 1624, Song Kwang-p'il and Yu Pi.[26] In 1625, Ch'oe Myŏng-gil spoke in behalf of the *sŏja*. He argued that the court could allow restrictions on some offices but that others ought to be opened to the *sŏja*. Although opposed by others, Ch'oe argued that there were "illustrious" offices and "important" offices and that the *sŏja* could be given the latter.[27] Nine years later Ch'oe again petitioned the throne to argue for liberalizations for *sŏja*. He said it had been over nine years since the king had established the rule of allowing *sŏja* to serve in the "important" offices, yet few appointments had been made. Ch'oe then pointed out the procedures for implementing the new rule and defined the "important offices" as including, among others, the lower offices (section chief level) within the Ministries of Finance, Punishments and Public Works. He asked that worthy *sŏja* be appointed forthwith. Whereupon the king appointed Shin Hŭi-gye and Shim Ir-un, both of whom had passed the exams within the year.[28] The

---

[25] *Kyusa*, 1:9b. See also Yi Sang-baek's article "*Ch'ilsŏ chi ok*," [The criminal case of the seven *sŏja*], *Yi Pyŏng-do paksa hwan'gap kinyŏm nonch'ong* (Seoul: Ilchogak, 1956), pp. 655-681.

[26] The Wagner-Song index: #5086 and #5105.

[27] *Kyusa*, 1:10b-13a. The *Kyusa* account is given in considerable detail and gives the arguments on both sides. As was often the case, the pro-*sŏja* side argued that in China's golden age men were employed on the basis of talent regardless of background. The opposition argued that without maintaining distinctions in social status there would be chaos in society.

[28] *Kyusa*, 1:18a. Shin is #5311 and Shim, #5335, in the Wagner-Song index. Two other *sŏja* passed the exam that year, #5345 Yi Kyŏng-sŏn, & #5356 Kim Yŏ-ryang. Yi is mentioned in a *Kyusa* footnote on p. 18a, along with #5425 Kim Koeng (1635) and #7051 Yi

100

*Kyusa* does not speak of the success of *sŏja* in exams under King Injo but the rosters list sixteen more who passed between 1635 and 1648 (13 years), one of the more successful periods of time for *sŏja*.[29] In the years from 1392 to 1623 (231 years) only eighteen men were labeled in the rosters as *sŏja*. The situation seemed to have improved.

In the next 126 years the rosters record the status of another 124 *sŏja*.[30] As another sign of a slightly improved situation for the *sŏja* in the seventeenth century, high and powerful ministers were still speaking out in their behalf. Song Shi-yŏl, who had one of the longest records of service in the 500-year dynasty and who was inducted into the National Confucian Shrine of the National Academy, argued that the limitations on *sŏja* were not proper.[31]

## Sŏja Status in the Household

The position of the *sŏja* in society, as discussed above, was important to the *sŏja* in the household because his position in society could be used to buttress his position as an heir in the household. In a few cases they were successful. In many more they were not.

In a case that reached the court in 1666, a sitting magistrate (of Yŏngp'yŏng county), Kwŏn Yŏn, attempted to have himself installed as the heir to his uncle, Kwŏn O, who had only a *sŏja* for an heir. The Censorate charged that Kwŏn Yŏn's attempt to wrest the heirship from the *sŏja* was wrong and recommended that Kwŏn be dismissed from office. After some

---

Hyŏn (1694) as having been given "important" appointments.

[29]Those who passed were:

| | | | | |
|---|---|---|---|---|
| Yu Myŏng-jŭng, | #5402, 1635; | | Pak Hong-ho, | #5382, 1635; |
| Kim Ki-myŏng*, | #5457, 1637; | | Yun Chi-nam, | #5437, 1636; |
| Yi Sun-nam, | #5488, 1639; | | Yi Chin, | #5465, 1638; |
| Kwŏn Ch'ik, | #5536, 1641; | | Min Sa-ryang, | #5523, 1639; |
| Han Tŭng-nyang, | #5553, 1642; | | Shim Il-chun, | #5541, 1641; |
| U Kyŏng-sŏk, | #5590, 1644; | | Kwŏn Kan, | #5566, 1642; |
| Pak An-gi, | #5675, 1648; | | Yang To, | #5609, 1644; |
| Kim U-jŏng, | #5696, 1648. | | Cho Chŏng, | #5676, 1648; |

*Kim Ki-myŏng is not labeled as a *sŏja* in the roster itself, but his father, Sŏng-il, is labeled as such in the Kyŏngju Kim-ssi genealogy (*Kyŏngju Kim-ssi sebo*, H-Y #K2290.5/8103.2; 4.2:55a).

These men were given section chief level (Sr. 6) or similar appointments in the central government. The highest was a county magistrate (Jr. 4). Some had passed preliminary exams, some held government positions already at the time of passing, and some were *yuhak* (without position). Some were sons of prominent officials.

[30]The data from the Wagner-Song index, mostly based on the *Munkwa pangmok* is summarized and included in a table in an article by Song June-ho, "Chosŏn sidae ŭi kwagŏ wa yangban mit yangin (I)" [*Yangban* and commoners in the examinations of the Chosŏn period (I)], *Yŏksa hakpo*, no. 69 (1976), p. 135.

There appear to be others such as those listed in the *Kyusa* and others found in genealogies.

[31]*Kyusa*, 1:18b-19a.

discussion and several appeals, the king concurred. Kwŏn was dismissed and the *sŏja*, who was never mentioned by name, was reinstated as the owner of the property and he resumed performance of the ceremonies, which they said he had performed for years.[32]

Also on the side of the ledger favoring *sŏja*, there was a ritual text published in this same late seventeenth century time frame that still held that the *sŏja* could, and should, serve as the heir. In a question-answer format, the question was asked: "One can adopt or one can promote one's *sŏja* to be an heir. Which is proper?" The answer was that one can either (1) use one's *sŏja*, (2) discard the *sŏja* and adopt an heir, or (3) retain the *sŏja* as one's own heir, but allow the lineage heirship to pass to a collateral line. The text, however, did go on to state that if one has a *sŏja*, one should not adopt. The second and third options outlined were simply custom and not sanctioned by the classics or etiquette; and which of the three alternatives to follow in a given case was left to the individuals concerned, it said.[33] In actual practice, more and more men, faced with the alternatives of retaining their own *sŏja* or adopting a nephew from within the patrilineage, chose to adopt.

On the social and political front, in the late seventeenth century several more petitions from *sŏja* were submitted to the king. In 1695, 988 *sŏja* from the Kyŏngsang area led by Nam Kŭk-chŏng presented their signed petition.[34] On the heels of the Kyŏngsang petition, Yu Il-sang, a *chinsa*, led a group of 1,000 from the Chŏlla province.[35] And then thirty years later, in the first year of King Yŏngjo's reign (1724-1776), *sŏja*, this time 5,000 strong, submitted a petition to the new king.[36] Yŏngjo responded favorably, but little was done by the administrative arm of the government. Forty-eight years into his reign, Yŏngjo complained that *sŏja*, who did manage to pass the exam, were not being employed. He urged the

---

[32]Hyŏnjong 7, 1666.12.*mujin*; rv. 16:25b (37:534). The censor, Min Kwang-suk, charged that a letter from Kwŏn O, which stated that Yŏn had been adopted (*shiyangja*), was forged in order for Yŏn to confiscate the property of the unnamed *sŏja* heir.

[33]*Myŏngjae ŭirye mundap*, by Yun Chŭng (1629-1714), as quoted in *RZS*, p. 23.

[34]*Kyusa*, 1:21b. The petition listed the worthy *sŏja* of the dynasty in matters of scholarship and in the wars of the last century and noted that once a person was labeled a *sŏja*, his descendants were stigmatized forever. And therefore, the document surmised, more than half of the country was descended from *sŏja*.

[35]*Kyusa*, 1:25a.

[36]*Kyusa*, 1:45b.

government officials to not only disregard limitations on *sŏja* but to actively search for qualified *sŏja* to serve.[37]

On the private front, Yi Su-dŭk, a minor military official, wrote about the effects that official limitations had on the *sŏja* in the household:

> The current prejudice against *sŏja* limits the subject in his relationship to the king and the son in his relationship to his father. It has become so extreme that men discard their own *sŏja* to adopt distant cousins that are no more than strangers passing by on the street.[38]

Although a close examination of the last two centuries of the dynasty is beyond the scope of this study, a brief look at the balance of the dynasty shows that the arguments of the Yŏngjo period were in essence the same as those repeated throughout the remainder of the dynasty. In the public sector, the *sŏja* was concerned with opportunities to serve and attain government positions. In the private sector, the *sŏja* became more and more concerned about being replaced in the household by his father adopting a nephew to be the heir.

Yŏngjo's grandson and successor, Chŏngjo (r. 1776-1800), took as positive a stance in favor of assisting the *sŏja* as any of the Yi kings.[39] He repeatedly urged the officials of the government to recommend *sŏja* for positions in both the capital and the countryside. At one point, he urged them to be sincere and employ *sŏja* on a wide scale, not just in a token way.[40] In the fifth, sixth, and again in the seventh year of his reign, Chŏngjo complained that the various organs of government were not complying with his directives to employ *sŏja*.[41] He stated that there was a tendency to give a *sŏja* one job and then never reappoint him.[42]

Chŏngjo was noted for creating the palace library, the Kyujanggak, and in regard to *sŏja*, he was noted for appointing several prominent *sŏja*, or men of *sŏja* sub-lineages, to a particular position in the library, the position of *kŏmsŏ* (junior librarian). Four of these successful *sŏja* became known as the *sagŏmsŏ*, the "four librarians." Their case is interesting in that it shows

[37]*Kyusa*, 1:59a. Perhaps Yŏngjo was particularly sympathetic to *sŏja* because he himself was born of a palace woman rather than the queen, making him a *sŏja* of sorts.

[38]*Kyusa*, 1:49a. Dated 1769.

[39]*Kyusa*, 2:1.

[40]*Kyusa*, 2:2b.

[41]*Kyusa*, 2:3a-b.

[42]*Kyusa*, 2:5a.

the sympathetic treatment given by Chŏngjo to them, in spite of prejudice against them.

The "four librarians" were Yi Tŏng-mu, Yu Tŭk-kong, Sŏ I-su, and Pak Che-ga. Only the last, Pak, was a first-generation *sŏja*, the others were second, fourth, or fifth generation *sŏja*.[43] Contrary to a common prejudicial view found in some sources, the four librarians were not limited to their *kŏmsŏ* positions. As scholars, known for their interest in China and the new school of philosophy growing in Korean known as *shirhak*, and as writers, active in writing and publishing, they also held mid-level government positions. All reached the level of county magistrate. Although eligible for appointments outside of the library, they certainly were handicapped in their access to higher and nobler offices. None of the late Chosŏn era *sŏja* enjoyed the level of success that some *sŏja* attained in the early years of the dynasty.

In 1791, Chŏngjo discussed the status of the *sŏja* with Yi Tŏng-mu. At the meeting they discussed the discriminatory seating practice for *sŏja* at ceremonies at the National Academy (Sŏnggyun'gwan). Seating order was determined by age, but an old *sŏja* had to sit behind the youngest of the legitimately-born in attendance.[44]

They not only discussed the public aspects of the discrimination against *sŏja*, but they also looked at the situation of the *sŏja* in the household. Chŏngjo noted that the position of the *sŏja* would be strengthened if adoptions were not allowed for men who had *sŏja*. He pointed out that although more often violated than obeyed, the Chosŏn Code stipulated that only those who had no heirs, either legitimate or *sŏja*, could adopt. Yi Tŏng-mu suggested that those who had *sŏja* should have their own offspring promoted to legitimate status rather than adopt.[45] There was precedent for doing what Yi suggested; Yi Yulgok had his *sŏja* designated as *sŭngjung*, a lineage heir. Some years after Yi Tŏng-mu made his

---

[43]Yu Tŭk-kong's great-grandfather, Sam-ik, was the first-generation *sŏja* (*Munhwa Yu-ssi sebo*, 12:32-58a; H-Y #K2290.5/4202.3). Sŏ I-su's great-great-grandfather was the first *sŏja* in his ancestral line (*Taegu Sŏ-ssi sebo*, vol. ŭl-1, p. 3a; H-Y #K2290.5/ 2947.12 or FK544). Yi Tŏng-mu's case was more difficult to confirm. His father was the youngest of six natural sons of a man who nevertheless adopted a lineal successor, a fact that can only mean all six natural sons were *sŏja*. (*Chŏnju Yi-ssi Murim-gun p'abo*, 1:130; H-Y #2290.5/4483.4). The case of Yi's mother is clearer. She was the daughter of Pak Sa-ryŏm who is listed in the 1723 *chinsa* roster as the brother of Pak Sa-yu. The listing indicates that Sa-yu was a *sŏja* (*ŏbyu*) and that Sa-ryŏm was of the same status. Therefore, Yi's mother was second generation *sŏja* thus making Yi a third generation *sŏja* on his mother's side and second generation on his father's side. Pak Che-ga is listed as the *sŏja* of Pak P'yŏng in *HIT*, p. 296.

[44]*Kyusa*, 2:7a-10b.

[45]*Kyusa*, 2:10b.

suggestion, the Ministry of Rites began to record a procedure whereby *sŏja* were made legitimate heirs through a process of petitioning the government to, in effect, adopt one's own *sŏja* as one's legitimate heir.

A government register, the *Suyang sŭngjŏk ilgi*, kept between 1843 and 1894, recorded the cases authorizing promotion (*sŭng*) to legitimate status (-*jŏk*) by adoption or fosterage (*suyang*).[46] In the final century and a half of the dynasty with the increase in the incidence of adoption, *sŏja* complaints were aimed at the practice which in effect supplanted them in their own households. They criticized the practice of adoption and argued, as seen above, for the alternative whereby they would be promoted to legitimate status. These arguments were seen in documents submitted to Kings Sunjo (r. 1800-1834), Hŏnjong (r. 1834-1849) and Ch'ŏlchong (r. 1849-1863).

During Sunjo's reign a petition from 9,996 *sŏja* repeated many of the arguments made earlier but emphasized the point that, according to the Code, only those who did not have an heir, by either wife or concubine, could adopt. If one had a *sŏja*, one should not adopt.[47] Some members of Sunjo's court agreed and made the following statement:

> *Kich'ul, ch'ŏnsogya;*
> *iphu, inhabya.*
> Being born is a phenomenon of nature;
> Making an adoption is an affair of men.[48]

The implication was that men should not interfere in the affairs of heaven; *sŏja* should not be replaced by adopted sons.

### The *Sŏja* Son versus the Adopted Son

In the first half of the dynasty the *sŏja*'s major battles were in the political arena, but in the latter half of the dynasty, as indicated above, the battle had two fronts, the private (or household) and the public (or political). Whereas the public arguments were basically the same in the early portion of the dynasty as in the later portion, the argument in the private sector, in the household, came to be centered on the concept of intralineage adoption. Those who opposed the advancement of *sŏja* in the public sector did not want them to hold government positions; in the private sector the

---

[46]The document is a single volume kept today in the Kyujanggak section of the Seoul National University library; catalog number 13038.

[47]*Kyusa*, 2:18a.

[48]*Kyusa*, 2:25b, line 3.

opposition was in the form of the patrilineal cousin adopted to be the heir responsible for the ancestor ceremonies and the inheritor of the household property.

In response to the petition mentioned above (from 9,996 *sŏja* in 1823) the *Kyusa* compilers in support of the *sŏja* position said:

> These days there are those who speak of the status of the mother being a commoner or a public slave or a private slave. But, if we follow the father, we do not follow the mother. Therefore, it goes without saying that whether the mother is a commoner or a government slave or private slave, her sons are all equally noble [as the other sons of the father].[49]

The petition went on to argue that the father of a *sŏja* ought to promote his *sŏja* to legitimate status—the *sŭngjŏk* system. It said that those *sŏja* recognized as heirs in noble households would be accepted in noble society.[50]

The opposing argument was:

> The household that opens the way for the *sŏja* to become legitimized (*sŭngjŏk*) will no longer be noble. If one family does it today, then another does it tomorrow, and within a few years, the whole situation will become a mass of confusion. Soon the distinctions will disappear. For this reason, the father should not take his *sŏja* to be his heir.[51]

In questions of inheritance of property and ritual prerogatives, the early dynasty offered a variety of options. Daughters, adopted daughters, adopted sons from the wife's kin group as well as from the husband's, and *sŏja* were all possibilities. Yet all of these alternatives proved to be unsatisfactory, including the option of promoting the *sŏja* to legitimate status, although this option remained marginally viable well into the late

---

[49]*Kyusa*, 2:25b.

[50]*Ibid.*, 25b-26a.

[51]*Kyusa*, 2:20b. This argument is contained in a long response on the part of students in residence at the National Academy. The *Kyusa* excerpt was part of a declaration issued on the occasion of a *kwŏndang*, an organized demonstration carried out by the entirety of the student body to express grievance or outrage. A synonymous term is "*konggwan*", literally, to "empty the hall" or in other words, a demonstration in the form of a walkout.

Chosŏn period.[52] Eventually, in the case where a son was not born into the household by the legal wife, the adoption of a legitimate patrilineal kinsman, an agnate, became the only acceptable recourse. In the next chapters, we will examine the development of the orthodox solution to the problem of heirship, beginning with the role of women in the process and eventually arriving at the orthodox procedure of adoption of a nephew from within the patrilineage.

---

[52]Pae Chae-hong, "Chosŏn shidae ch'ŏpchanyŏ ŭi chaesan sangsok kwa chonjae yangt'ae," [Inheritance of property by the children of *ch'ŏp* (secondary wives) in the Chosŏn period].

# 7

# Early Patterns of Adoption:
# The Roles of Daughters and Wives

The principle of adoption (both agnatic and non-agnatic) was espoused from the beginning of the Chosŏn period and was included in the first edition of the *Kyŏngguk taejŏn*, the Code, but few agnatic adoptions took place in the early dynasty. Non-agnatic adoption, that is to say maternal relatives, non-relatives, and sometimes daughters were adopted. Beginning in the sixteenth century, the number of people who practiced agnatic adoption increased dramatically. By the late dynasty, almost every member of the aristocracy, and many of the lower classes, who did not have a son adopted an agnatic nephew.[1] The percentage of men who were adopted began to increase at the onset of the mid Chosŏn period. (See Table 9.1, page 164, for a graph showing the increase in the rates of adoptions.)

In this chapter, we will examine the practice of adoption and its transformation in the early Chosŏn period. We will see that numerous alternatives were available to husbands and wives in the fifteenth century. As was the case with inheritance, as noted in section one, women played a greater role in early Chosŏn period adoptions, not only as wives and mothers, but also as adoptees, as daughters. After the second century of the dynasty, however, one seldom sees a female child adopted. And by the middle of the Chosŏn period, it was only the male child in the proper generation level within the patrilineage who was a candidate for adoption—classic agnatic adoption.

The *Kyŏngguk taejŏn* makes reference to adoption in a contradictory fashion, an indication that the writing of the dynastic code, on this point, was a compromise between those who espoused Neo-Confucian principles and those who held onto the "national practice" (*kuksok*), the indigenous

---

[1] Here, nephew means any candidate in the next lower generation of the lineage. It is used here in a classificatory sense, not merely to mean the son of one's immediate brother.

Korean way of doing things.[2] Under the section of ritual (*yejŏn*), there were two headings, *pongsa* and *iphu* that pertain to heirship, that is, succession to the rights to perform ceremony (*pongsa*) and privileges in regard to household or lineage leadership by agnatic adoption (*iphu*). Under *pongsa*, the ceremonies was the focus, under *iphu*, succession to the line was the focus.

Another section of the Code covers inheritance of property; the section of punishments (*hyŏngjŏn*), under the heading of private slaves (*sach'ŏn*) gives guidelines for the inheritance of property.[3] Therein one of the key issues concerning slaves was how slaves are passed on to the next generation—inheritance of property. In that section, the concept of an adopted son was mentioned; it refers to *suyangja* or *shiyangja* as potential heirs to property. In the early dynasty, before ritual concerns had grown to the prominence that they did later, a *suyangja* or *shiyangja* was a sufficient heir.

The ritual section, ignoring the two methods *pongsa* and *iphu*, was concerned with succession to ritual prerogatives and to the lineage heir status—inheritance of intangibles, of status. Therein an adopted son, the *kyehuja*, was quite a different person from the *suyangja*, the heir to property. Eventually, the agnatic adoptee, the *kyehuja*, would also inherit all the property, as well as the status. By the late seventeenth century, the conflict between *pongsa* and *iphu* was resolved by giving primacy to the *iphu* procedure, but during the fifteenth and sixteenth century there was conflict between adherents of both principles under ritual (*pongsa* and *iphu*) as well as adherents of the principles of property inheritance by adoption, *suyangja*. Disputes at court supporting multiple options were heard, and each had its own justification.

The two articles on ritual said nothing about property. And there was no mention of *suyangja* or *shiyangja* in the ritual section. The term *kyehuja* does not appear in the slave section of the Code until the 1746 amended version.

The article on agnatic adoption (*iphu*) states: "If one does not have a son by either his legitimate wife or his concubine, he may adopt a nephew

---

[2]Deuchler has clarified this issue by showing that *iphu*, what she prefers to call "jural succession," was the product of Neo-Confucian ideology that was only beginning to take hold in Korea; and *pongsa*, what she calls "ritual succession," was recognition of the older tradition of fraternal or horizontal succession. *The Confucian Transformation*, p. 141.

[3]Property was mostly reckoned in terms of slaves and land. In the sections concerning slaves it includes a note that says "it is the same for land" (*chŏnji tong*) and in sections concerning land, it says "same for slaves" (*nobi tong*). See *Taejŏn hoet'ong*, p. 713, Hyŏngjŏn [concerning slaves], p. 33; and p. 225, Hojŏn [concerning land], p. 11.

from within the lineage (*chija*) to be the heir."[4]  Thus, it provided for heirship by the concubine's son, a *sŏja*, in theory, but that was not an option that many were pleased to choose (see chapters five and six).  The *suyangja* or *shiyangja* was not included in the ritual section of the code because he was not often considered an heir to a lineage, but more importantly, in the early dynasty few families were organized into patrilineages[5] and thus, many families looked at a variety of choices in selecting the method for passing property, ritual, family name and status to the next generation. Lineages came later and with them came the complex duties of ancestor worship, a kind of glue that kept the lineage together.[6]

Eventually, by the later half of the Chosŏn period, the adoption (*iphu*) of a agnatic nephew (*kyehuja*), became the ideal solution to the problem of not having a son but the practice was seldom seen in the early period rather, heirship by daughters and other forms of non-agnatic adoption were practiced.

The cases here show how the transformation developed and reveal a complicated set of alternatives. We will examine a series of alternatives available to those who desired to adopt.  Under the heading for each alternative, we will begin in the early dynasty and move forward toward the most recent period when that particular alternative was still viable. The order will generally be from the oldest and/or short-lived to the recent and/or long-instituted.

## The Adopted Son Versus the Daughter

In the early Chosŏn period, daughters were on equal footing with sons in their rights to inheritance, as described in chapters one, two and three. As heirs, daughters could and did succeed to the family line both in terms of inheriting property and in terms of ritual inheritance. They did not inherit lineage headships because lineages did not exist.

---

[4]*Taejŏn hoet'ong*, p. 367; *Yejŏn*, p. 37.

[5]The Code provided for high officials to perform ceremonies for three generations of ancestors, lower officials for two, and non-officials for the parents (*Taejŏn hoet'ong*, p. 365; *Yejŏn*, p. 36a); yet the *Shillok* has citations that show even high officials were not complying (See Deuchler, *The Confucian Transformation of Korea*, p. 134ff). Compare that situation with what had developed even by the middle dynasty where three generations became a kind of minimum and many households provided ceremonies for a long line of ancestors.

[6]See Timothy Brooks, "Funerary Ritual and the Building of Lineages in Late Imperial China," and Patricia Buckley Ebrey, "The Early Stages in the Development of Descent Group Organization," for examples of lineage building and ritual in China. Mutsuhiko Shima, "In Quest of Social Recognition:  A Retrospective View on the Development of Korean Lineage Organization," addresses some of the same issues for Korea.

Exactly how satisfactory it was for a couple to have only daughters is a question because there were indications of son preference even at the time when daughters could be heirs. A 1535 inheritance document, one of the earliest extant documents of its kind, for example, shows that the parents' property was given to two daughters, but mention is made of the father's desire to have had a son. The property was given with the instruction that the ancestor rites were to be conducted by the *oeson* (a grandson by one's daughter, a non-agnatic grandson).[7]

That the term "*oeson*" generally refers to a male heir is implied in the inheritance document of Shin Saimdang and her four sisters, where the designated ritual heir, Yi I, is a grandson, a male *oeson*.[8] It would be difficult to measure the strength of son preference in early Chosŏn, but suffice it to say that although the daughter was guaranteed equal inheritance rights by law, it would not be safe to assume that parents would have always been satisfied with daughters as heirs. For one thing, the surname was conveyed by the father to the son, but a *oeson* had a different surname. Nonetheless, a daughter, as an heir to property and ritual obligations early in the dynasty, was an alternative to the adoption of a son. Cases of *oeson* heirship were numerous, but cases of agnatic adoption were rare.

## The *Yŏje*, State Ceremonies for Lonely Spirits

In 1516, attitudes toward daughters as heirs were revealed in a discussion of a ceremony called the *yŏje*, ceremonies sponsored by the state for lonely spirits, spirits of those who died without heir.[9] The *yŏje* had been performed since at least late Koryŏ times,[10] was adopted as one of the official state ceremonies by the new Yi court,[11] and was performed in the spring and autumn[12] at the national level by the king and in each county by the magistrate.[13] On this occasion in 1516, Nam Kon initiated the discussion by saying that the *yŏje* gave solace to lonely spirits that were often perceived as spirits of those who had died without heir. Nam argued

---

[7]This document is held in the Kyujanggak collection at the Seoul National University library and has been reproduced in a volume of old documents published by the library titled, *Komunsŏ chipchŏn*, 1972, p. 202. Also see page 30, footnote 32.

[8]See chapter one, p. 27, footnote #26.

[9]Chungjong 11, 1516.10.*kisa*; 26:45a (15:227) and *RZS*, p. 338.

[10]T'aejong 11, 1411.7.*kapsul*; 22:10b (1:595).

[11]T'aejong 1, 1401.1.*kapsul*; 1:76a (1:193).

[12]Sejong 12, 1430.2.*ŭlch'uk*; 47:20a (3:221).

[13]Sŏnjo 28, 1595.1.*kyŏngja*; 59:23b (22:426).

that it would be much better to make adoptions so there would not be as many lonely spirits.[14]

Shin Sang joined the discussion and offered the criticism that in Korea even the high aristocracy do not adopt, but rather their daughters carry out the ceremonies for them after they die. He said this was a great mistake, but fortunately the royal family had made adoptions for even small children who died and also for those who had been guilty of "crimes," such as Pang-bŏn and Pang-sŏk, sons of T'aejo who were killed by Pang-wŏn (T'aejong) in his takeover of the throne in 1398. Shin went on to say:

> There is goodness and virtue in the example of the royal household, but officials who have only daughters do not adopt an heir [but give their property to the daughters]. They fear that their property will fall into the hands of outsiders [meaning adoptees who are not literal descendants].[15]

State Councilor Shin Yong-gae agreed with Nam and Shin Sang and added the argument that "in our country, we are not following the ritual texts."[16] He noted that the contemporary practice of siblings carrying out ceremonies in rotation was not found in the ritual texts and was one of the most extreme examples of corruption. He urged that the Ministry of Rites be called upon to legislate against the practice. Of course, the discontinuance of holding ceremonies in rotation meant that women would be disallowed participation. Although pressure to cut down the prerogatives of daughters as heirs was growing, still in the early dynasty, women clearly held rights to both property and ritual participation. Examples of holding ceremonies in rotation, and providing inheritances for that purpose, were found well into the late seventeenth century.

## Mme Ch'oe, the Adopted Daughter of Kang Chu

The following case shows the status of a woman as an adopted heir in the early Yi period. Kang Chu and his wife, Mme Yi, adopted a daughter, the natal daughter of his sister who was the first wife of Ch'oe Sa-gang.[17]

---

[14]Chungjong 11, 1516.10.*kisa*; 26:45a (15:227) and *RZS*, p. 338.

[15]*Ibid*. Note that here the term "outsider" (*oein*) is used to mean one who is adopted; but in later times, the same term is used to mean the grandson by a daughter (*oeson*).

[16]*Ibid*., p. 45b.

[17]Sejong 25, 1443.11.*ŭlhae*; 102:29a (4:526), and *RZS* pp. 242 and 407. And also see *Andong Kwŏn-ssi sebo* of 1476, 3:60a. The Andong Kwŏn-ssi sebo is the oldest extant genealogy (*chokpo*) in Korea, records Tae-saeng and Sŏ-saeng [Se-saeng] as the sons of Kang Chu and labels them as "born to a secondary wife" (*pushilsan*). It also records the wife of Yi In as the daughter of Ch'oe Sa-gang, but as we would suspect since adopted

The young woman married Yi In, a member of the royal family (T'aejong's second son by a concubine) whose title was Hamnyŏng'gun. Later, Kang took a commoner woman named Pobae as a concubine. She bore him two sons, T'ae-saeng and Se-saeng.

Table 7.1
Kang Chu's Heirs

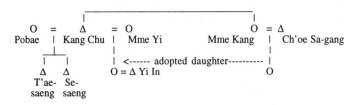

In 1443, two years after Kang died, the division of the property was contested, which brought the issue to the pages of the *Shillok*. In accordance with Kang's will, his adopted (*suyang*) daughter was given 150 slaves; his concubine, Pobae, 200 slaves; his *sŏja*, Tae-saeng, 200 slaves; and his *sŏja*, Se-saeng, 150 slaves.[18] Kang's first (legal) wife, Mme Yi, had given 18 slaves to her adopted daughter and 20 slaves to her husband. When Kang Chu died, Yi In seized 80 unallocated slaves and also the 20 slaves Mme Yi had once given her husband, Kang. He further forced Pobae to retrocede 20 slaves from her earlier allocation. Pobae sued to regain her property and, after considerable discussion at court, won. Yi In and his wife kept the property that had been given to her in the will of her adopted father and mother.

What is revealing about the practice of adopting daughters is found in Yi In's statement for the court in which he argued his claim to property held by the concubine. He said:

> My wife was adopted when she was seven days old and raised by Kang Chu and his wife. I became their son-in-law and lived in their house.[19] Even after he took a concubine and even after their sons were born, there was no moment in which

daughters are never listed in either old or recent *chokpo*, it does not show her adoption to Kang.

[18]*Ibid.* Note that the *RZS* account mistakenly says Se-saeng was only given 50 slaves rather than 150 as recorded in the *Shillok*.

[19]Note the uxorilocal marriage which was common at that time.

the feelings between us changed in the slightest and they treated us exactly as they had from the beginning. And when Chu died, we carried out every stage of the funeral as if he had been our natal father. In summary we did our utmost both when he was alive and after his death as well. As a matter of principle, slaves and property are only the concern of the family involved. Even if there are children by the primary wife, adopted children can also receive property if there is a close bond of emotion between them. This is the common practice these days.

The above case shows that even *yangban* of unquestioned standing considered the adoption of a daughter as an option in solving the childless dilemma in the early Chosŏn period. The permanence of such an adoption may be questioned, however, when one notes that the oldest extant printed genealogy, the *Andong Kwŏn-ssi sebo* of 1476, lists her only as the child of Ch'oe Sa-gang without reference to her adoption to Kang Chu.[20] In contemporary Korea there are reports of so-called adoptions that would be better called "loans" in that the natal parents keep the child recorded in their household register (*hojŏk*) when the child is temporarily "adopted" to a friend or relative for periods of months or years. Such may have been the case here. Regardless of the absence of record in the genealogy it is clear, however, that Mme Yi, Kang Chu's wife, considered the adopted daughter her heir since she gave her all of her property.[21]

## The Kim So Case

There was a significant case in 1481 in which a man set forth circumstances under which his son was to be disinherited and his property given to his two daughters.[22] Kim So had a son, Sŭng-sŏ, and two daughters. While So was alive, he rebuked his son in a written indictment charging him with three offenses. They were:

---

[20] It may be expecting too much to anticipate the adoption record in the *Andong Kwŏn-ssi sebo* since there are no adoptions, agnatic or non-agnatic, listed in this, the earliest of *chokpo*.

[21] See E.W. Wagner's article on seventeenth century household registers for an example of women passing the household headship to other women. One case shows property passing from a grandmother-in-law, mother-in-law, wife, and daughter. In "Social Stratification in Seventeenth-Century Korea: Some Observations from a 1663 Seoul Census Register," p. 43.

[22] Sŏngjong 12, 1481.2.*kapcha*; 126:7a (10:195) and *RZS*, p. 136.

First, while your parents are alive and you are under age forty, adopting a child [taking another's child as your *suyang* child] was your first offense; second, when taking up the post of county magistrate not performing ritual greetings [to your parents], was your second offense; and third, when you were angered at your mother for taking back a female slave with whom you had had relations, disobeying your mother was your third offense.

He further stated that he had desired to submit an indictment to the government but feared the damage to the father-son relationship and forbore. He concluded his directive by saying: "If, in the end, you have no legitimate children, I will not permit my property [that I have already given to you] to go to a *sŏja*; rather, I will give it all to my two daughters' posterity." However, when Kim So died, Sŭng-sŏ gave his slaves to Yi Yŏng-bŏn whom he had adopted as a *suyangja*.

At court both sides of the argument were presented. The first was that the father had stated that the two daughters should receive all his property. The second was that since the father did not say not to adopt (he said not to pass on his property to a *sŏja* but he did not specifically say not to give the property to an adopted heir), and since a *suyang* child is the same as one's own, then the property ought to be given to Yŏng-bŏn. Both arguments were said to be reasonable. The king decided: "We ought to follow the father's directive. The property should be given to the daughter's descendants."[23]

Sixteenth Century Cases

Seventy-five years later, in 1556, the viability of a *suyang* or *shiyang* adoption of either a son or a daughter was still recognized as is illustrated by the discussion found in the *Shillok* record of the sixth month of that year.[24] It was proposed that when a *suyang* adoption took place after one of the partners in a marriage had died, an adopted heir from the living partner's lineage would not be allowed to inherit all the property from the deceased partner. The adopted child was not considered a lineage heir (*kyehuja*) but rather an heir to the husband's or the wife's family (*chok*) and could be

---

[23]Ibid.

[24]Myŏngjong 11, 1556.6.*chŏngmi*; 20:60a-61a (20:346) and *RZS*, p. 383. The discussion took place in the context of preparing a commentary on the Code, but was finally recorded in a work titled *Sasong yuch'wi* [Various legal precedents]. It was originally published by Kim Paek-kan in 1585, and now found in a modern edition published in 1964 (Seoul: Pŏpche chosa wiwŏnhoe), p. 516 and pp. 520-1.

given a partial inheritance in order to perform the ceremonies (*pongsa*). Such a child could receive an additional fraction (either one-fifth or one-seventh) in order to carry out the ceremonies for the deceased parent. Since the child would not perform the ceremonies for the grandfather he or she would not receive all the ceremonial property. If, however, the child was adopted before the age of three, the law was interpreted, the child could inherit everything as though born into the household. The reasoning was that if the adoption was made while both partners in the marriage were alive, they both were party to the decision and the child represented both of them at the ceremonies.[25]

## Yun Ch'un-nyŏn as a Non-Agnatic Adoptee

In the same year, 1556, a *suyang* adoption by a maternal relative was described in connection with an issue of "avoidance of suspicion" (*p'ihyŏm*), the equivalent of modern-day "conflict of interest." The case mentioned the adoption in a matter-of-fact fashion implying that it was not questioned; but such an adoption would have been considered highly unorthodox if recorded in late dynasty documents. Yun Ch'un-nyŏn asked the king to be excused from adjudicating a case involving Hwang T'ang-gyŏng's wife, Mme O, in a dispute over inheritance by a *suyang* adoptee. Yun said that his own case was too much like that of Mme O's and that he could be accused of impartiality or conflict of interest. In stating his reasons for avoiding the duty he outlined his own case wherein he was adopted to Hong Chi. Hong had married a Mme Yun who was a sister of Yun Ch'un-nyŏn's grandfather and she, at the request of her mother-in-law, adopted him to be the heir to her father-in-law's fortune. Yun had been challenged by the illegitimate offspring of the Hong line; Hong Chi's father, Hong Yun-sŏng, had an illegitimate son whose posterity argued that they as *sŏja*, not Yun as a *suyang* adoptee, should be the heirs. Yun had won his suit thirty years earlier and the king (Myŏngjong, whose mother was a sixth-*ch'on* cousin to Yun) cited the "statute of limitations" (*taehan*) in saying it was acceptable for Yun to adjudicate the Hwang case.[26] Indication of Yun's adoption to Hong Chi would never be found in a genealogy, but fortunately it appears, incidentally, in the *Shillok*.

---

[25]Here, it is implied that the wife had autonomy in choosing an heir for her property and even had a say in the disposition of her husband's. Although this case implies equality of the two parties to the marriage, a case in 1492 concluded with the decision that the wife should only petition for approval of an adoption that her husband had decided upon before he died. See Sŏngjong 23, 1492.8. *kyemyo*; 268:5a (12:212) and also *RZS*, p. 323.

[26]Myŏngjong 11, 1556.8.*imja*; 21:20b-21a (20:357) and *RZS*, p. 163 and *MTP* A:255b,4d & 257a,3a & B:43b,2d.

### Yi Chong-nin becomes the Heir to Kwŏn Ch'an

Four years later, a dispute involving Myŏngjong's own brother, Ki, titled Tŏgyanggun, showed that the attitudes toward the acceptance of a daughter's son as an heir were changing.[27] [Yi] Ki's father-in-law, Kwŏn Ch'an, had no sons by either wife or concubine and had virtually raised Ki's eldest son, Chong-nin, from birth (probably because of a uxorilocal marriage). While Kwŏn was aged and on his deathbed Ki sought the king's permission for Chong-nin to perform the rites for his maternal grandfather (Kwŏn) so that he "not become a lonely ghost." Ki argued that if a stranger, adopted as a *suyang* before the age of three can perform the rituals, then surely a *oeson* adopted as a *suyang* can be permitted to perform the rituals. The king had the matter discussed by the Chief State Councilors and others and, after receiving opinions that it was proper, agreed.

The *Shillok* historians added a note saying that this was highly irregular. The next day the Censorate severely criticized the action.[28] Myŏngjong responded that this case involved the performance of mourning rites (*poksang*) by a *oeson* and that it was "unlike a case of lineage succession (*kyesa*)," therefore it was not necessary to change the earlier decision and it was not necessary to interrogate-under-suspicion the rites officials for the opinion they rendered. Myŏngjong rejected the Censorate's criticisms.

In the view of the Censorate, the case was irregular in two regards. One was the *oeson* factor—the adoption (or, in other words, the appointing) of one's daughter's child as the heir. The other was the generation factor—a grandfather adopting a grandson as his direct heir, in effect, skipping a generation. There are other examples of both. Examples of the first factor will follow directly. Concerning the second, the importance of the correct generation, cases showing an increased concern for maintaining the proper generation level when adopting will be shown below in chapter nine.

### A Late Sixteenth Century Hallmark Case

King Sŏnjo (r. 1567-1608) had a clearer perception of the impropriety of heirship by daughters than did any of his predecessors. In 1587, he reversed the decision in a case arbitrated by the Ministry of Rites. Yi Cha

---

[27]Myŏngjong 15, 1560.10.*shinmi*; 26:60a (20:569), *RZS* p. 235, & *MTP* A:50a,1a-d. It may be significant that the 1535 *Munhwa Yu-ssi sebo* (hereinafter *MYS* ) (9:16b) in listing Ki as the son-in-law of Kwŏn Ch'an also, in rare fashion, lists Ki's son, Chong-nin. Perhaps this was an indication of the adoption described here. Ki and Chong-nin are also listed, in the usual fashion, in their own patrilineage (10:55a).

[28]Myŏngjong 15, 1560.10.*imjin*; 26:60a (20:569), and *RZS* p. 236.

had a son, Pae, who married the daughter of Han Yong but had no children. Pae's wife proposed the (*shiyang*) adoption of one of her relative's daughters as an heir. The daughter of Yi Cha, Pae's sister, argued that she, herself, ought to be the heir.[29] The Ministry of Rites agreed with her and drew up a document for the king to approve authorizing the daughter to be the ritual heir (*pongsa*).

Sŏnjo challenged the decision arguing that although it was more appropriate for a biological daughter to be an heir than for a daughter-in-law to adopt a female relative, when women perform ceremonies, he reasoned, they do so out of emotion. In this case, a patrilineal nephew of Pae ought to be found and adopted to serve as an heir to Cha and the ancestors, Sŏnjo concluded. A nephew, Yi Yu-hu, was later adopted. By the late sixteenth century, heirship for adopted daughters was no longer a practical alternative.

<u>The Song Versus Yi Dispute</u>

A long series of disputes that began in the sixteenth century and were settled in the late seventeenth century shows the weakening of the daughter's line and particularly the weakening of the position of a woman, in most cases a widow, to initiate the adoption of one of her relatives. The former high official, Song In-su (1487-1547), had a son, Ŭng-gyŏng, who had no heir; therefore, he adopted his cousin's son, Sŭng-jo. Ŭng-gyŏng had one daughter who was the first wife of Yi Chŏng-hyŏng; they had one daughter. Ŭng-gyŏng's wife, the daughter of Yi Chin, loved her granddaughter and gave her all of the property. The granddaughter had married So Ha-jin but had no children and therefore adopted (*shiyangja*) a grandson of her father, Yi Kyŏng-yŏng, by another wife (not her own mother). Yi Kyŏng-yŏng inherited all the property, but in Injo's time (r. 1623-1649) was sued by the kinsmen of Song Sŭng-jo, the adopted son of Song Ŭng-gyŏng. The Song lineage won the suit and all the property. Later, Yi T'ae-gi, the grandson of Yi Kyŏng-yŏng, allegedly using factional power ties, sued and won back the property. In 1681, with another shift in factional power, the court was

---

[29]Sŏnjo 20 1587.5.*ŭlmyo*; 21:7b (21:433) and *MTP* A:9la,2a,b,c. Although the *Shillok* states that Pae was the son of Cha, the *MTP* shows an intervening generation, Ch'u. On examination of the genealogy, *Hansan Yi-ssi yangdo kongp'a sebo*, Yi Cha indeed had a son, Ch'u, who had a son, Pae. Cha also had three daughters, the third of whom married a royal family member, Yi Man-nyŏn, titled Pongnŭng-su. The *Shillok* makes reference to Cha's daughter who married a man with the title Pongsŏng-su. The *Shillok*'s version is probably in error since the *MTP* (A:18b,4d) and the genealogy agree in presenting Yi Man-nyŏn with the title Pongnŭng-su (although each uses a variant form of the *nŭng* character) as the son-in-law of Yi Cha.

asked to return the property to the Song line and to prosecute Yi T'ae-gi. King Sukchong (r. 1674-1720) concurred.[30]

Table 7.2

Diagram of the Song Versus Yi Dispute

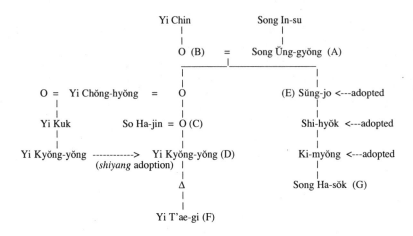

Schematically (see table 7.2), the property of Song In-su was first given to his son, Song Ŭng-gyŏng (A); then Ŭng-gyŏng's wife (B) gave it to her daughter's daughter (C); and she passed it on to her adopted son, Yi Kyŏng-yong (D). The adopted son of Ŭng-gyŏng, Song Sŭng-jo (E), sued for the property and won, but then his descendants lost it in a suit to Yi T'ae-gi (F) who finally lost it to the descendants of the Song line (G).[31]

The property changed hands several times; each side won and lost as the judgment was based on one set of values and then another. Ultimately, the daughter's line lost and the adopted line won. This case is similar to that of the one involving the dispute between the Ma and the Chin lineages covered in chapter three (pages 59-61). The major difference is that one dealt with the adoption of a female relative as the heir (Song-Yi), and the other

[30]Sukchong 7, 1681.8.*kyŏngin*; 12:10a (38:546) and *RZS*, p. 164.

[31]Actually, the Song line included several adoptions. Not only was Sŭng-jo adopted but his son and grandson were also adopted into the line. See *MTP* B:184b,2a,b,c. This line is fairly closely related to Song Shi-yŏl one of the most powerful officials of the dynasty. Sŭng-jo's adopted son was an eight-*ch'on* cousin to Song Shi-yŏl, and Sŭng-jo's adopted grandson was the natural brother of Song Shi-yŏl's adopted son.

dealt with inheritance by the lineal descendant of a female (Ma-Chin). The former preceded the latter by a century.

In summary, in the above cases we have seen that the adoption of a female child and the adoption of a female's relatives were once accepted but became problematic. Daughters could still inherit property equally with sons in the majority of households and wives still held authority in such matters as inheritance and the selection of an adopted heir; but a wife could no longer suggest the adoption of a female heir nor could she suggest the adoption of a male heir from among her relatives. She could, however, assist in the selection of an appropriate nephew from her husband's lineage as the concept of the lineage developed. The involvement of a category of widow, known as a *ch'ongbu*, in matters of adoption became, however, problematic during the sixteenth century. Below we will retrace some of the chronological space already covered above, but we will focus on the status and role of the *ch'ongbu*.

### The *Ch'ongbu*

A *ch'ongbu* (the wife of the eldest son) when widowed claimed the right to perform rituals in her husband's stead. Since women in the early dynasty could perform the ceremonies, and since when their husbands were alive they apparently performed them together, it must have been appropriate for the widow to perform those rituals alone after her husband's death.

The *ch'ongbu* occupied an interesting position in the transition. In the early contours of the argument, she represented the lineal principle (*chongppŏp*); she derived her privileges from her husband, the eldest son. She argued that she, as surrogate for her husband, had priority in holding the ceremonies over the younger brothers of the husband who argued for *hyŏngmang chegŭp* (when the eldest brother dies, the younger brother succeeds). But as time went by, gender became the determining factor, and the *ch'ongbu* was excluded from ritual heirship.

The status of the widow became an issue in 1473 when Shin Suk-chu argued that if the eldest son did not have an heir, his property and ritual obligations should be given to the second son. But, he pointed out, when the eldest son's wife was still alive there were often fights over who should occupy the main house. The king, Sŏngjong, tabled the issue at that time.[32]

---

[32]Sŏngjong 4, 1473.11.*muja*; 35:13b (9:69).

Forty-three years later, Chungjong brought up the case of Chŏng Su. The case had come up before and was not to reach a final resolution until another four years had passed (see below). The king stated that Chŏng Su's widow had petitioned for an adoption and one had been authorized by the Ministry of Rites, but that the Censorate had objected saying that since the *ch'ongbu* was alive, it was not possible for Chŏng Su's widow, as the mother-in-law, to name an heir.[33]

Table 7.3
Chŏng Su's Lineage Diagram

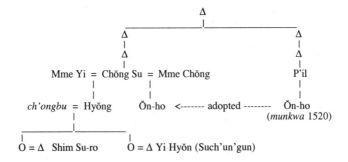

Shin Yong-gae, who was the Minister of Rites when Chŏng Su's widow applied for an adoption, responded that he had done the right thing:

> Chŏng Su died without heir [since his only son, Hyŏng, had predeceased him and left no heir]. A man should not be without someone to perform ceremonies for him; therefore, his second wife [Mme Chŏng] desiring to name an heir petitioned the Ministry of Rites. For this reason I authorized the adoption. The Censorate, however, objected and said I was wrong and that when a *ch'ongbu* is alive, it is not possible for a second wife [Mme Chŏng] to name an heir. It seemed to me that since Chŏng Hyŏng [Su's son]'s wife,

---

[33]Chungjong 11, 1516.10.*kisa*; 26:45b (15:227).

although living, did not have a son, there was nothing wrong with authorizing Chŏng Su's second wife to adopt.[34]

Kong Sŏ-rin representing the Censorate entered the discussion and in his argument provided an explicit explanation of the contemporary view of the *ch'ongbu*:

> Although Chŏng Su's son, Hyŏng, has died, Hyŏng's wife is still alive and is a *ch'ongbu*. Since Hyŏng has no sons it is his wife who can name an heir. It is permitted for Su's second wife to report to the Ministry of Rites that Hyŏng's wife, the *ch'ongbu* who should name the heir, had not named an heir. But it is certainly not permitted for her to name the heir herself.[35]

Shin Yong-gae entered the fray on behalf of the first wife, Mme Yi, by emphasizing that Chŏng Hyŏng had died without heir and by challenging the Censorate's position that Su's second wife could not name an heir as long as the *ch'ongbu* was alive.

The king entered the discussion saying:

> If the *ch'ongbu* [Hyŏng's widow] were to adopt a kinsman there would naturally be someone to perform the ceremonies for Chŏng Su. This is not far removed [from the intent of the classics]. On the other hand, having a *ch'ongbu* is not different from having a daughter. Yet this is what the Censorate advocates. I fear that in the future those who have daughters will never adopt.[36]

Kong Sŏ-rin responded:

> The classics [in their advocacy of adoption] cannot be discarded. To not make an adoption just because of one's household's goods, one's land and slaves, [which one would rather leave to one's daughter] is totally wrong. But Chŏng Su's second wife ought not make an adoption on her own.[37]

---

[34]*Ibid.*
[35]*Ibid.*
[36]*Ibid.*, p. 45b-46a.
[37]*Ibid.*, p. 46a.

The discussion moved on to the original issue of ceremonies and the Chŏng family was not discussed again in the *Shillok* record until four years had passed. In the second month of 1520, the Ministry of Rites reported to the king that they could not come to a decision and they called for the king to solicit opinions of high officials and adjudicate the matter.[38] Mme Chŏng was the second wife of Chŏng Su and she had petitioned the Ministry of Rites to adopt Ŏn-ho, the son of Su's fourth-*ch'on* cousin, P'il (see table 7.3), nine years earlier and was granted permission.[39] The Censorate said this amounted to discarding the legitimate heir, Hyŏng. Hyŏng's name had already been inscribed on Su's spirit tablet; and although he had no sons, he was the heir. The *ad hoc* council of high officials agreed with the Censorate; if an adoption was to be made, it should be made to Hyŏng, not Su. The *ch'ongbu* prevailed and so did a principle that Chosŏn society was eventually to honor exclusively.

### The *Ch'ongbu* and the *Ch'aja*

In 1547, midst a list of issues of relatively minor concerns, Yun Wŏn-hyŏng, the infamous maternal uncle of Myŏngjong, raised the problem of conflict between the *ch'ongbu* and the *ch'aja* (the younger brother [of the deceased husband]). He said:

> In our country, when the eldest son dies without leaving an heir, at times his wife, the *ch'ongbu*, will survive him. At the same time a second son's son may perform the mourning rituals for the grandparents for a three year period [implying lineage heir status] in some cases. At other times, the second son's son does not. This is a major ritual, but since the country lacks a fixed law it causes anxiety. I request that the court widely discuss this issue and settle it.[40]

A month later Myŏngjong indicated to the Ministry of Rites that in situations where the grandfather had lost his eldest son, and where the eldest son had no heir, even if the eldest son's widow was still alive, the eldest

---

[38]Chungjong 15, 1520.2.*chŏngch'uk*; 38:32b (15:623).

[39]See *MTP* A:235a,4d and 235b,1a,2a; also see *Yŏnil Chŏng-ssi soksu sojong sebo*, 1:10b, Central National Library catalog no.: *han* 58 *ka* 24-51. The *Munhwa Yu-ssi chokpo* lists Chŏng Su both in his own lineage (*MYS* 2:48A) and as the son-in-law of Yi Pa (*MYS* 5:67A); in both places it states Chŏng Su had no heirs (*muhu*).

[40]Myŏngjong 2, 1547.9.*chŏngsa*; 6:17b-18a (19:527).

grandson by the second son should be allowed to mourn for three years.[41] Such a decision appears to have been the end for the *ch'ongbu* as an exclusive heir to ritual responsibility, but she remained active in lineage affairs and still participated in rituals on a rotational basis. The *ch'ongbu* was to have a few more victories as well as losses before the battle was over.

## The Ch'ongbu and the Adoption Prerogative

The rights of the *ch'ongbu* came to be challenged by the deceased husband's younger brother (the *ch'aja*) or the younger brother's widow in two cases, one in 1551 and one in 1552. The *ch'ongbu* not only claimed the right to perform ceremonies after her husband died but also claimed the right to determine who would be the adopted heir if she had no children. The right of the husband's younger brother derived from the concept known as *hyŏngmang chegŭp* (if the elder brother dies, the younger brother succeeds). The alternatives contain classic elements of conflict not only between the eldest son's widow and the younger brother or his widow, but also between the eldest son's widow and the mother-in-law. The mother-in-law preferred to see her second son become the ritual heir in both the 1551 and 1552 cases, but the *ch'ongbu* argued that she could adopt a patrilineal nephew to be the heir. In both cases the *ch'ongbu* won.

Table 7.4
Yi Kwi-su's Lineage Diagram

---

The 1551 case concerned a member of the royal family, the descendants of King Sŏngjong's twelfth secondary son (a son born to a palace woman rather than the queen), Chong, titled Musan'gun.[42] Chong married a Mme Shin and had seven sons but the eldest, Kwi-su (Yŏngsŏn'gun), and the second, Mi-su (Yŏngch'ŏn'gun), had no heirs. Kwi-su's widow, Mme An, initiated procedures to adopt Su-bang, the second son of the sixth brother, Sŏk-su. The issue was brought to Myŏngjong for a decision. Several high officials including Yun Kae, Shin Kwang-han and Kim Kwang-jun argued that the rule of *hyŏngmang chegŭp* should apply. They quoted the section of the Code under the article on ceremonies (*pongsa*) which stated that if the eldest son had no heir, then the next son should perform the ceremonies.[43] They argued that since Kwi-su died without heir and Mi-su was still alive, that Mi-su ought to be considered the principal heir. Mme Shin, the mother, agreed with this point of view. On the other hand, Yun Sa-ik pointed out that even though the second brother, Mi-su, had already performed the ceremonies, he was without heir. Yun argued that it would be improper to adopt a son to Mi-su and leave Kwi-su, the eldest, without an heir. He argued that the adoption initiated by Mme An as the *ch'ongbu* ought to stand. The king agreed.

The 1552 case was structurally the same as the 1551 case except that it involved an aristocratic, not royal, family and more importantly, the second brother had a son. Yŏ Hŭi-nyŏng had three sons, Maeng-on, Chung-on, and Se-on. The eldest, Maeng-on, died without heir. Chung-on had a son, Mun-mang, and Se-on had a son, Ŭi-nam. When Yŏ Hŭi-nyŏng's wife died, Mun-mang began to prepare to do the mourning for her when Maeng-on's widow forbade him, claiming the right to initiate an adoption. Thereupon she declared that she intended to adopt Ŭi-nam (literally, to have him succeed to the position of ritual heir [*sŭngsa*]).[44]

The case came before the king, who asked Left State Councilor Sang Chin for an opinion. Sang replied that the eldest son of the second brother, Mun-mang, should perform the rituals—according to the rule of *hyŏngmang chegŭp*. The Censorate (OCG) objected and stated that the "law of the *ch'ongbu*" was in effect in Korea. They cited a decision of the court five

[42]Myŏngjong 6, 1551.8.*chŏngmyo*; 12:3b-6b (20:35) and *MTP* A:46b,2b-c and *RZS*, p. 330.

[43]*Taejŏn hoet'ong*, p. 365.

[44]Myŏngjong 7, 1552.4.*kabin*; 13:26a-b (20:80) and *MTP* B:219b,1b-d and *RZS*, p. 333 and Kim Tu-hŏn, *Han'guk kajok chedo yŏn'gu*, p. 271.

years earlier wherein it stated: "The right of adoption (*iphu*) resides solely with the *ch'ongbu*."[45]

The Censorate referred to the case of Yi Kwi-su, cited above, wherein the right of the *ch'ongbu* to initiate an adoption had been reaffirmed the previous year.

Table 7.5
The Yŏ Mun-mang Lineage Diagram

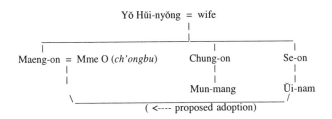

Myŏngjong said he would confer with his mother. (He was only eighteen years old and conferred with his mother often on state affairs.) That same day he responded that the Yŏ Mun-mang case was no different than that of Yi Kwi-su; it was permissible to deny Mun-mang heir status.[46] The right of the widow to participate in ritual matters and to decide the issue of who was to be adopted was upheld by the mother of the king.

### Erosion of the *Ch'ongbu*'s Prerogatives

Three months later, the female prerogative that had been vouchsafed in the above decisions came under attack. The Ministry of Rites argued that widows were abusing their prerogatives in setting up adoptions.[47] They stated that the law said close relatives should be adopted, but some were choosing distant relatives even when close relatives existed. The Ministry of Rites asked that a council of high officials be convened to establish laws that would prevent such abuse. The king concurred.

In 1554, the Censorate submitted a long memorial defending the role of the widow to perform ceremonies. Their argument was that although

---

[45]*Ibid.*

[46]*Ibid.*

[47]Myŏngjong 7, 1552.7.*pyŏngshin*; 13:54b-55a (20:94).

moral principles were constant, the customs of Korea were different from China's.

> We have an aristocratic system and they do not. We have a slave system and they do not. Does this mean we should abolish the aristocratic system and the slave system? According to the texts of etiquette, the wife comes to the groom's house, but in our country the groom goes to the bride's house. Attending the grave for three years is not according to ancient [Chinese] customs, yet we do it. Does this mean we should marry at the groom's home and abolish the grave-side mourning system? There are many cases like this so why should we uniformly follow Chinese institutions?[48]

The memorial went on to say that there is a basis found in the ritual texts for the widow to take charge of the rituals. If she has no sons and her husband dies, she performs the ceremonies. There are those, the Censorate said, who would expel such a woman from the household and argue that she would not qualify to carry out the ceremonies. As it says in the *Analects*, "The linen cap is prescribed by the rules of ceremony, but now a silken one is worn. It is economical and I follow the popular practice." And Master Cheng said in his commentary, "If there is no harm to the intent in such matters, I follow the local custom."[49]

The Censorate concluded its memorial by paraphrasing Master Cheng's commentary: "Now in this law of the *ch'ongbu* there is no harm to the intent; thus to follow the local [Korean] custom seems appropriate." They also asked that Myŏngjong call a conference of the high officials to decide the matter, since opinion in the court was divided.[50] Myŏngjong agreed to do so and twenty-four days later the Censorate attempted to clarify usage of the term "*ch'ongbu*" by stating that there were two categories of widows who come to be responsible for the ancestor rituals. The first looses her husband (an eldest son) after his parents have died; the ceremonies have already become the son's responsibility and then she assumes the ritual obligations. The second occurs when the husband dies while his parents are still alive. In that case the ritual responsibility has not yet become the

---

[48]Myŏngjong 9, 1554.9.*ŭlch'uk*; 17:44a-45b (20:235).
[49]*Ibid.*, 45b.
[50]Myŏngjong 9, 1554.9.*ŭlch'uk*; 17:44a-45b (20:235).

son's, therefore, the widow cannot claim responsibility to perform the rituals and all that goes with it.[51]

On the second day of the eighth month two years later, Myŏngjong addressed a communication to the Royal Secretariat saying:

> In the discussion about the *ch'ongbu*, there has been no consensus and we have continually changed the statutes. This is not correct. We ought to examine the precedents and the Code and settle this matter.[52]

The response of the three State Councilors and Myŏngjong's powerful maternal uncle, Yun Wŏn-hyŏng, was quoted in the *Shillok*. They argued against adoption (as preferred by the *ch'ongbu*) and in favor of the *sŏja* if one existed by making the point that there were two references to inheritance in the Code; one referred to rites (*pongsa*) and the other to adoption (*kyehu*). In both sections it was indicated that if one does not have a legitimate son but does have a son by a concubine, then the concubine's son becomes the heir and performs the ritual, and there is no need for adoption, the argument said. They continued by saying that the importance of distinguishing between legitimate and illegitimate is overly emphasized at times; if a first wife is widowed and childless but the husband had children by a concubine, the widow should not discard the *sŏja* in order to adopt a kinsman of her husband. As the argument developed it returned to the subject of the *ch'ongbu* by arguing that, by definition, the *ch'ongbu* was a widowed legitimate wife who had children. If she was childless, she could not inherit the ceremonies. The entry concluded by addressing Myŏngjong's initial comment that the Code was inconsistent and by arguing that there was no particular need to revise and clarify any of these issues. "The Code and the Royal Decrees are sufficient as they stand," was the recommendation of the State Council and Yun Wŏn-hyŏng. The king adopted their recommendation which favored *sŏja* and went against the *ch'ongbu* and her preference, adoption of an heir.[53]

---

[51]Myŏngjong 9, 1554.10.*chŏnghae*; 17:51b-52a (20:238). In making their clarification, the Censorate lamented the fact that many do not make the distinction between the two categories.

The Censorate's conclusion was not new. Nine years earlier Myŏngjong had already decreed basically the same thing, that a widow did not have *ch'ongbu* status if her husband died before his parents died. *Sugyo chimnok* [Collected edicts] (Seoul: Chosen Sotokufu Chusuin, 1943), p. 23, Myŏngjong 2, 1547.10.26.

[52]Myŏngjong 11, 1556.8.*muja*; 21:11a-12b (20:353).

[53]*Ibid*., p. 12b. Myŏngjong was manipulated by his mother and her brother, Yun Wŏn-hyŏng, during the early years of his reign. This is a good example of the court and king bending to Yun's will. See chapter six, p. 94-95, for more on Yun.

Finally, this was the death knell for the *ch'ongbu* and her participation in the mourning rituals as the principal heir. Although widows, wives, concubines, and other women were involved in adoption matters after this point in history, the word "*ch'ongbu*" does not appear again in the *Shillok* and seldom in other sources.[54] She lost her prerogative to participate in the ceremonies herself, but the alternatives of recognizing a *sŏja* and *hyŏngmang chegŭp* were not to be winners either. The decision was rendered by king Myŏngjong at a time when he was influenced by his maternal uncle, Yun Wŏn-hyŏng, in a way that fell short of the Neo-Confucian ideal; and although the Myŏngjong court was favorable to *sŏja*, subsequent courts were going to make decisions in a manner that was more orthodox, more Confucian. The *ch'ongbu* lost, but that for which she argued, the adoption of a [husband's] nephew, agnatic adoption, was to be the eventual winner.

Conclusions

The early dynasty saw women as heirs, not only as daughters, but as adopted daughters and daughters-in-law. The word heir was not limited to one person, but multiple heirs were possible, each sharing property and the prerogative of participation in rituals. We have seen that adoption did not normally take place if there were daughters born to the family, but that as time went by there was a concern for adopting an heir who carried on the name and membership in the patrilineage. Yet there were adopted daughters who acted as heirs, many of whom were related affinally. We saw a case where a daughter was preferred over a (*suyang*) adopted son; and yet a *suyang* adoptee had full rights of heirship if the adoption was made while both parents were living. We saw that there were numerous cases of non-agnatic adoption, most of which involved some kind of matrilineal or affinal connection. In the late sixteenth century, the king began to catch the vision of the agnatic principle and urged the Ministry of Rites to reject both the daughter's claim and the *shiyang* adoption; and ordered them to find an agnatic adoption. We saw a long complicated case that revealed heirship by daughters and non-agnatic adoptees, but in the end of a series of lawsuits the

---

[54]If the word was used again in the *Shillok*, it was not picked up by the compilers of the *Shillok* index. The term "*ch'ongbu*" does appear in the *ŭirye yusŏl* [Explanations of questions about propriety] by Shin Kŭn, published in 1792, wherein Yi T'oegye (1501-1570) is quoted as saying that if the *ch'ongbu* were disallowed to participate in the ceremonies, she ought not be thrown out into the streets. We should see to it that she has a place to go, he said. Aside from this citation, the use of the term "*ch'ongbu*" seems to all but disappear from the Korean sources after the sixteenth century.

agnatic principle won and all the property was confiscated and given to the lineage heir of the patrilineage.

We saw that women were not only heirs as daughters and as adopted daughters, but also as daughters-in-law. As the patrilineal principle began to take hold, the daughter-in-law was in a weakened position as an heir, but she could still arrange for adoption of males heirs connected by female ties (matrilateral or affinal). Eventually, when the lineage principle (*chongppŏp*) became more firmly entrenched, widows (*ch'ongbu*) played important roles in arranging for preferred agnatic adoptions. She endured criticisms as a woman, a non-agnate, and eventually she became established as the one who, in consultation with lineage elders, decided which one of several nephew-generation candidates would be selected as the agnatically adopted heir at a time when heir came to mean one, and only one, person responsible for ceremonies for the lineage segment, and who would inherit all the property necessary to carry out the all-important ceremonies.

# 8

# Early Patterns of Adoption:
# Rivalry Between Sons

From the fifteenth through the seventeenth century, the patterns of adoption gradually changed. Initially several options were available; as we have seen in the previous chapter, even the adoption of a daughter was possible. Even when restricting one's choice to sons, there were several options to choose from, in the early period, but by the end of the seventeenth century the choices narrowed to agnatic adoption. In this chapter we will look at some of the rivalries that were possible in the process.

In the mid fifteenth century, backtracking for a century from where we left off in the previous chapter, there were controversies over which son should be the principal ritual heir. Although inheritance was equilateral, the trend to have the eldest son regarded as the primary ritual heir (*chongja* or *chongson*) was growing stronger. Eventually the conflict was resolved in giving the eldest son control of both property as well as ritual. First ritual primogeniture developed gradually through the fifteenth and sixteenth centuries, then economic primogeniture fell in line with the changes in inheritance practices in the late seventeenth century. Here, again, we see the influence of the Confucian ritual texts and their emphasis on the eldest son. Movement toward recognition of the eldest son was not without fits and starts, however. Those who held onto the concepts of equilateral inheritance and equal footing for siblings in rights to property and ritual would often cite the Code, whereas those who argued for a strengthening of the role of the eldest son would cite the ritual texts.

We will begin with cases from the fifteenth century concerning the disinheriting of the eldest son; in the discussions therein are revealed conflicting attitudes about the importance of the eldest son versus the equality of sons.

## The Cho Kŭn Case

The *Shillok* outlined the Cho case:

Cho Mal-saeng viewed his eldest grandson, Yŏng, as incompetent and in his place had the name of his third son, Kŭn, written on the ancestral tablet of his deceased wife [indicating that he was to be the ritual heir]. He also wrote a document in his own hand indicating he had changed his principal heir. . . . The provision in the Code that states that another son (*ch'aja*) should attend the rituals speaks to the case where the father dies without a will. In the case of Cho Mal-saeng, he clearly indicated how the heirship should be. The fact that Yŏng was not qualified is known to everyone. This cannot be called a case of breaking the law because of loving one son and hating another.[1]

The most important factor in the case is that the father had the authority to change his heir. The fact that he did it, and did so in writing, rationally, and without emotional partiality, left the result unchallenged. That he chose his third son, rather than the next in line, the second son, was not an issue. At this point in the fifteenth century, primogeniture was still an alien concept.[2]

## The Kim Kyŏn-su Case

General Kim Yŏn-ji had three sons, Ik-su, Kyŏng-su and Kyŏn-su. Kyŏng-su had two children and then died while his father was still alive. Yŏn-ji did not want Ik-su, the eldest, to be his principal heir and wrote a document in his own hand designating Kyŏn-su as the ritual heir. Ik-su died and shortly thereafter Yŏn-ji died. Ik-su's widow [Mme Song], arguing that Yŏn-ji had not petitioned the government for permission to change the

---

[1]Sejo 4, 1458.8.*shinsa*; 13:38b (7:291) and *MTP* B:78b,4d. The *Shillok* entry emphasized the incompetence of the first son:

Moreover, if there was not a problem of competence, how could a father, on the basis of love or hate, go against all convention and law to try to disinherit his firstborn. Clearly, there is no error in this matter. The parents of an incompetent heir would take their sorrows to the grave. If they could not change the heirship, then would the laws that govern both the living and the dead be just?

[2]The fact that King T'aejong had abdicated before his death in order to pass the throne to his third son, Sejong, in 1418, may have been an obvious precedent. Later in the dynasty it is clear that the royal family was run on a set of precedence different from the aristocracy, but in the early dynasty that may not have been the case; what was fair for the king's family was fair for those who had helped put the king on the throne, e.g., the Cho Mal-saeng family.

heirship, filed suit with the Ministry of Rites. The Ministry, upon examination of the case, found that Yŏn-ji had already discussed the issue with his sons and sons-in-law, had written the document in his own hand, had witnesses to it, and had indicated that all the ritual property from his family and his wife's family was to go to Kyŏn-su. This was not a case of a senseless, senile old man changing the property on the basis of affection for the youngest child, they said; and although there is a regulation that these matters should be reported to the government, Yŏn-ji's document is dated before the enactment of that regulation and should therefore not be disregarded. Mme Song did not observe the written will of her father-in-law and in filing the suit strayed from her responsibility as a virtuous wife. She has violated basic moral precepts, they concluded, and recommended that the king follow the father's intent and recognize Kyŏn-su as the principal heir. The king agreed.[3]

Mme Song, although the term was not used, was a *ch'ongbu* and might have had a case had one condition been different. Structurally, her case was not much different from that of Mme An, the wife of Yi Kwi-su or that of the wife of Yŏ Maeng-on (see pages 123 and 124). But, unlike her counterparts of 76 years later, Mme Song lost her case. The critical factor in this case, too, seems to have been the will, the written intention of the father-in-law, which indicated a procedure different from that outlined in the Code. But since it was written by the father the document was considered valid and was implemented. The precedents set in both the Cho Kŭn and the Kim Kyŏn-su cases were specifically cited in the following case.

## The Shin Sŭng-min Case

At issue was a conflict between Shin Sŭng-min and Shin Chong-nyŏn. Sŭng-min had been a favorite of his great grandfather, Shin Hyo-ch'ang, and had apparently been designated the lineage heir by him. Chong-nyŏn disputed that point and argued that he, the grandson of the second son, should have priority over the grandson of the third son. The first son's descendants were out of the picture because of their *sŏja* status.[4]

Twenty of the highest officials of the day representing the State Council, the Six Ministries, and the Censorate were called to arbitrate the case. The basic premise was that the eldest son performs the ceremonies,

---

[3]Sŏngjong 6, 1475.2.*kyemi*; 52:4a (9:191) and *MTP* A:198a,1c-d.

[4]Sŏngjong 10, 1479.8.*kabo*; 107:7a (10:43); *RZS* p. 114; *MTP* B:43b,4b-d and *MTP* S:347,4a-c; and *MYCP* 2-63a,64a.

they said, but the Code also provides for the second son to perform the ceremonies if the first son has no heir.

Table 8.1
Shin Lineage Diagram (I)

The *Shillok* stated:

Shin Hyo-ch'ang's eldest son, Cha-gŭn, had no legitimate heir but has a *sŏja*. The second son, Cha-gyŏng, has many sons and grandsons. It is proper that he be the heir to Hyo-ch'ang. But Sŭng-min desires to be the heir and has testaments written by his great-grandfather and by his great uncle, Cha-gŭn. In the testament of Hyo-ch'ang it says: "In 1415, I gave orders to my son Cha-gŭn that Cha-su be made the adopted heir (*suyang kyehu*).[5] In 1434, I took my second son Cha-gyŏng's son, Yun-dong, as heir; but in 1439 when Yun-dong died, then I chose the wisest of my grandsons to be my heir."[6]

---

[5]The usage of the term *suyang kyehu* is unique and somewhat odd, but the usage tells us that the society of the time used such terms in an ambiguous and imprecise way when compared with later times. *Suyang* means adoption in a general sense, but specifically it is the adoption of a baby under the age of three, who is not an agnate, and who may have his surname changed to that of the family. *Kyehu* is a term that means adoption in the sense of "continuing the lineage" for those in the scholar/official class. See chapter one, p. 22, for definitions of these terms. Using these two specifically defined terms in the above context was unique in the *Shillok* record, and reveals that the thinking of the time was less than precise; exactly the kind of thinking that led to the dispute. Also see these terms in the glossary.

[6]Waltner quotes a late Ming commentary on the Code to indicate that the Chinese justified adopting a distant relative on the basis of *hsien*, the same term Shin Hyo-ch'ang chose (Korean: *hyŏn*) which can be translated as wise, or worthy. See *Getting an Heir*, p. 50, *passim, Ta Ming lü chi-chieh fu-li*, vol. 2, 4/11b, p. 558.

Based on this information, we see that Hyo-ch'ang first wanted Cha-su to be his heir but in the end wanted to be succeeded by the wisest of his heirs. This seems to have been his basic intent. Cha-gǔn, in line with his father's wish, desired to see Yun-gwan, who was Cha-su's son and as a descendant of his [Cha-gǔn's] father, made the heir. This is possible both on the basis of law and emotion; but Cha-gǔn, himself, could not fulfill the wish because he had a *sŏja* for an heir.[7]

In this situation, as the *Shillok* explained it, Cha-gǔn had a *sŏja* who could perform ceremonies for him; Cha-gyŏng had a son who could perform ceremonies for him; Cha-su had a son, Yun-bo, who could perform the ceremonies for him; and the grandfather, Hyo-ch'ang, had his grandson, Yun-gwan, who could perform the ceremonies for him. But in this arrangement, "Hyo-ch'ang does not have a son, and Yun-gwan does not have a father."[8]

In this early period, the concept of a lineage heir was not well developed as is seen in the attempt to have one son perform ceremonies to his father while the other is designated the principal heir to the grandfather. There were those in that period who argued that "this not only destroys the generational order but is also without basis both in natural feelings and law. From ancient times to the present, in the whole realm, there has never been a basis for making such an arrangement."[9]

Hyo-ch'ang's will indicated that he wanted his wisest descendant to be his heir. Although Sǔng-min claimed that that referred to him, the high officials asked how one determines whether Sǔng-min or Chong-nyŏn was wise or not.

This case is different from those of Cho Kǔn and Kim Kyŏn-su [cited immediately above]. Both were made heirs to their grandfathers, but both were linked to their grandfathers through their fathers. There was no

---

[7] *Ibid*. *MYCP* lists *muhu* (no heir) for Cha-gǔn. Yun-gwan is the third of five sons in *MYCP* 2:64A.

[8] *Ibid*.

[9] *Ibid*. 7b. This was a statement set forth by twenty officials listed by name who were all the senior officials of the court including the chief state counsel, the heads of the six ministries and the heads of the censorate.

directive like that of Hyo-ch'ang's in either case and neither was like Yun-gwan regarding his grandfather as a father.[10] One side argued that the matter of Hyo-ch'ang's heir should be settled by the Code by simply designating Cha-gyŏng's eldest son, Chong-nyŏn, the heir. The other side emphasized the importance of a man's will. They also noted that Sŭng-min had been performing the ceremonies for several years. "To change a son's status in one morning and give [the heirship] to another would violate the grandfather's will." The matter was left unresolved that day.[11]

Ten days later the same high officials were summoned and ordered to take up the case again. Some suggested that the Shin Sŭng-min affair was like that of Cho Kŭn and Kim Kyŏn-su, and Sŭng-min should be the heir. He had already been carrying out the ceremonies, they pointed out. But more of the officials outlined reasons for naming Chong-nyŏn the heir. The cases of Cho Kŭn and Kim Kyŏn-su were labeled as exceptional and should not be cited as precedents, they said. They interpreted the rule of heirship by the second son (*hyŏngmang chegŭp*) to mean that when the first son is disqualified, the responsibility devolves to the second, not the third son's line. The king said he would take the matter under advisement.[12]

The next day a compromise solution was proposed:

> The concept of the eldest being the primary heir has been an accepted practice from antiquity to the present. Human emotions and heavenly principles ought to be exercised together without sacrificing one to the other. It would not be right to give all of Sŭng-min's property to Chong-nyŏn. Can the property be divided between them?[13]

Other high officials agreed, arguing that since the father's directives were conflicting, perhaps the ritual responsibility, along with the property,

---

[10]*Ibid.* In the early period there are numerous cases of one heir-one ancestor; a certain heir is designated to perform ceremonies for a certain ancestor. As time went by one heir would perform ceremonies for the whole ascending line. This criticism of Yun-gwan skipping a generation and performing ceremonies for only the grandfather, is a criticism ahead of its time in terms of "lineal thinking."

[11]*Ibid.*

[12]Sŏngjong 10, 1479.8.*kapchin*; 107:12b (10:45). The concept of heirship of the second son is the essence of what Deuchler describes as horizontal inheritance, common in the Koryŏ period, which was eventually replaced by the Neo-Confucian inspired vertical inheritance, or the implementation of the *chongppŏp*. See Deuchler's *The Confucian Transformation of Korea*, p. 45, p. 140, and p. 207.

[13]Sŏngjong 10, 1479.8.*ŭlsa*; 107:15 (10:47).

could be divided. Sŏngjong decided that the property could be divided equally between the two disputing descendants.[14]

In 1483, four years after the unfortunate Shin Sŭng-min had to share his inheritance with a cousin, he was again involved in an inheritance dispute. This time the issue was slightly different. It was not a question of whether the second or third brother should be the heir when the eldest son had no heir, but rather should the adopted son of the second brother have priority over the adopted son of the third brother.

Table 8.2
Shin Lineage Diagram (II)

The Censorate proposed that Sŭng-yŏn, an adopted cousin to Sŭng-min, should be the primary heir to Cha-su. Sŭng-min challenged the decision.[15] In the discussion, it was noted that Cha-su's eldest son, Yun-bo, had no heir and neither did the second son, Yun-jŏ.[16] Therefore, Sŭng-min, as the adopted heir to the third son, could carry out the lineage ceremonies (sŭngsa taejong). Sŏngjong's decision was in favor of Sŭng-yŏn because both he and Sŭng-min had the same basic qualification—both were direct descendants of Cha-su—but Sŭng-yŏn was adopted to the second son whereas Sŭng-min was adopted to the third.[17]

---

[14]Ibid. Note that this method of dividing the ritual heirship was radically different form that used after the seventeenth century when primogeniture was the modus operandi.

[15]His argument was that Sŭng-yŏn had forged the adoption documents. The Censorate agreed that the documents looked suspicious, but upon checking with Yun-jŏ's widow, Mme Yi, they confirmed that she intended the adoption to take place.

[16]MYS 2-63a,64a indicates that Yun-bo had three daughters and two sons, but his first son had only a daughter and the second is labeled muhu (without heir). It also indicates that Yun-jŏ was muhu.

[17]Sŏngjong 14, 1483.1.chŏngyu; 150:3b (10:424) and MTP B:43b,4b-d and MTP S:347, 4a-c.

<u>The Pak Kon Case</u>

Forty years later, crossing the line into the sixteenth century, a similar case is found, the case of Pak Kon. The difference between the Pak case and the second Shin case above was that the heir to the third son was biological, not adopted (and in both cases the heir to the second son was adopted). A distinction was drawn between *iphu* (jural succession) and *pongsa* (ritual succession). The discussion was theoretical and nonspecific, initially.[18] The next day the specifics of the case came to the fore. The dispute was between Pak Hwi, the son of a third brother, and Pak Kon, the adopted son of the second brother.[19]

The widow of Pak Sung-ye, Mme Yi, adopted Kon, a son of her husband's cousin. Hwi took the ancestor tablet of his grandfather, Pak Ni, from the ancestor shrine by force, claiming the right to perform the ceremony (*pongsa*). In the process Hwi broke down the gate of the ancestor shrine.

Table 8.3
Pak Lineage Diagram

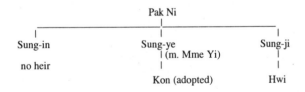

The Ministry of Rites stated that if the eldest son is without an heir but has an adopted son (*kyehuja*), and if the adopted son is the biological son of the adopting father's sibling, then he can offer the ceremonies. But if he is a clan-cousin (*sojok*), a cousin that does not share a common natural grandfather, then he can offer the rites to the father and mother to whom he is adopted, and the son of the second son can properly perform the ceremonies for the grandparents. The king declared that the genealogical relationship between Kon and Hwi should be verified: if Kon was a

---

[18]Chungjong 15, 1520.12.*imin*; 41:14b (16:7).

[19]Chungjong 15, 1520.12.*kyemyo*; 41:15a (16:8); *RZS*, p. 371; and *MYS* 6-38b, & 10-82ab,83ab.

descendant (*ch'inson*) of Pak Ni, then he can offer the ceremonies; but if not, then Hwi should.[20]

Three days later, the court discussed the issue again. Although the *Shillok* does not record a decision, the king spoke in favor of the adopted son, Kon, in spite of the fact that he had said earlier that Kon should not perform the ceremonies if he were not a direct descendant. Kon was classified as a "clan-cousin" (*chokson*), whereas Hwi was classified as a direct descendant (*ch'inson*), but the king and the court favored the adopted son and spoke of the criminality of Hwi in breaking into the shrine, taking the spirit tablet and proceeding to inappropriately perform ceremonies.[21] Although Hwi's alleged criminality overshadowed the case, still the court was inclined toward the adopted son of the second brother over the natal son of the third brother.

In the above cases we see an interesting transition. In the cases of Cho Kŭn and Kim Kyŏn-su, the third brother's son won. In the first Shin Sŭng-min case, the dispute was settled by a fifty-fifty compromise. In the second Shin case and forty years later in the Pak case, the third brother lost to the second brother's line.

The alternative of having a second or third son serve as the ritual heir was problematic and short-lived in application. Gradually, the eldest son came to have full rights and authority in regard to heirship of both property and ritual rights. In the cases above the first son was disinherited: in the first case for incompetence, in the second because of early death, and in the third because he had only a *sŏja* heir. In the fourth and fifth, a dispute between sons adopted to the second and third brothers ignored the possibility of adopting an heir for the eldest brother. By the latter half of the dynasty, an heir would certainly have been adopted for each of these eldest sons in prominent lineages.

## The Kyech'uk Decree

In 1553 (the *kyech'uk* year in the traditional calendar), while emphasizing the point that only close kin should be adopted,[22] the court discussed the case of Yi Sŏn:

---

[20]*Ibid.*

[21]Chungjong 15, 1520.12.*pyŏngo*; 15:15b (16:8) and *RZS*, p. 372.

[22]The *Analects* were quoted wherein it states that for a non-descendant to perform the ceremonies is flattery, meaning such performance of ceremonies would be an attempt to curry favor from a prominent deceased person. *Analects*, II.xxiv.1; p. 154 in the Legge edition. Waltner also makes reference to this passage in China.

Yi Sŏn, who had no heir adopted his nephew, Yi Han-wŏn, by petitioning the Ministry of Rites according to law. Thereafter, his second wife, Mme Yi, gave birth to a son. After Sŏn died, the same Mme Yi petitioned for a dissolution of the adoption. This was wrong. The Ministry of Rites should have disapproved the petition because the father-son relationship had been fixed. They followed an inappropriate precedent in dissolving the adoption. Not only was this completely wrong by law and righteousness, but according to the Ming Code, one should adopt a nephew [a relative of the proper generation level]. One should look first among close relatives then gradually to more and more distant relatives to find an adoptable son. Only in that manner can one go to a distant relative.[23]

The degree of kinship involved in the adoption was a minor point in this case. The more important element, a son born after an adoption was made, became the basis for the *Kyech'uk* Degree. The decree stated:

An adopted son becomes a man's son. From ancient times until the present, this has always been true and should not be changed once it is done. A man who has no heir adopts a nephew as his heir. Once an adoption is made, one certainly ought not simply dissolve the adoption by petition to the government on the basis of emotion. . . .

If after the adoption is made, a son is born, the property should be divided equally between them, but the biological son should perform the ceremony and the adopted son should be the "second son" (*ch'aja*). This is the basic intent of the Ming Code which should [be followed to] eliminate fights based on misinformation and personal opinion. In the case at hand, even if Yi Sŏn were alive he could not have dissolved the adoption. Mme Yi, as one who does not know the principles of righteousness, has asked for a dissolution of adoption. And the Ministry of Rites's authorization of such an act is wrong in the extreme.

Based on the Ming Code, one ought to proceed slowly and carefully in dissolving adoptions. From this time forth

---

[23]*Sugyo chimnok*, no. 48, 1553.4.20, p. 26. There is only a partial account in the *Shillok*: Myŏngjong 8, 1553.4.*imjin*; 14:47a (20:131).

this shall be an unchanging law. In order that there be no disputes in the dissolution of adoptions this decree is given to the Ministry of Rites.[24]

The *Kyech'uk* Decree was controversial from the outset, and the more it was argued the wider its impact was felt. Five months after the original decree, while its interpretation was still being argued, a test case emerged involving not a conflict between an adopted son and a later-born legitimate son but one between an adopted son and a *sŏja*.

## The Nam Cho-wŏn Case

The following case is long and complicated. It is one of the most detailed cases of controversy over heirship in the *Shillok*. It contains several significant elements highlighting the issues which were important at the time. Although the initial controversy centers on the eligibility of a *sŏja* to serve as the ritual heir, a subject explored in chapters five and six, the argument turned to the subject of adopting an heir and raised the question of which candidate, among the range of kinsmen, would be most appropriate. The role of the widow, a subject discussed in chapter seven, is also noteworthy.

### Table 8.4
### Lineage Diagram of Nam Cho-wŏn

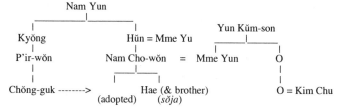

The Censorate set forth the case by first outlining the dilemma of using a *sŏja* as an heir. "... although the *sŏja* is of low status, he has the same blood as a legitimate son, ... yet a man's widow hates the *sŏja*."[25]

---

[24]*Ibid.*

[25]Myŏngjong 8, 1553.9.*shinhae*; 15:19a (20:155). Deuchler also analyzed this case; "Heaven Does Not Discriminate," p. 131.

Nam Cho-wŏn had no heir but had two *sŏja*. After his death, his widow, Mme Yun, discarded the *sŏja* and adopted her husband's fourth-*ch'on* cousin's son, Chŏng-guk. After Mme Yun died and he completed the three-year's mourning [for her], the *sŏja* brothers wanted an equitable share of their father's property. Chŏng-guk, in anger, created a document alleging that Hae [the *sŏja*] and his brother had committed numerous crimes and submitted it to the Censorate which office arrested and imprisoned Hae.[26]

The case was complicated by the fact that one of the censors who raised the issue, Kim Chu, was a relative by marriage (his wife's mother was a full sister) of Mme Yun.

The *Shillok* historians added the following interlinear comment:[27]

> [Nam] Chŏng-guk's elder brother, Chŏng-bang, died without a son; therefore Chŏng-guk ought not to have become another's heir, yet he coveted the property of Cho-wŏn. He induced his older brother's widow to adopt a distant cousin to her line while he, for his part, sought to become the heir of Mme Yun [Nam Cho-wŏn]. Concerning his dispute with his *sŏja* brothers, Hae, et. al., he gave large bribes to Yun Wŏn-hyŏng and Kim Chu. The high officials thus were inhibited by Yun; that is why this turned out the way it did.[28]

The issue surfaced again three days later.

> Concerning the matter of Nam Cho-wŏn, he performed *chesa* for his grandfather, the Provincial Governor Nam Yun, but he had only *sŏja* who are not qualified to serve *chesa* to Nam Yun. Cho-wŏn's younger brothers, Ŭng-wŏn and Sŏb-wŏn, did not have sons. Therefore, in 1535, Mme Yi, Cho-wŏn's mother, requested as an adopted heir Mong-dŭk, the son of Cho-wŏn's fourth-*ch'on* cousin, Sung-wŏn. But Mong-dŭk died, and Mme Yun, the wife of Cho-wŏn, petitioned (Mme Yi had died so that it was Mme Yun who petitioned) asking that another fourth-*ch'on* cousin (P'ir-wŏn)'s son, Chŏng-guk, be adopted to serve the *chesa* to

---

[26]*Ibid.*, p. 19b.

[27]*MTP* B:153a,1b. See *MYS* 3-97B for Nam's lineage data; 8-96a for his marriage to Yun Kŭm-son's daughter; and 9-91b for Kim Chu's marriage. Kim Chu and Yun Kŭm-son both passed the highest civil service exam (serial sequence numbers in the Wagner-Song index are #2823 and #1725, respectively).

[28]Myŏngjong 8, 1553.9.*shinhae*; 15:19b (20:155).

Nam Yun. This is proper according to the law of offering *chesa* in the Code. It is not that Mme Yun hated the *sŏja* and did this to suit her own fancy, moreover, Cho-wŏn is the eldest legitimate heir of Nam Chae, a *kaeguk kongshin* [merit subject at the founding of the dynasty]. If Cho-wŏn has no heir then the ceremonies for Nam Chae will be cut off. Not only should Mme Yun seek an heir but moreover it is appropriate that the state also should select an heir for Cho-wŏn so that the *chesa* can be served to Nam Chae. Cho-wŏn had no heirs and his younger brothers had no heirs either. Two fourth-*ch'on* cousins, Ch'i-wŏn and Sung-wŏn, each had only one son. Another fourth-*ch'on* cousin, Chun-wŏn had no heirs. Only P'ir-wŏn had two sons. His second son is Chŏng-guk. For the sake of the ceremonies to Nam Yun, the primary line great-grandson of Nam Chae, Mme Yun had no choice but to make Chŏng-guk the heir and adopt him.

Chŏng-guk's recent petition to this office [the Censorate] states that Nam Hae had said Chŏng-guk's adoption documents were forged and presented as part of a stratagem; therefore, this office has obtained the Ministry of Rites register[29] and compared it to the data in Nam Hae's allegation. We found a petition dated 1548 from Mme Yun which stated that Mong-dŭk once had been adopted but had died and that she desired Chŏng-guk to be the heir to offer *chesa*. Special royal permission was granted. Nam Hae's suit, stating that Chŏng-guk's adoption certificate had been forged, is, in our judgment, not credible; therefore, we view Nam Hae's crime as extreme.[30]

It was recommended that Hae be prosecuted, not for contending legitimacy and fighting for property but for calling the king's authorization a forgery. This, it was charged, was tantamount to ridiculing the king himself.[31]

---

[29]This register was likely the *Kyehu tŭngnok* [The register of adoptions] that is kept in the Kyujanggak. The extant volumes begin with one numbered "volume two" in 1618. The above case could well have been recorded in the missing volume one. For more on the register see chapter nine.

[30]Myŏngjong 8, 1553.9.*kabin*; 15:21a-b (20:156) & *RZS* p. 363.

[31]*Ibid.*, p. 21b.

As preface to the above case, the Censorate presented a discussion in which the terms "*pongsa*" and "*iphu*" were defined and used to argue for adoptions of distant relatives in a theoretical sense and specifically in the Nam Cho-wŏn case. In the interpretation presented, *pongsa* was defined as ceremonial responsibility to the great-grandfather, grandfather, and the father, or in other words, lineage heir status. *Iphu* refers to one generation, they argued, and was an adoption with responsibility to serve the father only. They said *pongsa* was for the lineage (*chong*), which was defined as three generations; whereas *iphu* was said to be for one individual (*ilgi*).[32]

The definitions were useful to the Censorate in making their argument at that point, but in fact, as time went by, the line between the two terms, "*pongsa*" and "*iphu*," became quite indistinct. Both terms came to refer to lineage status, and as the concept of lineage grew deeper after the middle of the dynasty, the concept of adoption for the lineage came to mean much more than the three generations outlined by the Censorate in 1553. And, in fact, in the Nam Cho-wŏn case, the importance of continuing the *chesa* for Nam Chae, a sixth-generation ancestor, was given greater stress. But at that time, as the concept of lineage was growing stronger in Korean society, the above argument including its distinction between the various types of heirs was one of the first statements of the necessity to adopt more distant kinsmen.

Continuing from the above citation, the Censorate went on to say that since the *pongsa* heir performed ceremonies for the father, grandfather and great-grandfather, that if one's sibling's son could not be found as a candidate for adoption, then a fourth-*ch'on* cousin's son, a blood descendant of one's grandfather, could be selected. And if not a fourth-*ch'on* cousin's son, then the son of a sixth-*ch'on* cousin, the descendant of one's great grandfather, could be selected.[33] Thus the rationale was developed and justified to select increasingly more distant kinsmen as adopted heirs. The more distant, vertically, the ancestor to be honored, the more remote, horizontally, the "nephew" that was eligible to be adopted as an heir.

Two months later, the State Council issued a statement concerning the adoption case of Nam Cho-wŏn in which they criticized the handling of the case by the Censorate. They reviewed the decision and quoted again the same passages of the Code that had been quoted in the presentation of the

---

[32]Myŏngjong 8, 1553.9.*kabin*; 15:20b (20:155). This categorization of the terms "*iphu*" and "*pongsa*" mirror that found thirty-three years earlier in the reign of King Chungjong. See Chungjong 15, 1520.12.*imin*; 41:14b (16:7).

[33]*Ibid.*, 21a.

case earlier, but drew a distinction between close and distant relatives. They argued that:

> [The descendants of] the grandfather are close but [the descendants of] the great grandfather are distant. In making adoptions, one ought to choose those who are close. This is the intent of the Code.[34]

Concerning the selection of heirs for ancestors who were illustrious or meritorious subjects, the Chief State Council stated that one need not necessarily choose a fourth-*ch'on* cousin's son as long as one selects the senior-most among all of the man's descendants to perform the ceremonies to the ancestor. They requested that this matter be turned over to the Ministry of Rites for detailed discussion and a decision.[35]

As with many cases of change and innovation, there were those who proposed the change and those who were against it. In 1553 the Censorate, manned by younger officials, represented those who saw the need to go to more distant relatives to find heirs for adoption, but the State Council, manned by senior statesmen, was opposed. Eventually the State Council's position would not be able to withstand the tide; beginning at this point Chosŏn period Koreans began to adopt more and more distant members of the patrilineage as heirs to property and ceremony. And indeed, their perceptions of kinsmen in terms of patrilineal groupings began to grow more distinct.

### The Debate of 1556

Three years later, the *Kyech'uk* Decree and the precedent set that year became a matter of discussion at court. Hong Sŏm, the Minister of Rites, proposed in a lengthy memorial that the issue of adoption and heirship be settled and that the *Kyech'uk* Decree be clarified. He said:

> In the *iphu* section of the Code where it says, "If a man does not have an heir by either his wife or concubine, then he may request permission of the government to adopt a nephew," it means that if one has a *sŏja*, one cannot adopt someone else's son. But the Code also says, "Although one has a *sŏja*, if one desires to adopt his younger brother's son, he may petition." Now this means that when the *sŏja*'s father is still

---

[34]Myŏngjong 11, 1553.11.*kapchin*; 15:52a (20:171) and *RZS*, p. 364.
[35]*Ibid.*

alive, one does not want to "eat from the hands of a *sŏja*" [how much less would one, as a departed spirit, want to receive offerings from a *sŏja* after one's death]. But if this father is already dead, the *sŏja*'s "legitimate mother" [the dead man's widow] cannot discard her husband's *sŏja* and adopt one of the husband's nephews, that is clear. In recent years, the laws have not been strictly observed. There are numerous cases where the widow, out of jealousy and not wanting to see the ceremonies performed by the *sŏja*, petitions and receives special permission to adopt one of her husband's nephews.

In the last *kyech'uk* year [1553], the views of the State Council and of the officials of the Ministry of Rites were obtained as follows: "In a case where the eldest son has only a *sŏja*, he may not adopt anyone but the son of his younger brother." Since this decree was issued, there have been numerous petitions to the Censorate or to the Ministry of Rites from *sŏja* who were unable to become their father's heirs, requesting that a sixth-, eighth-, or tenth-*ch'on* adoption be dissolved. We would like to do as they wish, but when the adopted son has already worn the mourning clothes and mourned for the adoptive parents, can they again revert to being nephews? This is a serious and difficult matter. We would like the already decided matter not to be changed, but then not only would a son [*sŏja*] be unable to treat his father as his father, but also the provision of the Code that only he who is without a concubine's son can adopt is violated; and the *Kyech'uk* Decree will not be carried out.

Now, are all those pre-*Kyech'uk* Decree cases of those who long ago became heirs to be changed one after another in accordance with the high officials' interpretation [of the *Kyech'uk* decree], and thereby return the heirship to the *sŏja*? Or should it apply only to those who adopted since the decree was issued? Let us call another council and settle this matter to avoid future disputes.[36]

After thus criticizing the practice of adoption as it was developing at the time, particularly in cases where a *sŏja* was ignored, Hong went on to lay blame at the feet of the widows who tried to bypass their husbands' *sŏja*.

---

[36]Myŏngjong 11, 1556.2.*pyŏngjin*; 20:13b (20:323) and *RZS*, p. 367-370.

In his statement, one sees the powerful influence of the widow in the selection of an adopted heir:

> The legitimate wives always point out that there are limitations on the *sŏja* in that they are allowed to perform the *chesa* for the parents' generation only and they do not want to see *sŏja* become heirs. In searching out the basic intent of this matter in the Code, we find the commentary on the article, "*Sŏja* promoted to lineage heir [*sŭngjung*]," which says, "the *sŏja* who has been promoted to lineage heir performs the ceremonies for his own mother in a private room and the observation of the ceremony is limited to her [and none of her ancestors]. . . . For a *sŏja*, although his personal status is elevated to that of lineage heir, his mother is still base, therefore he performs the ceremonies for her in his private room and the ceremonies stop with her. But there is no doubt that he ought to perform the noblemen's ceremonies for the father and grandfather for whom he is heir. But these days, the widows do not want to see the *sŏja* promoted to lineage heir status. It is necessary to obtain testimony on this point as well [as that mentioned above], because we hear some arguments that coincide with this view and some that do not. Please call a conference and decide this matter.[37]

Myŏngjong agreed to call the conference. Opinions must have varied outside of the State Council but there was unanimity among the three State Councilors and Yun Wŏn-hyŏng. The State Council was all in line with Yun on the subject. Among them, Chief State Councilor Shim Yŏn-wŏn stated:

> Previously when we spoke of permitting only the son of one's brother to be adopted, it was because one's younger brother's son is a bloodline grandson of one's father. Thus, he can succeed to the rites for his grandfather and the more distant ancestors and become their successor. The more distant relative is not a descendant of that grandfather and is therefore not qualified to succeed. If we know that "the spirits will not partake of offerings from those who are not descendants," then

---

[37]*Ibid.*, 14a.

what is the point of even discussing who is first and who is last in [terms of] the law?[38]

Second State Councilor Sang Chin spoke out in support of *sŏja* but indicated concern about repealing adoptions that had been made prior to the enactment of the *Kyech'uk* Decree. He suggested that only violations made since the decree should be corrected.[39] Third State Councilor Yun Kae echoed the sentiments of the other State Councilors and stressed the father-son relationship as one of the great moral relationships of society:

> It clearly states in the Code that if a legitimate son does not have an heir, he should have his *sŏja* perform the ceremonies. This cannot be changed in a hundred or a thousand generations.[40]

He went on to criticize the Ministry of Rites for allowing adoptions when they should not, as in cases where there is already a *sŏja* who could serve as the heir.

Myŏngjong's maternal uncle, Yun Wŏn-hyŏng, summarized the position of the State Council by saying:

> It is clear that the entry in the Code which states, "He who has no heir by either wife or concubine, may adopt a nephew to be his heir," means that if one has a *sŏja*, one should not adopt. It is true that at times high officials with *sŏja* have strongly wished to make a nephew their heir and have petitioned for and received special permission to adopt. But such has been a temporary prerogative of a high official; it should not be considered a precedent applicable to everyone. How much more so for the widow who lives alone and discards her deceased husband's *sŏja* and on her own makes a special request to adopt her husband's distant kinsman—this is a severe violation of the law. Even if one can obtain special permission, the lineage elders ought to obey the law and block attempts to petition the throne, thereby "firmly fortifying the dikes of the paddies." A law often ignored becomes like water over the dike. The intent of the *Kyech'uk* Decree was to fortify the dike. For those who made an adoption before the

---

[38]*Ibid.*

[39]*Ibid.*, 14a-b.

[40]*Ibid.*, 14b.

*Kyech'uk* Decree, since the sons have already worn the mourning clothes and the father-son relationship is established, it would be improper to make changes now. What about those adoptions enacted after *kyech'uk*? When it says, "commoners only perform ceremonies for the father and the mother," it refers to the fact that the parents are not aristocrats . But when we refer to a *sŏja* who is made a lineage heir, we should use the precedent of the aristocrats and then there will be no doubt that he should perform ceremonies for his father and grandfather.[41]

Myŏngjong, taking his cues from his powerful uncle, said:

We will carry out the principles of the *Kyech'uk* Decree. But we need not change those adoptions made before the decree was issued, and neither can we change the cases of those high officials who asked for special royal permission even though permission was sought after the issuance of the *Kyech'uk* Decree.[42]

The court of Myŏngjong, which in 1553 and again in 1556 held fast to its support of the *sŏja* as heir and to its rulings which limited the scope and frequency of adoption, was fighting a losing battle. Only a few high officials outside of the State Council felt supportive of the pro-*sŏja*, anti-adoption position. One reason for the State Council's intransigence, as was pointed out in chapter six, was the unique position of Yun Wŏn-hyŏng. As the king's mother's brother he held unusual power, and as one who sought to open the road to legitimacy for his children by his concubine, Nanjŏng, he fought strongly against the tide. Yun's advocacy was eventually more of a detriment than an asset because of his infamy. He was exiled and executed, with his concubine, upon the death of his sister, Myŏngjong's mother. And thereafter, he was known as one of the villains of the Chosŏn period.

## Sŏnjo and the *Kyech'uk* Decree

Twenty four years later, Sŏnjo was faced with the problem of interpreting the wide ranging and ambiguous *Kyech'uk* Decree. The case that brought the issue to the court was that of the adoption of Yu Hwa.

---

[41]*Ibid.*, 14b-15a.
[42]*Ibid.*, 15a.

Hwa was adopted to Yu Sa-sang who was the son of Yu Pu. Sa-sang later sired a *sŏja* named On. Sa-sang petitioned to have the adoption of Hwa dissolved and have On perform the ceremonies. The king asked that the court discuss the case in light of the Ming Code which stated that if a son is born after an adoption, the later-born son should perform the ceremonies and the adopted son should be considered a second son.

The court was divided but did not consider dissolution of the adoption proper, rather they argued either that the adopted son should be the heir or that the later-born *sŏja*, as a biological son, should be the primary heir (like a first-born son) with the adopted son taking a subordinate role (like a second son). Those who subscribed to the second view argued that Hwa was a *shiyangja*, not a *kyehuja*. As the institution developed, a *kyehu* adoption (also known as *iphu*) was for the sake of an ascending line of ancestors, and the son had full rights to property as well as the rights to participate in the ceremonies; but the *shiyang* adoption was merely for one parent or the other and did not serve the ancestors.

Table 8.5
Yu Lineage Diagram

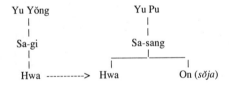

Sŏnjo decided that the *sŏja* should perform the ceremonies for the ancestors and the adopted son was restricted to performing the ceremonies for Sa-sang, the father. The Censorate, defending the adopted son, strongly challenged Sŏnjo's decision on the spot, but the king cited the Ming law as part of the basis for his rejection of the Censorate's position.[43]

Three months later, the Censorate raised the issue of Yu Hwa's adoption and questioned the decision of the court. Censor Ki Tae-jŏng argued that the adopted son should have continued as the primary ritual heir, but the king held to his decision.[44]

---

[43]Sŏnjo 13, 1580.10.*imja*; 14:17b-18a (21:367-8).
[44]Sŏnjo 14, 1581.1.*shinmi*; 15:1b (21:370).

Twenty nine days later the high officials again discussed the case of Yu Hwa's adoption. Some argued that an adoption made should not be dissolved. Others argued that the biological son had primacy. Others cited the *Kyech'uk* Decree which stated that a biological son should perform the ceremonies and the adopted son should be treated as a second son (*chungja*) and the property should be divided equally.[45] Sŏnjo shifted his position, and citing both the Ming law (to support the *sŏja*) and Korean custom (to divide property equally), decided to divide the property between the two sons and consider the adopted son as a *shiyangja*.[46]

### The Shim Chi-wŏn Case and the *Kyech'uk* Decree

A precedent-setting confrontation on the issue of a son born after an adoption was made, a so-called *husaengja*, was set before King Hyŏnjong (r. 1659-1674) in 1662 and discussed at court on no less than fourteen different occasions over the next seven years.

The central figure in the case was Shim Chi-wŏn, who had adopted a son, Ik-sŏn, but who after his wife died, remarried and had a son, Ik-sang.[47] The controversy centered on the question of which of the two sons, the adopted or the biological (the *husaengja*), should be considered the ritual heir. Each had his advocates.

The Censorate, led by Min Chŏng-jung, submitted a memorial saying an adopted son is like a real son. If a biological son is born after an adoption is made then the biological son should be regarded as a second son. This view is in keeping with the decree made by King Injo, he argued. He cited the Chinese case of Hu An-guo and said that this is also what the former Chief State Councilor Ch'oe Myŏng-gil did. Those who say the ritual heir must be the blood heir pose an affront to human morality, he argued. He advocated that the Ministry of Rites be directed to clarify this matter and correct all the cases since the Injo decree. The impetus for the Censorate's action at this time was a response to charges that Shim Chi-wŏn had tried to discard his adopted son, which, his accusers said, should not be allowed.[48]

Four days later the issue was raised again and the other side of the question was presented. The opposition did not argue that the adoption

---

[45]Sŏnjo 14, 1581.2.*kyŏngja*; 15:5a-b (21:372).

[46]The final decision was recorded in an interlinear comment added by the *Shillok* compilers at the location of the first entry concerning this case. Sŏnjo 13, 1580.10.*imja*; 14:18a (21:368).

[47]*MTP* B:117b, 4b-c.

[48]Hyŏnjong 3, 1662.9.*kyemmi*; 6:3b (36:346).

should not be dissolved but rather that the adopted son ought to be considered as a second son, with the biological son performing the eldest son role, as was outlined in the Myŏngjong decision known as the *Kyech'uk* Decree.

In response, those who argued for the primacy of the adopted son cited a decision made in the Injo period. The argument was that the adoption was to remain in force with the adopted son acting in the role of the primary heir and the later-born son was to be considered as a second son. The Injo period decision cited the Ch'oe Myŏng-gil case as precedent. Ch'oe had kept his adopted son in spite of the fact that another son was born later. He had cited as precedent the two Chinese sages, Hu An-guo and Chu-ke Liang, who similarly kept their adopted sons even after sons were born later to them.[49]

The next day various officials argued the merits of each of the conflicting decrees.[50] And five days later, Min Chŏng-jung argued that although the Myŏngjong decree forbade the dissolution of an adoption, it made a temporary expedient of what should be an unchangeable relationship. The more constant rule is that which was decreed by King Injo, he said.[51] Three days later, Yi Kyŏng-sŏk also argued for following the Injo decree. He said that ritual laws can be changed as they were in 1553 with the Myŏngjong decree and again later in the Injo period. He recommended that the Injo decree be honored but that the court not go back and force rectification of all cases between Myŏngjong's and Injo's time. Hyŏnjong responded that the elderly statesman's opinion was reasonable and agreed that that was the way it should be.[52]

At this point it would appear that the adopted son had the support of the king and the high officials. In fact, the support of the pro-adopted-son faction was so strong at that time that eight days later Hyŏnjong was asked to force all in violation of the decree of King Injo to correct the situation, i.e., to reinstate adopted sons who may have been disenfranchised after a son was born into the home.[53] The king's response was not recorded but two days later Chief Censor Yi Hong-yŏn asked again that the Injo decree be enforced. He lamented the fact that there were certain sectors of the society

---

[49]Hyŏnjong 3, 1662.9.*chŏnghae*; 6:5a (36:347) and *RZS*, p. 198.

[50]Hyŏnjong 3, 1662.9.*muja*; rv.7:44a (37:288). The abbreviation "rv." indicates the revised version of the *Shillok* which is available for the Hyŏnjong period. The revised version is the modern volume 37, whereas volume 36 is the original non-revised version.

[51]Hyŏnjong 3. 1662.9.*kyesa*; rv.7:45b (37:288).

[52]Hyŏnjong 3, 1662.9.*pyŏngshin*; 6:7b (36:348).

[53]Hyŏnjong 3, 1662.10.*kapchin*; rv.7:50a (37:291).

that feigned obedience but tried to get around the royal decrees. He asked that all those who were in violation be forced to correct the situation retroactively. Hyŏnjong denied the request.[54] Nothing appeared in the record for the next six months, but when the issue surfaced again, Hyŏnjong waffled on the issue. Nam Ku-man and other censors petitioned the king saying, again, it was wrong for a child born after an adoption was made to be treated as the eldest son. Hyŏnjong called for the register wherein the Injo period decree was recorded, but he was told that it had been destroyed in the Manchu invasions. They pointed out, however, that fortunately the contents were preserved in the text *Ŭirye munhae* (Answers and analysis of ritual questions) written by Kim Chang-saeng. Hyŏnjong responded that he did not have sufficient information to make a decision.[55]

Two days later, Hyŏnjong asked about the nature of the decree issued during Injo's reign. Wŏn Tu-p'yo responded that for a royal decree to be official it had to be formally approved by the Censorate and printed, implying that the Injo decree may not be binding since it was only verbal.[56]

The next day, another censor, Wŏn Mal-li, stated that the king's disinclination to reinstate adopted sons was not good. The evidence, he said, was clear when Injo permitted Ch'oe Myŏng-gil to let his adopted son be the primary heir. Wŏn stated that he would not be able to serve a king who did not follow the former kings. Chŏng Kye-ju proposed that Wŏn Mal-li be dismissed. The king approved.[57]

Two months later, the Ministry of Rites made a policy statement which was to put the matter to rest, at least for a while. They stated that once an adoption is made, it ought to remain even if a son is born later. The adopted son is the ritual heir and the natural son plays the role of a second son. This is in accordance with Injo's decree, and the decision the king (Hyŏnjong) made in the tenth month of last year, they said. Therefore,

---

[54]Hyŏnjong 3, 1662.10.*pyŏngo*; rv.7:51b (37:291).

[55]Hyŏnjong 4, 1663.4.*musul*; 6:33a (36:361).

[56]Hyŏnjong 4, 1663.4.*kyŏngja*; 6:34b (36:361). Chŏng T'ae-hwa supported Wŏn Tu-p'yo's assertion with his own recollection of the event. He recalled a time when the king held an audience with noble officials wherein he asked how many children each had. Ch'oe Myŏng-gil answered that he had an adopted son and then was fortunate enough to have a biological son. But he indicated to Injo that he intended to use his adopted son as his principal heir. Injo gave his approval. Chŏng indicated that he understood the decree was never committed to paper and that it was only a verbal authorization.

[57]Hyŏnjong 4, 1663.4.*shinch'uk*; 6:34b (36:361).

the Ministry of Rites recommended that this simply be accepted as the regulation. Hyŏnjong agreed.[58]

Five years later, the issue surfaced again, and again the Shim family was specifically mentioned. Shim Ik-sang, the biological son of Shim Chi-wŏn, was appointed to a minor position in the Crown Prince Tutorial Office. The Censorate was divided in its view of the matter with Chief Censor Chang Sŏn-jing supporting Ik-sang's appointment, but a junior censor, Yun Kyŏng-gyo, opposing on the grounds that Ik-sang had stolen the legal heirship from his adopted brother, Ik-sŏn.[59]

A *Shillok* commentary explained that support for Iksang was based on Myŏngjong's decree, and although it was not in accord with the Injo period precedent, it was not a crime to ignore the later precedent and go back to an earlier precedent, the one associated with Ch'oe Myŏng-gil. It was just one option, the commentary argued. The reason for the criticism of Ik-sang was rather that he tried to take the primary heirship only after his father had died and his adopted brother had already performed the mourning rituals. Moreover, Ik-sang acted on his own without any legal action or authority. For these reasons, Ik-sang was criticized by the Censorate. The next day the Censorate discussed Ik-sang's appointment again and recommended he be dismissed. Hyŏnjong denied the request twice, but when it was submitted a third time he relented, and Shim Ik-sang was dismissed.[60]

The issue still was not settled. Four months later, Kim Man-jung stepped forward to say that Shim Ik-sang's removal from office was inappropriate. His being charged with stealing legitimacy was based on a great misunderstanding.[61]

Two months later, seven years after the dispute began, the final word on the subject—at least in Hyŏnjong's time—was uttered by the powerful official, Song Shi-yŏl. He reviewed the case and stated that Shim Chi-wŏn had an adopted son, Ik-sŏn, but later bore a son, Ik-sang, who performed the ceremonies. He then judged that handling the matter in this way violated propriety. After a discussion, the king agreed that the adopted son should be the heir.[62]

---

[58]Hyŏnjong 4, 1663.6.*chŏngmi*; rv.8:52b (37:320). For the reference to the tenth month of the previous year, see footnote #53 above.

[59]Hyŏnjong 9, 1668.7.*mushin*; rv.19:20a (37:615).

[60]Hyŏnjong 9, 1668.7.*kiyu*; rv.19:20b (37:615).

[61]Hyŏnjong 9, 1668.11.*pyŏngjin*; rv.19:57a (37:633). The Kim Man-jung here is the same man who went on to author one of Korea's greatest novels, *Kuunmong* [The nine cloud dream].

[62]Hyŏnjong 10, 1669.1.*musul*; rv.20:15 (37:642).

## The Puan Kim *Husaengja* Case

The large cache of documents from the Puan Kim lineage that proved so valuable in examining Chosŏn dynasty inheritance practices in chapter two, also provides some insight in examining cases of adoption. The first occurred in 1675, shortly after the time of the Shim Chi-wŏn case but unlike the Shim case, the Kim's did not attempt to dissolve an established adoption. The lineage heir, Myŏng-yŏl, had two sons, Pŏn and Mun. Pŏn had no children, initially, and Mun died in his thirties, but did have one child, Su-jong.[63] In 1675, when Su-jong was four years old, he was adopted by Pŏn. The adoption was certified by the Ministry of Rites.[64]

The Puan Kim inheritance document dated 1688, signed by Pŏn, stated in its preface that an interesting turn of events had taken place in the intervening thirteen years since the adoption of Su-jong.[65] Pŏn's wife had died, he had remarried, and had two sons. Faced with a choice of dissolving the adoption and sending Su-jong back to perform the ceremonies for, and inherit the property of, his biological father, Mun, on the one hand, or maintaining the adoption, on the other, they chose the latter. The adoption made, stayed. They did, however, decide to send the elder of Pŏn's later-born sons, Su-ch'ang, to Mun as a posthumous adoption.[66] The 1688 inheritance document stated in its preface:

> For over forty years, we have not had an heir born to our family. Unavoidably, therefore, I petitioned the Ministry of Rites and adopted the only son of my deceased younger brother making him the heir to the generations of ancestors.

---

[63]We do not know Kim Mun's dates of birth and death, but we do know that his older brother was born in 1639. Therefore, a birth date in 1640 would be the earliest possible year. He was mentioned as deceased in the adoption document of 1675, wherein Su-jong was adopted to Pŏn. His son, Su-jong, was born in 1671. Therefore, Mun was between 30 and 35 when he died.

[64]The format of certificate was in the standard format described below, in chapter nine, issued by the Ministry of Rites and dated the first month of 1675. It is found in PKK #1 (p. 170). There is one curious aspect to the document. We know from the other Puan Kim documents that Su-jong was the first grandson born to Myŏng-yŏl, see PKK #11 & #12 (pp. 203-4) (1672.1.11). Yet in the adoption certificate, he is referred to as the second son of Mun! Was there an earlier son who died young and was excluded from the genealogy and other documents? Did they choose to consider the daughter born first as the first child, and the only boy, as the second child/son? Or did the family falsify their application fearing that a request to adopt an only son would be rejected? I suspect the latter.

Another curious aspect of the document is that it stated, in the typical formulaic way, that the son had indicated his own desire to be adopted. As noted above, most sons were adults at the time of the adoption, but Su-jong was only four years old.

[65]For more on the 1688 inheritance document, see chapter two, p. 44.

[66]The Ministry of Rites certificate for the adoption of Su-ch'ang to Mun, if it ever existed, is not found in the collection.

Thereafter, my wife died and I remarried and had two sons. The ritual heirship has already been decided; it will be handled by my adopted son, Su-jong, since he is certainly the eldest son. Since my deceased brother had no children and there is no one to perform the ceremonies for him, I have given my son, Su-ch'ang, as an adopted son to serve ceremonies to him.[67]

There was, in effect, an exchange of sons. The important difference between them was that Su-jong was designated the lineage heir and was assigned to manage the ritual property.[68]

Table 8.6
Kim Su-jong's Adoption

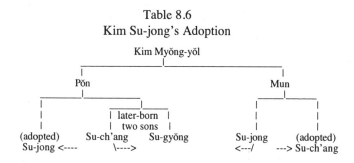

The above cases, the Shim Chi-wŏn case and the Kim Pŏn case, show the preference for maintaining rather than dissolving an adoption. Although both of the above cases ended in maintaining the adoption, in the late dynasty there were numerous cases of dissolution; in fact, there appear to have been more and more as the dynasty wore on. As with the issue of making an adoption, since there were few in the beginning of the dynasty, there were few cases of dissolution; but as adoption became more common, cases of dissolution became more frequent. The Code provided for dissolution in cases of the death of the brother left in the natal family and in cases of criminal misconduct, but in the atmosphere of the late dynasty, adoptions were dissolved for a variety of reasons. (Dissolution of adoption will be covered in chapter nine.)

---

[67]PKK #29 (pp. 213-17), dated 1688.3.7.

[68]Su-jong was obviously a capable man. He passed the *chinsa* exam in 1710.

*Hyŏngmang chegŭp* (Lateral Inheritance)

By the seventeenth century the alternatives for providing an heir had narrowed. Options available in the first half of the dynasty gradually came to be considered inappropriate. What was to become the ideal form of adoption, that of adopting an agnatic nephew, was being clothed in orthodoxy. Still, in the first half of the seventeenth century, much of the old order persisted with much of the new. Here, we will examine a hold-out—one of the last gasps of the pre-Confucian past.

Primary in its day but declining under the onslaught of the Neo-Confucian ideals, *hyŏngman chegŭp* (when the elder brother dies, the younger brother succeeds), the last remnant of lateral inheritance, had lost out in arguments in the sixteenth century but was still being argued in the early seventeenth century.[69]   Prior to the establishment of the lineage principle (*chongppŏp*) of Neo-Confucianism with its emphasis of vertical or lineal descent, under the concept of *hyŏngman chegŭp,* when the line of the first son ends (this is often seen in the early portion of genealogies), then the second son takes over the responsibility of the eldest son.   The appearance of the term is limited primarily to the late fifteenth and sixteenth century, the early transition period.   The term may have been used before and after that time, but it was featured as a principle in the argumentation put forward during the early transition time.[70]   The concept is important in that it contains elements of both the pre-Confucian as well as the Confucianized practice.   Specifically, it contains the element of equality among siblings on the one hand (it functioned at a time when inheritance was equally divided), but it articulates the Confucian ideals of one heir, male, who alone is responsible for the ceremonies.   Although property was still being divided equally, the sharing of ritual responsibility (*yunhaeng*) was being abandoned, and in its place, the eldest son's role became featured.   In the post-transition phase, the eldest son could not be replaced by a lateral move, by a brother, but rather, the line was accentuated and an agnatic adoption was the recourse, rather than the line coming to an end, if the eldest son did not have an heir.

---

[69]The subject is treated in Yi, Kwang-gyu, *Han'guk kajok ŭi sajŏk yŏn'gu*, p. 310ff, although he does not discuss the transitory nature of this practice;  Yi's presentation implies that it was viable before and after the period of transition.  See also Yi Su-gon's preface to *Kyŏngbuk chibang komunsŏ chipsŏn* (KCKC), p. 80 & 91; and examples in documents on p. 235 & 629.

[70]See the cases at the conclusion of chapter seven (pp. 126 & 130), wherein *hyŏngman chegŭp* is found in opposition to the will of the *ch'ongbu*, and early in chapter eight (p. 146) where *hyŏngman chegŭp* is cited as a principle to argue that one of the sons other the than eldest should be the heir.

In addition to the cases mentioned above (both at the end of chapter seven, and here in chapter eight) the highlighting of one more case, perhaps the most complicated of cases that cites the precedent of *hyŏngman chegŭp*, will complete our picture of the role this concept played in the Confucianization process.

### The Hwang Ik-son Suit

A lawsuit, actually more of an appeal, was filed by Hwang Ik-son (1695-1764) in about 1760; at issue was a decision made much earlier. The document containing his allegations is an extremely long one; it is written in classical Chinese and contains over 7000 characters. The scroll is over fifteen feet long and nearly three feet wide. Therein is outlined the history of six generations of a lineage segment resident in North Chŏlla province, and the alleged wrong-doing of one sub-segment of the lineage.[71] Although the suit was filed in about 1760, the heart of the argument was the use of the *hyŏngman chegŭp* concept as applied in their lineage in the mid seventeenth century, three and four generations earlier.

### Table 8.7
### Lawsuit of Hwang Ik-Son

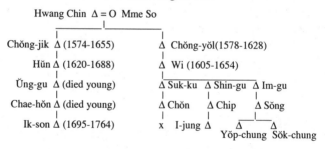

Hwang Ik-son's lawsuit was filed against his tenth-*ch'on* cousins Yŏp-chung, I-jung, and others, claiming that his own line was the rightful line to carry on the rituals for Hwang Chin, an *Imjin* War hero. He charged that the collateral line had stolen the rights three generations earlier, and now they were about to pass the privilege to an adopted son within their

---

[71]*Chŏnbuk chibang ŭi komunsŏ (1)* [Ancient Documents from the North Chŏlla Province, part one]. Chŏnju: Chŏnbuk hyangt'o munhwa yŏn'guhoe, 1993, p. 207, document #19.

sub-segment of the lineage. He elaborated that his great-grandfather, Hŭn, had had to flee the area because of a "murder case" (the details were not given). Hŭn's uncle, Chŏng-yŏl, and cousin, Wi, claimed the rights to perform the ceremonies (and the property that went with it) on the basis of *hyŏngmang chegŭp* (lateral inheritance—if the elder brother dies, the younger brother is the successor). Ik-son charged that *hyŏngmang chegŭp* was an incorrectly applied principle, as he presented his case showing that there were several errors underlying the action that resulted in the transfer of the property and ritual rights to the collateral relatives.[72]

The document was not only extremely long, and detailed, but at the end of the document there was a list of twelve items submitted in support of the lawsuit, such as copies of the pertinent pages of the Code, inheritance documents, a copy of the allegedly falsified genealogy, and two copies of statements by prominent philosophers concerning proper ritual. Concerning *hyŏngmang chegŭp,* the document argued that at an earlier time lateral inheritance may have been permitted, but in more recent times the ritual responsibility and the property should be passed on through the direct line. Since the other side argued that the ceremonies needed to be performed for an ancestor (who was a war hero) whose spirit tablet was "immovable" (and therefore should have memorial services forever), Ik-son's strategy was to use their argument against them by saying that if the line of descent (rather than the sharing of inheritance) was most important, then he, as the eldest son's eldest son for five generations, should have the rights. There was an implied recognition of the fact that at an earlier time lateral inheritance may have been acceptable, but in these later times vertical inheritance was correct. The argument was over which of the vertical lines was appropriate.

The magistrate's judgment was not written on the scroll (often the magistrate's handwritten decision is written on such documents), but we know from an examination of the other documents in the collection, Ik-son

---

[72]Among them were: (1) The stronger line stole the rights from the weaker line and only thereafter tried to justify what they had done on the basis of *hyŏngmang chegŭp*; but if one looks at the death dates of those concerned, *hyŏngmang chegŭp* does not apply. Hŭn's father, Chŏng-jik, outlived both his brother, Chŏng-yŏl, and his nephew, Wi; whereas *hyŏngmang chegŭp* means the younger brother succeeds in event that the elder brother dies, Chŏng-jik outlived his alleged heirs. (2) In order to claim the *hyŏngmang chegŭp* principle, Suk-ku, the compiler of the 1723 edition of the genealogy falsely recorded the date of Chŏng-jik's death as twelve years early in order to give justification to their claim. (3) The other side's claim that grandfather Chŏng-jik himself awarded heirship to Wi has never been documented. (4) The document that fifth-generation grandmother So allegedly wrote awarding heirship to Wi has never been seen.

did not win his suit;[73] the other side held onto the property that they obtained by means of *hyŏngmang chegŭp* but retained by means of vertical inheritance including the use of agnatic adoption. In much the same way as other arguments that ran over the course of several generations, the Ma-Chin (p. 60) case and the Song-Yi (p. 120) case, here the eventual winner was the one arguing for agnatic adoption, but it took several generations to settle on the "correct" procedure. These three long-running cases stand as symbols of the three major alternatives defeated by the lineal principle which included at its heart agnatic adoption. The Ma-Chin dispute was between the agnatic line and the *oeson* or non-agnatic grandsons; the Song-Yi dispute was between agnatic line continued via agnatic adoption and the daughters line continued via non-agnatic adoption; and now the Hwang dispute was between agnatics lines one of which claimed descent through the primary line and one that first relied on *hyŏngmang chegŭp* but later established their claims to vertical lineage heirship by means of agnatic adoption.

## Conclusion

By the late seventeenth century, agnatic adoption was becoming firmly established as the norm. Moving into the eighteenth century, daughters had gradually been excluded from the ceremonies and only a few still retained rights to property inheritance. *Sŏja*, although not completely acceptable as heirs, were still holding onto a place in the household. The emphasis on the eldest son was taking over as the controlling principle in both inheritance and ritual. The Confucian ritual texts placed great importance on the eldest son.

In this chapter we have seen that agnatic adoption eventually surpassed all other options. In the previous chapter, we saw agnatic adoption eventually supplanted non-agnatic options, including adoption of daughters, and the adoption of affinal males. Here we have seen that even among agnates, until the principle of the eldest son was established, there were still several options.

---

[73]*Ibid.*, page 218. Song June-ho, the editor of the collection and author of the analytic comment on this document, concluded that the petitioning side not only lost, but that, since the magistrate's judgment is not found written on the document, it may not have ever been submitted. Indeed, many preserved documents, (like the draft memorial to the throne as seen on page 98, note 22) were carefully drafted, for whatever reason never submitted, and yet kept in the family's cache of documents anyway.

Song also pointed out that there is some evidence that the real issue, aside from what was stated in the document, was one of *sŏja* versus legitimate son. Hŭn, although he passed the *chinsa* exam, may have been a *sŏja*, and his posterity, as was typically the case, may have been stigmatized. If this were the real issue, it was not explicit.

We saw that in the fifteenth century, sons other than the eldest son were selected as the principal heir. The cases of Cho Kŭn, Kim Kyŏn-su, and Shin Sŭng-min showed that on the basis of *hyŏngmang chegŭp*, the second or third son, could be assigned to take charge of the rituals. We saw that only a select few families were concerned with maintaining ceremonies for a line of ancestors. Resolution of conflicts depended on written wills as much as on points of law, and that sharing responsibilities, or splitting duties between contestants was possible.

In the sixteenth century, the Pak Kon case has shown us an inclination toward the second son as the one next in line, when there was a problem with the first son. In this 1520 case, we also saw an attempt to deal with the contradiction built into the Code, that between *iphu* and *pongsa*. *Iphu* contained the seeds of the patrilineal, vertical concept and *pongsa* contained the seeds of the older horizontal concept.

Then the Yi Sŏn and Nam Cho-wŏn cases, both in 1553, became factors in the decree of that year, the *Kyech'uk* Decree.[74] At issue was a dispute, not based on the death (or disqualification) of the eldest son (*hyŏngmang chegŭp*), but, in the former case, the birth of a natural son after an adoption had been concluded, and in the later case, a challenge by a *sŏja* son. In the former case, a Solomonesque compromise, splitting the inheritance was the solution, similar to the compromise solutions seen in the fifteenth century. With partable inheritance practiced all around them, it was easy to conclude with a division of responsibility; but after the implanting of primogeniture, we will not see such divisions of rights and property. The *Kyech'uk* Decree kept the adopted son in the household.

The Nam Cho-wŏn case concerned heirship by *sŏja* but in the discussion therein emerged an attempt to sort out the difference in practice between *iphu* and *pongsa*, again. *Pongsa* meant service for three generations of ancestors, but *iphu* was originally only for one generation, it was concluded. As time went by *iphu* was going to end up as succession to multiple generations and supplant*pongsa* as as an important*modus operandi*. More importantly, *iphu* would come to mean taking a brother's or cousin's son as one's own—agnatic adoption. *Pongsa* would come to mean offering of ancestor worship by either an adopted or biological son.

The debate over the *sŏja* as heirs was re-opened by the Nam Cho-wŏn case in 1556, when the young King Myŏngjong, under the influence of his

---

74Deuchler points out that there was abnormal weather in the early summer of 1553 which led to King and court reflection on morality and rectification of morals, which took the form of supportive action for the sake of the unfortunate *sŏja*. See "Heaven Does Not Discriminate," p. 134.

"villainous" uncle, Yun Wŏn-hyŏng, tried to protect the fading rights of the *sŏja*, by attempting to curtail the tide of momentum favoring agnatic adoption. Myŏngjong, echoing Yun's proposal, argued for agnatic adoption—only agnates of close degrees of kinship could adopt. Rather than stemming the tide, Yun's association with the pro-*sŏja*, anti-adoption, side of the argument discredited that position when Yun's career ended in disgrace.

The first test case of the *Kyech'uk* Decree to emerge in the reign of the late sixteen century monarch, Sŏnjo, was that of Yu On (*sŏja*) versus Yu Hwa (adopted). Although the adoption was an ideal agnatic adoption, the king preferred to grant lineage heir status to the *sŏja* and treat the adopted son as a lesser status *shiyangja* with rights to only one generation of ceremonies. Forced into a compromise, the king agreed to split the heir status and property between the two contestants.

In the late seventeenth century in the Shim Chi-wŏn case (citing the Ch'oe Myŏng-gil case) and in the Puan Kim case (Kim Su-jong) the decision was to honor the adopted son while the later-born son took the role of the subordinate, second son.

We concluded by returning to where this chapter began, with *hyŏngmang chegŭp* (the remnant of lateral inheritance) by looking at the Hwang case, a lawsuit based on a seventeenth century use of the concept. Most of the cases in this chapter concerned adoption of lineage members or close patrilineal kinsmen in the early Chosŏn, pre-lineage times. The controversies were over which candidate should be the primary heir. Even among agnates there were options.

Eventually agnatic adoption came to be linked with the concept of primogeniture. Theoretically, it may appear that agnatic adoption could exist in a situation of equal division of inheritances among all sons. And any son without a male heir could adopt an agnate. But when all sons have equal access to inheritances, lateral inheritance is the option. It is only when primogeniture is practiced that agnatic adoption, for the sake of the eldest son's line, is found. Thus the term agnatic adoption implies primogeniture.

This chapter has shown that the road to the ideal was not well-paved; there were several rough spots along the way, still by the end of the seventeenth century, Korea came to view the role of the eldest son as dictated in classic Confucian ritual texts as the ideal. And agnatic adoption was the best way to attain that ideal when a man had no heirs or had only daughters. In the next chapter we will see that even with a solid commitment to agnatic adoption and primogeniture there were still wrinkles in the social fabric that needed ironing out.

# 9

# Agnatic Adoption

With the alternatives to agnatic adoption fading, chapter seven covered the decline of non-agnatic adoption and chapter eight covered the problems in attempts at non-primogeniture agnatic adoption, the late transition period, from the late seventeenth century onward was the time for the perfection of the system. But there were still problems. How were adoptions authorized and documented? What role did the government play in authorizing and certifying adoptions? What happened when an adoption did not work out? Could an adoption be dissolved? Which nephew should be chosen? Did *sŏja* continue to be considered as heirs? What of commoners; did they also practice agnatic adoption? These questions will be addressed in this chapter. The documents for this chapter will primarily be a series of registers kept by the government, the Ministry of Rites. There were four different registers; each served a different purpose, and each helps us answer one of the questions above and reveals the status of the practice of adoption in the latter half of the dynasty.

The following chart shows how dramatic the rise in agnatic adoption rates were beginning in the middle of the dynasty. Toward the end of the dynasty virtually all, among the upper class and many of the lower classes as well, who did not have a son adopted. The examination rosters used to determine the following rates showed only those who had become adopted by the time they passed an exam; there were at least some who were adopted later in life, after they had passed the exam, but nonetheless, although the figures are conservative, the percentages of those involved in adoptions were close to the percentages of those who biologically did not sire a son.[1]

---

[1] Jerry Dennerline states that 20% of men adopted an heir in China, "Marriage, Adoption, and Charity in the Development of Lineages in Wu-hsi from Sung to Ch'ing," p. 202. Jack Goody in "Strategies of Heirship," *Comparative Studies in Society and History* quotes a study in India that concludes 22% of couples did not have a son. In other areas, he states the figure is between 15% and 30% (p. 4-5). He also states that societies with horizontal inheritance have more options than those with vertical inheritance because they

Table 9.1

Increase in the Practice Of Adoption

Percentages are based on records of candidates in state exams who were adopted, specifically the exams were *sama* exams, both *saengwŏn* and *chinsa*. Here they have been grouped in fifty year blocks to level out the peaks and valleys of individual years — see Appendix 3 for detailed statistics.

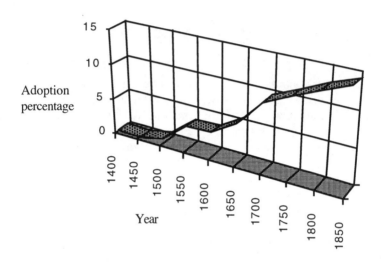

The Ideal

    The *Kyŏngguk taejŏn* states: "If one does not have a son by either his legitimate wife or his concubine, he may adopt a nephew (*chija*) from within the lineage to be the heir." The commentary to the Code states: "If both fathers agree, then the adoption is ordered. If the father is deceased, then the mother petitions."[2]

    Petitioning the government meant submitting documents to the Ministry of Rites by every party involved in the adoption. The following were almost always included in the documentation: the adopting father (or his wife if he were dead), the biological father (or wife), the son to be adopted, and the representatives of the lineage (the meaning of which changed over the course of the dynasty). That the two fathers would have to submit documents stating that they concurred in the arrangement is not at

---

can turn to collaterals (p. 3). This factor applies to Korea as well and helps illustrate the type of transition the Korea had gone through, from "lateral inheritance" to a high rate of adoption.

[2] *Taejŏn hoet'ong*, p. 367; *yejŏn*, 37a.

all surprising, but the fact that the son himself was a party to the proceeding and that he had to state his willingness to be adopted may be surprising until one realizes that adoptions generally took place when the son was a fully grown man. Usually the adopted son was between twenty and forty years of age.[3] It should be noted that in many cases an agreement to adopt, a tentative adoption, was worked out long before the parties involved went to the government to formalize the matter. The ages of the two fathers at the time of the adoption is also noteworthy. Most were old, beyond normal child-rearing age, and close to fifty percent were deceased.[4]

## Certificates of Adoption

Once all the parties to an adoption submitted the appropriate documentation, the Ministry of Rites would examine the case and if everything was in order would issue a certificate of adoption. The following is a translation of a typical certificate.

### A Certificate of Adoption

Among those items presented to the King, there was the following:

Ch'oe Ik, a *t'ongtŏngnang* (Sr. 5 rank), is without heir and thereby requests the adoption of Kyŏng-yu, the second son of his eighth-degree cousin (8-*ch'on hyŏng*), Ch'oe Chun, to be his heir. We have examined and verified the census registration of both sides.

The request of Ch'oe Ik stated he is without an heir by either his wife or concubine, and that he desires to adopt, Kyŏng-yu, the second son of his eighth-degree cousin (8-*ch'on hyŏng*), Ch'oe Chun, to be his heir; both sides have agreed and submitted appropriate documents.

The request of the *t'ongtŏngnang* Ch'oe Chun stated that since his eighth-degree cousin (8-*ch'on che*) is without an heir by either wife or concubine, his second son, Kyŏng-yu, desires to become the heir; both families have agreed and have submitted appropriate documents that support this request for adoption.

---

[3]See my article, "Adoption in Korean Genealogies", *Korean Journal* 14 (1) (January, 1974):28-35.

[4]*Ibid.*

The affidavit of Ch'oe Ik has been verified wherein he stated he is without an heir by either his wife or concubine, and that he desires to adopt Kyŏng-yu, the second son of his eighth-degree cousin (8-*ch'on hyŏng*), Ch'oe Chun, to be his heir; both sides have agreed and submitted appropriate documents.

The affidavit of Ch'oe Chun has been verified wherein he stated that since his eighth-degree cousin (8-*ch'on che*), Ch'oe Ik is without an heir by either wife or concubine, his second son, Kyŏng-yu, desires to become the heir; both families have agreed and have submitted appropriate documents that are in accord with this adoption.

The affidavit of the *saengwŏn*, Ch'oe Yŏng-nyŏn, who is the lineage representative of Ch'oe Ik and Ch'oe Chun, has been verified wherein he states that Ch'oe Ik is without an heir by either wife or concubine, and that Kyŏng-yu, the second son of his eighth-degree cousin (8-*ch'on hyŏng*), Ch'oe Chun, desires to become the heir, and that both families have discussed this matter and have submitted appropriate documents.

The above requests and affidavits, have been examined in the context of the adoption article in the Code which states: He who is without heir by wife or concubine may petition the government and adopt a lineage nephew to be the heir; and in a commentary it adds: If both fathers agree then the adoption is made.

It is proposed that Ch'oe Kyŏng-yu be made the heir of Ch'oe Ik as recorded above.

Dated: *Kang-hsi* 31.12.4 [1692].

Official in charge: Shim Pŏl.

Royal permission is hereby granted; the adoption is to be carried out as outlined above.

[Signed and sealed by the Second Vice Minister of Rites and the second secretary.][5]

---

[5]The original document is in the author's possession and is reproduced as the underlay beneath the title page of this book.

If the adoptive father was already deceased, as indicated in the Code, the adoptive mother had the right to submit the application. The following is a typical example:

### A Certificate Issued by the Ministry of Rites

The Twelfth Year of the *Chia-ch'ing* [Chinese] Emperor (1807), second month:

This is a certification of adoption. In response to the request submitted by Mme Yi, the wife of the deceased scholar Chŏng In-gwang who resided in Kŭmsan, wherein she proposed the adoption of Mun-ju, the second son of her husband's first cousin [*sach'on*], T'ae-hwi. The census registers of both sides have been verified.

In Mme Yi's affidavit she states that her husband died without an heir by either wife or concubine. Mun-ju, the second son of her husband's cousin, T'ae-hwi, desires to become the heir. Both sides of the family agree and have submitted their requests that the adoption be authorized.

The affidavit of Chŏng T'ae-hwi, a scholar residing in Kŭmsan, stated that his cousin, Chŏng In-gwang, died without an heir by either his wife or concubine. His second son, Mun-ju, desires to become the heir. Both families have agreed and have submitted appropriate documents.

The statements in the letter of Mme Yi that her husband died without an heir by wife or concubine and that Mun-ju, the second son of her husband's cousin, T'ae-hwi, desires to become the heir, and that both sides of the family have discussed this matter and have submitted appropriate documents have been verified.

The statements of Chŏng T'ae-hwi that his cousin, In-gwang, died without heir by wife or concubine and that his own son, Mun-ju, desires to become the heir, and that both sides of the family have discussed this matter and have submitted appropriate documentation have been verified.

The affidavit of the scholar Chŏng Uk, who is the lineage representative of Chŏng In-gwang and Chŏng T'ae-hwi, which states that Chŏng In-gwang died without heir by either wife or concubine and that his wife submitted a request stating that Mun-ju, the second son of her husband's cousin, T'ae-hwi, desires to become the heir, and that both families have discussed this matter and that they have submitted appropriate documents has been verified.

The above affidavits, letters, and documents have been examined in the context of the adoption article in the Code which states: He who is without heir by wife or concubine may petition the government and adopt a lineage nephew to be the heir; and in a commentary it adds: If both fathers agree then the adoption is made. If the father is dead then the mother may petition.

It is proposed that Chŏng Mun-ju be made the heir of Chŏng In-gwang as recorded above.

Dated: *Chia-ch'ing* 12.2.19 [1807].
Official in charge: Song Chi-gyŏm.

Royal permission is hereby granted; the adoption is to be carried out as outlined above.

[Signed and sealed by the Minister of Rites.]6

*Kyehu Tŭngnok*, the Register of Adoptions

Abstracts of authorizations issued by the Ministry of Rites were recorded in the *Kyehu tŭngnok*, the register of adoptions. The abstract of the above certificate was recorded as follows:

In a list of royal authorizations given to this Ministry was the following: The deceased scholar from Kŭmsan, Chŏng In-gwang, had no heirs and thereby his wife, Mme Yi, asked that Mun-ju, the second son of her husband's first cousin (*sach'on*), T'ae-hwi, be adopted. The lineage elder, Chŏng Uk, has agreed and has submitted supporting documentation. Can the adoption of Chŏng Mun-ju to Chŏng In-gwang be authorized?

Dated: *Chia-ch'ing* 12.2.19 [1807].
Official in charge: Song Chi-gyŏm.

Royal permission granted.7

---

6The original document is held by a descendant, Chŏng Chu-yŏng, a man active in Sŏnggyun'gwan activities and Confucian and lineage associations; a photocopy is in the possession of the author.

7*Kyehu tŭngnok*, hereafter *KHTN* [The register of adoptions] kept by the Ministry of Rites (1618-1894). The first eighteen volumes, with some gaps in the record but covering the period from 1618 to 1863, is held in the Kyujanggak collection of the Seoul National University Library, catalog no. 12869. The last volume (1864-1894) is kept at the Ch'angsŏgak collection at the Academy of Korean Studies. There are no page numbers, but

Only the bare facts are listed in the *Kyehu tŭngnok*, whereas the adoption certificate itself gives a more detailed picture of how complicated and serious the matter of adoption was. To change one's father was said to be tantamount to changing heaven. "There is only one heaven, and a man can have only one father."[8] Changing one's father was a serious matter and, in principle, only the king could grant such approval.

In the above case, the adopting father was deceased; therefore the adopting mother initiated the paper work which was appropriate according to the *Kyŏngguk taejŏn*. The matter was slightly simpler if the adopting father initiated the action.[9] But it was considerably more complicated if both adoptive parents were dead. Since the Code does not say what should be done in such a case, action initiated by surviving relatives was handled in a special way.

Such entries are found in the *Pyŏl kyehu tŭngnok*, the register of special adoptions, which is also known as the *Pŏboe kyehu tŭngnok*, the register of extralegal adoptions. In many instances, the *Pyŏl kyehu tŭngnok* is much more instructive than the *Kyehu tŭngnok* because the boundary between what is permissible and what is not is more evident, more at issue. Cases of adoption requests for a man and wife who have both died are seen frequently therein, as well as a wide range of exceptional situations, some of which result in adoption and some not. Both registers offer important insights into the social and family values of the later Yi dynasty. Both were apparently extant before the *Imjin* invasions, but the records that predate the war were destroyed. The *Kyehu tŭngnok* is preserved mainly in the Kyujanggak collection at Seoul National University but there are a few volumes kept in the Changsŏgak collection at the Academy of Korean Studies.[10] The oldest extant volume has "Volume Two" written on the

entries are identified by their dates. The document cited here is found under the listing in 1807, *Chia-ch'ing* (the Ch'ing China reign period) 12.2.19.

[8]The original quotation says, "Heaven does not have two suns; a nation cannot have two sovereigns." By extrapolation, it is also said that a man cannot have two fathers. This rationale was used to argue that one should call his adopted father simply "father" and his biological father his "natal father" (*saengbu*). One should not call the adopted father "*yangbu*" (adoptive father).

[9]For examples of other adoption certificates, see *KCKC*, pp. 488, 543, 548, 603, 606, and 618; or see PKK, p. 170-171, nos. 1, 2, and 3; all of which are covered herein: #1, page 155, and #2 & #3 on page 174.

[10]Until recently, it was assumed that all the volumes of the *Kyehu tŭngnok* were kept in the Kyujanggak; see Ch'oe Chae-sŏk's table showing which years are covered by which extant volumes in *Han'guk kajok chedosa yŏn'gu*, p. 591-593. Recently, this author discovered two additional volumes, one *Kyehu tŭngnok* and one *Pyŏl kyehu tŭngnok* kept in the Changsŏgak (housed at the Academy of Korean Studies).
According to Ch'oe's tables, the missing *Kyehu tŭngnok* volume would be number 39, the last volume (beyond what had assumed to be the last volume, number 38, that dates from 1856 to 1863). The lost volume is thicker that previous volumes by double; therefore, it

cover; its first entry is dated 1618.[11] The *Pyŏl kyehu tŭngnok* covers the period from 1637 to 1753.[12]

These registers provide a comprehensive picture of the principles and practices of adoption, particularly when used in conjunction with other sources such as the *Shillok* and printed genealogies (*chokpo*).

## Dissolving an Adoption

Adoptions made can also become adoptions dissolved. The Code outlines the bases for dissolution. The earliest version of the *Kyŏngguk taejŏn* stated:

> If the natal parents of the adopted son lose their heir, the adoption may be dissolved and the son may return to his natal home. The adopting parents may then arrange for another adoption.[13]

An example is recorded in the *Pyŏl kyehu tŭngnok*:

---

may have been two separate volumes at one time, but is now bound in one cover. It covers the period from 1864 to 1894, virtually the reign of King Kojong at end of the dynasty.

Ch'oe's table and supporting text (p. 590) indicates that of the 38 volumes listed, twenty are listed as extant (in the Kyujanggak collection) and eighteen volumes as missing. However, in addition to the newly-discovered volume, from the nineteenth-century-end of the chronology, there is evidence that the *Kyehu tŭngnok* was being kept as early as 1553. See the Nam Cho-wŏn case in chapter eight above, p. 143, footnote 29, for a reference to an adoption register that could well have been the *Kyehu tŭngnok*. There could have been more than one volume that pre-dates the earliest extant copy (dated 1618). Ch'oe's table, if updated, should therefore include at least 41 volumes, one (or more) missing from the sixteenth century or earlier, and two volumes (actually one double-sized volume) newly discovered, dated from the nineteenth century.

[11]Ch'oe Chae-sŏk has a table (p. 592) showing that the first two volumes (the one with "Volume Two" written on the cover, but labeled volume one by the modern catalog, and the one with the modern label of volume two) were not kept in an orderly chronological fashion. Volume one has cases dated from 1618 to 1636, and volume two have cases dated from 1618 to 1630. One possible explanation for the overlapping coverage is that the binding on both of them came undone and they were rebound in haphazard fashion. All the remaining volumes were kept in more-or-less chronological order. Certainly the chaos of the period contributed to the disorder; it was the time immediately following the disastrous Japanese invasions of 1592-1598, and actually overlapped with the Manchu invasions of 1627 and 1636.

[12]The recently-discovered volume of the *Pyŏl kyehu tŭngnok* is a thick volume covering the dates from 1717 to 1732. On Ch'oe Chae-sŏk's table (p. 593) there were thirteen total volumes, but four are listed as missing. Volumes 9 and 10, dated from 1719 to 1735, fit the time frame of the one, thicker-than-average volume.

The two volumes recently found at the Changsŏgak (one *Kyehu tŭngnok*, see footnote 9 above, and one *Pyŏl kyehu tŭngnok*) were both double-sized compilations and would have been four volumes by the standard of the other registers kept at the Kyujanggak.

The author acknowledges the assistance of David Thompson in finding the volumes heretofore uncited and unknown in their out-of-place holding at the Changsŏgak.

[13]*Taejŏn hoet'ong*, p. 367.

Ch'oe P'il-sun originally had three sons. The first, named Sŏk-cho, was adopted out to his father's fourth-*ch'on* cousin, P'ir-yŏng. Unfortunately, the other two brothers died and there is no one to perform the ceremonies. In examining the ritual section of the Code, it says that when an adopted son's original parents have no heirs, then it is permissible for the adopted son to return to his home. Sŏk-cho has indicated that he would like to return to his natal family. The Code indicates that it is permissible for a son to return to his natal family and royal decrees have also indicated that this is permissible. Can we dissolve this adoption?

Dated: *K'ang-hsi* 25.2.5 [1686].

Official in charge: Yi Ŏn-gang

Permission granted.[14]

The framers of the Code were shortsighted from the perspective of late dynasty ideal practice. Underlying the dissolution provision was the assumption that the son who was adopted out had a brother who stayed at home and performed the ceremonies for the natal parents. If that son died, the Code stated, the adopted son was to return home. But the dissolution of a relationship, a relationship that was said to have been established with the approval of heaven, was not without its problems. The adoptive parents would have to make new arrangements, and the deceased son could not be ignored. He sometimes needed an adoption made for him. Eventually, the late dynasty practice was to leave an adoption in place, and if the heir at home died without an heir, an adoption would be made for him. The early dynasty was concerned with having an heir for the short-term objectives of the ceremonies at hand; the late dynasty was concerned with every male having an heir.

In the early period, the law was restated by King Myŏngjong:

After an adoption is made, should the biological parents suddenly lose their heir, the adoption can be dissolved and the adopted son returned to his natal home. The adoptive parents can then adopt another son. Had the adoptive parents died, the son can perform ceremonies to both sets of parents.[15]

---

[14]The *Pyŏl kyehu tŭngnok* (*PKHTN*), 1686.2.5.

[15]*Sugyo chimnok*, p. 28, #51; Myŏngjong 9, 1554.2.14.

Myŏngjong's statement coincided with a commentary to the Code which stipulated that if the adoptive parents were deceased, the dissolution provision could not be applied, but rather the living son should perform the ceremonies to both sets of parents.[16] And as late as the late seventeenth century adoptions were dissolved without much ado. Gradually, however, adoptions were not dissolved for reasons as mundane as the demise of a set of parents. Rather, an additional adoption was set for the only son left at home. The solution was not to go back on an adoption, but to go forward in setting up more adoptions. Eventually, nothing short of the direst circumstances called for the dissolution alternative. Criminal conduct and disobedience were bases for dissolving adoptions in both the early and late dynasty. Eventually, a related issue, whether an adoption should be dissolved if the adoptive father later sired a son, became a controversy in the mid Chosŏn period.

Dissolution of Adoption in the *Kyehu tŭngnok*

The *Kyehu tŭngnok* lists several cases of adoption that were dissolved for a variety of reasons. As indicated above, the Code allowed for dissolution if the only son left in the natal family died. There were two such cases listed in the register, one in 1635 and one in 1640.[17] There were also two cases in which the adoption was dissolved because the biological parent had not given permission. In the first case, in 1634, the papers submitted by the biological father were discovered to have been forged.[18] In

---

[16]*Taejŏn hoet'ong*, p. 367-8. The note explained that the ceremonies for the adoptive parents could be combined with those of the adopted child's natal parents. The child would "temporarily" perform ceremonies for both sets of parents. In practice, this option was only rarely exercised in Korea, but was rather common in China. Many Chinese genealogies show one heir designated to carry on the lines of two and sometimes three "fathers".

[17]The first case is *KHTN*, 1635, *Chung-chen* 8.9.16; "Dissolution of the adoption of Kim Yŏng-su." Abstract:
Kim Yŏng-su had two sons. His younger brother, Sŏk-su, adopted the second son, Pyŏk, in 1619. In 1630, the elder son died and Yŏng-su, being the lineage heir, therefore, sought the return of his second son through the dissolution of the adoption.
The second is *PKHTN*, 1640.4.20. Abstract:
The adoption of Yi Shi-sŏng, the son of Yi T'ae-nam, to Yi Ch'ŏng-nam should be disallowed because he is an only son. He had a brother who died leaving him the only son.

[18]*KHTN*, 1634,*Chung-chen* 7.i8.16. Translation:
Song Kyu was without heir so he adopted Tŏng-nip, the second son of his eighth-*ch'on* cousin, Song I-gi, without discussing it with I-gi. He submitted a forged application document making it look as if the biological father had agreed.
In adoption both families must approve it; if not it violates the law. Adopting from a

the second, in 1703, the other parties to the adoption simply did not consult the biological father.[19] Apparently, the adoption had been authorized by the government on the assumption that the man had died; his wife had submitted documentation which usually happened only in the case of the demise of the biological father.

In 1724, an adoption authorized in 1709 was dissolved because of the criminal conduct of the adopted son.[20] The *Kyehu tŭngnok* also mentions one case wherein the king initially gave special authorization for the adoption of an only son, but after Chief State Counselor Kim Su-hang criticized the action, the adoption was dissolved. Interestingly, the *Kyehu tŭngnok* makes the statement that the adoption of an only son would be authorized in the case of merit subjects or luminaries, but for this candidate, Kim Man-gil, although the king said he was personally sympathetic, but the government officials argued that Kim was not a luminary and the adoption was dissolved.[21] Late in the dynasty an only son was often adopted if his biological father was a number two or three son, and the eldest son need an heir. As a lineage head, he would claim the eldest son of a younger brother, even if the son were an only son. The biological father would then adopt the second or third son of his brother or cousin. In effect, there were two adoptions to solve one problem.

<u>Long Distant Adoptions</u>

Another aspect of the institution of adoption was the tendency, in the late dynasty, to make more adoptions of remote kinsmen. Although the Code specified that a close relative should be adopted, either the son of a brother or a close cousin, as the dynasty wore on, adoptions of more and more distant relatives became common.[22] This is best seen in the *Kyehu tŭngnok* but can easily be detected in any genealogy.

distant relative is also a crime. Whether Song Kyu falsely signed Song I-gi's name or whether someone else did, we do not know, but it is clear that Song I-gi did not give his permission. The adoption certificate obtained by Song Kyu must be retrieved and canceled. The criminality of the case must be investigated.

[19]*KHTN*, 1703, *K'anghsi* 42.11.18. Abstract:

Song Cho submitted a petition saying that Mme Yi, the wife of his eighth-*ch'on* cousin, Song Hwi, in collaboration with a fourth-*ch'on* cousin, Song Chin, had applied for and received permission to adopt his son, Kap. But they had not consulted him, Song Cho said. Since the law requires that the biological parent of the adopted child be consulted, this was an improperly authorized adoption and should therefore be canceled. The king agreed.

[20]*KHTN*, 1724.7; "A cancellation of an adoption made in 1709" [listed in *KHTN*, 1709, *K'ang-hsi* 48.8.3]. Abstract:

Yi Kang adopted Kong-jŏng, the second son of Yi Ch'ŏl. It was canceled in the seventh month of 1724 for unspecified criminal conduct.

[21]*PKHTN*, 1686.7.21.

[22]Peterson, "Adoption in Korean Genealogies," pp. 28-35.

174

The development of distant-kinsman adoption is revealed by returning to the Puan Kim documents. Above, we saw the adoption of Su-jong; there were several adoptions in subsequent generations. Su-jong had a son, Pang-gil, who did not have a son and died at the age of twenty-seven; consequently an adoption was made for him the year after he died. The adoption certificate, dated 1743, was written by the natal father, Pang-bo, the son of Su-gyŏng, the second of the later-born sons of Pŏn. Pang-bo stated that Pang-gil, his fourth-*ch'on* cousin, died without heir and that Pang-gil's wife, Mme O, requested an heir since her husband was the lineage heir (*chongson*). The adopted son, originally named Hyŏn-dŭk, was later renamed Tŭng-mun.[23]

Table 9.2
Kim Tŭng-Mun's Adoption

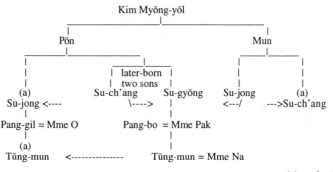

(a) = adoption

There was nothing unusual about the Tŭng-mun adoption. It was, in fact, ideal in many respects. The adoption was between close kin of the proper generation level. The two fathers were recorded as fourth-*ch'on* cousins but were biologically sixth-*ch'on* cousins since Su-jong, the adoptive grandfather, had also been adopted. The problems arose with the adoption in the next generation.

Tŭng-mun, himself adopted at the age of eleven, died at the age of thirty-five and did not have a son. His widow, Mme Na, requested the adoption of Chŏng-ha, the third of four sons of Mme Min, the widow of

23Puan Kim document PKK #2 (p. 170).

Kim Tong-ŏn, a twentieth-*ch'on* cousin.[24] In the meantime, Tŭng-mun's biological father Pang-bo had arranged the adoption of a grandson, Ŭng-p'yo, who was described as an eighth-*ch'on* adoptee. A dispute arose between Ŭng-p'yo and Chŏng-ha. Mme Pak, the wife of Pang-bo and the biological mother of Tŭng-mun, took the part of her adopted grandson, Ŭng-p'yo.

Table 9.3

The Adoptions of Chŏng-ha and Ŭng-p'yo

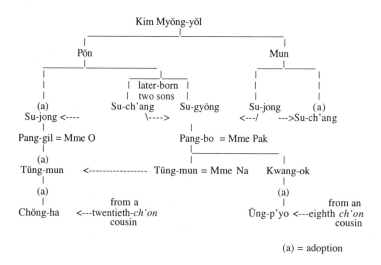

(a) = adoption

We have only the deposition written by Chŏng-ha which was apparently one in a series of arguments and counter-arguments. Chŏng-ha's deposition (in abstract) said:

> Midst many family tragedies, I have been entrapped by Kim Kwang-ok and his [adopted] son, Ŭng-p'yo. Ŭng-p'yo

---

[24]The adoption certificate issued by the Ministry of Rites is found in PKK #3 (pp. 170-1), dated 1768.9. Also in the collection is a document addressed to Mme Na signed (actually sealed) by Mme Min wherein Mme Min agreed to send her third son, Tar-hyŏn (later renamed Chŏng-ha), to be the heir to Kim Tŭng-mun, Mme Na's deceased husband. (Tŭng-mun died in 1767.) Dated 1768.7.15, Mme Min's statement was apparently part of the necessary documentation submitted to the Ministry of Rites. It is found in PKK #10 (p. 203).

was adopted in as my eighth-*ch'on* cousin. Kwang-ok should restrain his son from immoral acts but rather has seemed to encourage him. (My great-grandfather, Chinsa'gun [Su-jong], was an adopted son to his natural father's elder brother [Pan]. After the adoption, however, his wife died and he remarried and had two sons. The older [Su-ch'ang] was adopted to Chinsa-gun's natural father [Mun]. The younger [Su-gyŏng] is the great-grandfather of Ŭng-p'yo by adoption.)

Our common great-great-grandfather [Su-jong] divided his property equally between his heirs and the document still remains in my possession. Now time has passed and without basis there are accusations that the property was not divided equally. If Ŭng-p'yo had a basis in fact, he would say a specific piece of property or a specific slave were his, but he does not. Rather, he makes vague, general accusations. By this we can see that he has no basis in fact, but rather he is scheming. Since the documents exist this can all be proven.

Furthermore, Ŭng-p'yo has said that I have driven him and his adoptive grandmother out into the streets to beg!, but this is absolutely untrue. In addition, I have been accused of not acceding to Grandmother Pak's request to bring over the inheritance document so that the property can be redivided. Clearly this shows that I have the documents. I did not take them to Grandmother Pak, not because I wanted to ignore her, but because, one, she cannot read, and two, she is not the eldest grandmother and does not have the authority to redivide the property. I know the request did not originate with Grandmother Pak, but rather Ŭng-p'yo is behind all of this.

Furthermore, I have been accused of blocking the sale of Ŭng-p'yo's house. In reality, when a buyer came from Chŏnju to look at it, I encouraged him to buy it.

In principle, a family should have its inheritance documents. We have ours. By examining them one can see that Ŭng-p'yo's accusations have no basis. In reality, much of my property has fallen into his hands, but I have not tried to retrieve it because it is used to maintain Grandmother Pak. And yet Ŭng-p'yo makes these accusations of me. At this time, I am in mourning and have not yet been able to carry out the burial of my father. I do not care if I win or lose this property suit. Examine the documents and make your judgment.25

The cause of the dispute, in addition to greed, was probably the fact that Chŏng-ha was adopted in from a distant relative while Ŭng-p'yo was adopted in from a fairly close relative. Mme Pak may have disapproved of Mme Na arranging to adopt the son of Mme Min rather than one of her (Mme Pak's) own descendants. The collection of documents does not reveal the final resolution of the dispute, but it may have ended in the dissolution of Ŭng-p'yo's adoption; he does not appear in the genealogy.26 The long distant adoption remains as part of the genealogical configuration to the present.

Irrespective of the guideline in the Code indicating that one should adopt a close kinsman, as time went by more and more adoptions were established between more and more distant relatives. The Puan Kims were typical. But there were several calls for clamping down on those who overlooked the close in favor of the distant.

The *Kyehu tŭngnok*, which usually recorded only cases of adoption, in rare fashion also recorded a memorial from the Border Defense Council (Pibyŏnsa) in 1680 which criticized the Ministry of Rites for authorizing too many exceptional cases of adoption. The argument was multifold, but the points were that there were (1) too many cases of adoption when a *sŏja* already existed, and (2) they criticized the practice of adopting distant nephews often selecting candidates on the basis of talent. The document, written by Im Ch'ŏk, stated:

> In many cases people without sons who make adoptions
> often do so without following the law. Why is this so? The
> law states: if a man is not a primary line heir then "if he has
> no heir by wife of concubine then he may adopt." But now
> people are swayed by their wife's words, and they discard their
> *sŏja*, and take other people's children. And in the case of the

---

25PKK #20-1 (p. 139), undated but circa 1767, based on the statement that the author, Chŏng-ha, was in mourning for his father, Tŭng-mun, who died in 1767. The document itself is damaged in places so that not all the characters are complete. Therefore, I have rendered an abstract rather than a translation although in many places it is fully translated.

26*Puan Kim-ssi taebo* [The grand genealogy of the Puan Kim lineage] (Taejŏn: Hoesangsa, 1981), 2 vols. 2:12. Neither Ŭng-p'yo nor his father, Kwang-ok, appear in the *chokpo*. It is possible that they both changed their names, but there are no adoptions listed by any other name either.

primary line heir who adopts, he must, according to the law, take his younger brother's son but many do not. These days those who adopt look to see whether an adoptable son is bright or stupid, handsome or homely, and adopt a son from distant cousins. This custom harms relationships and destroys virtue.[27]

## Opinions on Adoption Found in *Munjip*

In addition to official opinions, such as that above, several scholar-officials, men whose writings were considered important enough to be collected and printed (*munjip*), wrote on the practice of adoption as they saw it.

Sŏng Man-jing (d. 1711), decried the adoption of distant kin in an essay dated 1692:

Most people in selecting an adoptable heir, even if their brother has a son, adopt a distant nephew. I think that although there may not be restrictions on a second or third son [since their adoptee serves only them], the heir to the father or the grandfather should definitely adopt from within his descent group. The reason for this is that if a second son adopts he can look for a talented heir whether he is close or distant. But for the grandfather, when there is a descendant, to adopt a non-descendant violates human feeling. "Everyone calls his son his son whether he has talents or not";[28] therefore, if one has a descendant perform the ceremonies, there will be no regrets in regard to the spirits or to human feelings.

How can one know whether a good son will have a bad grandson or a bad son can have a good grandson? For example, in a household where the eldest son dies, leaving a widow, she and her husband's younger brother may have just a slight disagreement whereby she will not refer to the basic principle [of adopting a close relative] but will go to a distant relative to adopt. In a worse case, there are law suits and family disputes. Nothing could be sadder. That is why I say

---

[27]*PKHTN*, 1681.1.13. See also footnote #38 below. Note here the pro-*sŏja* sentiment still extant in the late seventeenth century. For more on the *sŏja* part of this order, see p. 184, below.

[28]A quotation from the *Analects*, p. 239 in the Legge edition.

that in this case neither the giving nor the taking [of distant relatives in adoption] is good.[29]

As the trend continued, there were those who were still calling for a return to the basic principle of adopting a close relative a century later. Yi Wŏn-bae (1745-1802) said:

> The Ming dynasty emperor instructed that all those who seek adoptions should not discard the closely related in favor of taking a distant relative. Only when there are no heirs among the close relatives does one go to the distant relatives. Only after one has searched among all who would wear mourning clothes does one seek an adoption from among those who do not.[30]

A more liberal view, one that reflected the reality of the times, was expressed by Pak Mun-il (1822-1894) nearly another century later: "If a man has no heir, shifting the main line to his younger brother is not right. If the eldest son has no heir, he ought to adopt." As for whom the man ought to adopt, Pak said that the custom and the law clearly stated that an only son should not be adopted, therefore, the elder brother should look to a more distant relative for an adoption.[31] He did not advocate adopting distant kinsmen when close ones were available; no one could openly make such an advocacy, but in practice as the dynasty moved on, the choice of a kinsman for an adoption at times extended to more and more distant kinsmen although there were closer ones available.

Why did some choose to adopt a distant nephew when a more closely related kinsman existed? One likely explanation is that adoptions, particularly adoptions of distant kin, were a match of talent. For example, one who passed an exam often adopted a son who passed an exam. A prominent man without an heir was not likely to accept an heir who was not as promising as he himself had been as a youth. For the father it was a form of insurance, the best guarantee that his estate would be in good hands, would be used to take care of him in his old age, and would continue for generations to provide the wherewithal for the ceremonies for him and his

[29]Sŏng Man-jing, "Treatise on Adoption, 1692", Ch'udamjip, vol. 7, p. 10a.

[30]Yi Wŏn-bae, Kwiamjip, vol. 6, p. 34b.

[31]Pak Mun-il, Uamjip, vol. 8, p. 64b.

ancestors after he died. For the son, it was a chance for social mobility and opportunity. A good example comes from the late Chosŏn period. Kim Ok-kyun, the famed leader of the abortive 1884 coup, was adopted to a wealthy uncle. The promising young man thereby received a good education, passed the high civil service exam, and was eventually appointed to a series of important government offices.[32]

### Chŏng Yag-yong's Statement on Adoption

Chŏng Yag-yong (1762-1836), the famous *shirhak* philosopher, saw the dissolution of adoptions as a great social ill and argued that the problem could be avoided by allowing only posthumous adoption. He said:

> These days many people make adoptions while they are living; this is the cause of numerous abuses and malpractices. There are cases where a wife dies and out of sorrow an adoption is made. That adopted son performs the ceremonies for his deceased mother and then the father remarries and has a son. If the father dissolves the adoption then what happens to the ceremonies the son has observed? If he keeps the adopted son, then he is prolonging the days of his mother after she is dead. The relationship between mother and son and between older and younger brother worsens and they become antagonists.
>
> In other cases, the ceremonies in the adopted son's natal family are cut off. If the adoption is dissolved then the parent-child relationship of ten years can become that of strangers in one morning.
>
> In other cases, the son is adopted from a poor household into that of a wealthy household. The boy is taken with the wine, women and song of his new life and this is the source of numerous afflictions. If the adoption is then dissolved the man is broken and dejected.
>
> In other cases, a poor man works hard to find an adopted son, and the son dies young leaving the man even more deprived of the security he so desperately sought.

---

[32]Harold Cook, *Korea's 1884 Incident: Its Background and Kim Ok-kyun's Elusive Dream* (Seoul: Royal Asiatic Society/ Taewŏn Publishing Co., 1972). Note also that Kim's antagonist Yüan Shih-k'ai, was also adopted to a wealthy uncle.

In all of this there is adoption and dissolution of adoption, death and discontinuity [of family lines], life and continuity. The parent-child relationship is confused and the moral order if obfuscated. Even the best authorities cannot give answers as to how to deal with the resulting disorder. If we are to find the root of all these problems, it is in making adoptions while one is still alive.

If we were to ask any of the superior men of our society, they would say that one should not adopt while alive, but if one must, then resolve not to call each other father and son. In this we can follow the well-conceived laws and practices established by the former kings and sages, and there will be few regrets.[33]

In spite of the force of Chŏng's argument and in spite of his eminence as a commentator on social values, his view was not widely accepted. The tendency to adopt while yet alive continued to grow throughout the late Chosŏn period. The percentage of posthumous adoptions declined, and the number of adoptions that were dissolved continued to rise.[34]

### *Sŏja* as Adopted Heirs—Cases from the *Kyehu Tŭngnok*

How did *sŏja* fare as heirs in the seventeenth century and thereafter? As seen in chapters five and six, the plight of the *sŏja* was not a happy one, but it was not one of total despair, as we saw in chapter seven (p. 130 & 131); there were some kings and officials who took their part. Consider the case of Chŏng Sŏk-ki, a *sŏja* descendant of Chŏng Ch'ang-sŏ, adopted to become the heir in the primary line. He was originally an heir in a lesser collateral line. The issue was decided in 1634 when the king ruled favorably on a petition from the widow of Chŏng Ch'ang-sŏ. The entry in the *Pyŏl kyehu tŭngnok* said:

Heading: A special heir is established for Chŏng Ch'ang-sŏ by promoting a *sŏja* to lineage heir status.

The petition of Mme Kim, the widow of Chŏng Ch'ang-sŏ, states that her husband, by wife and by concubine,

---

[33]*RZS*, p. 31, quoting *Yŏyudangjip* vol. 35.

[34]Peterson, "Adoption in Korean Genealogies," pp. 28-35.

had neither son nor daughter and her husband's line ended because there was not anyone within the family who qualified for adoption. [The text of her petition follows.] During the Sŏnjo reign, in response to a petition, it was firmly decided that the *sŏja*, Kuk-saeng, would be specially promoted to be the lineage heir to Ch'ang-sŏ's father, Chŏng Se-ho, the deceased (posthumous) Chief State Councilor. After which, in 1586 when Ch'ang-sŏ died, Kuk-saeng performed the three-year ritual mourning. . . . After Kuk-saeng died, his eldest son, Pang-yŏl, died without heir. Therefore, by law it is proper that Sŏk-ki now succeed him. In 1629, the queen dowager decreed that the *sŏja* of a *sŏja* serving as a lineage heir was disquieting. She said one should make an appropriate adoption from within the lineage to serve the primary line. . . . Since I [the widow of Ch'ang-sŏ] viewed Ŭich'ang-gun, the widow of Kwang-yang, and Chŏng Kwang-jŏk as the lineage heads, I asked them but they responded that there was not an appropriate candidate in the main line and if there was not an appropriate candidate among the distant lines, then utilizing any *sŏja* was the same as using Sŏk-ki. Therefore, the property owner must decide as best he can.

In accordance with the dowager's decree, Sŏk-ki who is not only well-educated but extremely sincere and filial should receive the certification as the heir to the main line. But now, Sŏng-myŏng, the grandson of my husband's younger brother, Hong-su, an ignorant and immoral man, has dared to conspire to confiscate the property of the ritual heir. He calls himself a *yang* [good, commoner] *sŏja*. But Sŏng-myŏng's grandmother was a public slave in the *naeja* [government] warehouse. On the other hand, Sŏk-ki's mother was a private slave who was manumitted and became a commoner. Government slave or private slave, a slave is a slave. There are numerous cases where even a mean concubine's son is designated as a ritual heir. A legitimate branch line, let alone a commoner concubine's son, cannot take it away. Kuk-saeng was designated the heir over sixty years ago by Sŏnjo and by his queen. Sŏng-myŏng's plan to take over the ritual position is irrational in the extreme. For this reason, the Ministry of Rites issued a certificate to Sŏk-ki naming him as the ritual heir for the main lineage. [End of petition by Mme Kim.]

[The Ministry of Rites official said:] if we examine the above petition, Chŏng Ch'ang-sŏ, the eldest son of the (posthumous) Chief State Councilor Chŏng Se-ho has been designated as the heir. Ceremonies to him, whether by legitimate or *sŏja* heir, ought to be carried out by the descendant of Ch'ang-sŏ. The descendant of a brother of Ch'ang-sŏ, even though legitimate, has no authority to take the ceremonial privilege unto himself. Moreover, Sŏng-myŏng is an illegitimate descendant of Ch'ang-so's brother, and even more importantly, Kuk-saeng was, from the beginning, designated the heir by the queen. How can a member of the family try to change a royal decision? Even more so, how can Sŏng-myŏng, himself a base *sŏja*, attempt to carry out such a plan? To characterize Sŏng-myŏng's offense, it is nothing less than immorality and disrespect for the king.

The above mentioned Mme Kim, the widow of Chŏng Ch'ang-sŏ, is eighty years old and realizes that death is imminent. Fearing conflict over the estate after her death, she desires to see a clear resolution to this matter and therefore submitted her petition.

Since this matter deals with the inheritance of the in-laws of the former kings, it is not like unto other matters of the aristocracy.[35] Therefore, it cannot be submitted to anyone but the king. Is it permissible for the Ministry of Rites to issue a certificate designating Sŏk-ki as the ritual heir for the primary lineage?

Dated: *Sung-ch'eng* 7 (1634).4.30.
Official in charge: Sixth Royal Secretary, Yi.
Royal permission granted.[36]

The above case illustrates several important points. Although there was pervasive prejudice against *sŏja*, under special circumstances, such as royal approval, a *sŏja* could become a lineage heir. It is interesting to note

---

[35]Chŏng Se-ho's daughter married Tŏkhŭng Taewŏn'gun, the father of Sŏnjo. Se-ho was Sŏnjo's maternal grandfather. Chŏng Ch'ang-sŏ was, therefore, Sŏnjo's uncle. See also *HIT*, p. 228.

[36]*PKHTN*, 1634.4.30.

the argument of one *sŏja* that he was of higher status since his mother was a commoner not a slave. In any case, since only a few *sŏja* attained lineage heir status, one can conclude that a *sŏja* named as an heir had to have backing from others within the lineage. Throughout the latter half of the dynasty there were cases of men promoting their *sŏja* to legitimate status. In the *Kyehu tŭngnok*, several such cases were listed in the seventeenth century. In addition to the above complicated case, several other cases were recorded in a simple, matter-of-fact manner in 1627, 1629, and 1657.[37] In 1680, the Border Defense Council issued a special memorial through the Ministry of Rites emphasizing the importance of maintaining the position of the *sŏja* rather than adopting:

> If we are to correct this situation, we must completely follow the law. He who has a *sŏja* should not be allowed to adopt. The primary line heir should not be allowed to adopt distant cousins at will. Both these practices should be forbidden and thereby stop all these noisy law suits.

The Ministry of Rites commented on the Border Defense Council memorial:

> According to this memorial from the Border Defense Council, if those allowed to adopt be only those who have no heir by wife or concubine, then we will be in compliance with the law; but today there are many who adopt by special permission [as exceptions to the law], and this is the cause of lawsuits and disputes. If we are to correct this situation, then the Ministry of Rites must be instructed to follow the law in authorizing adoptions.
>
> The king concurred.[38]

---

[37]The three entries from the *Kyehu tŭngnok* are:
*KHTN*, 1627.7.15: Kim Ch'oe adopts Pyŏn, the *sŏja* son of his eighth-*ch'on* cousin, Kim Shi-ryang.
*KHTN*, 1629.1.20: Yun Shi-sŏng adopts Ho, the seventh *sŏja* of his elder brother, Yun Shi-shim.
*KHTN*, 1657.6.4: Chŏn Sŏl adopts Tŏng-nyun, the third *sŏja* of his fourth-*ch'on* cousin, Chŏn Ong.

[38]*PKHTN*, 1681.1.13. This passage is a continuation of the Border Defense Council's criticism of long-distant adoption. See page 178, footnote #27.

Five years later the *Kyehu tǔngnok* recorded another case of heirship by a *sǒja*. The case concerned the heir of Yi Yulgok who did not have a legitimate son but who indicated before he died that his *sǒja* was to be his heir. The great-grandson by adoption did not have a son. The problem was that he and his wife had both died and there was no one to petition for an adoption. The chief state councilor requested that the king authorize the adoption of a fourth-*ch'on* cousin who also would have been a descendant of the *sǒja* heir of Yulgok.[39]

Unlike the practices of inheritance and adoption, for the practice of using a *sǒja* as an heir, either by his own father or by an adoptive father, there is no consistent increase or decline to be seen over the course of the dynasty but rather there are short-term dips and recoveries, slightly down, then slightly up, over the course of the dynasty.[40] Inheritance clearly changed from a system of equal distribution for sons and daughters to one where the eldest son received the largest amount. Adoption gradually increased in frequency as the importance of the eldest son as an heir grew. But utilizing a *sǒja* was always an applicable alternative, although there were always limitations on his ability to function. At points in the dynasty when it looked as if the *sǒja* was losing ground, he reemerged with new strengths and new backing.

The number of cases where *sǒja* were utilized as adopted heirs as recorded in the *Kyehu tǔngnok* declined in the latter portion of the record, the late seventeenth through the eighteenth and into the nineteenth century.

---

[39]*PKHTN*, 1685.2.19; "A special adoption for the descendant of Yulgok." [Yulgok was enshrined in the National Confucian Shrine (Sǒnggyun'gwan) in the fifth month of 1682.]

On the tenth of this month, Chief State Minister Kim [Su-hang] met with the king and talked of the former minister, Yi I, who had no children by his first wife but has had the ceremonies performed by *sǒja* descendants. The great grandson, Hu-shi, had a son, Kye, but he died young and without heir. To make an adoption for Kye is difficult since all of his nephews are young. There is no one to perform the ceremony for the former great minister, Yi I, and the ceremony is in abeyance. The lineage has indicated that they would like to see Chǒng, the son of Hu-su, a fourth-*ch'on* cousin of Hu-shi, adopted to Hu-shi. The senior statesman Song Shi-yǒl has been involved in the discussions and agrees to this procedure. But since both Hu-shi and his wife are deceased, this matter must be decided by special, royal permission.

The king authorized a special adoption.

[40]Pae Chae-hong has concluded that the situation for *sǒja* gradually improved over the course of the dynasty. Liberalizations in terms of access to examinations, office, stipends, and wealth were not greatly improved, but overall there were some slight betterment of their situations. "Chosǒn shidae ch'ǒpchanyǒ ǔi chaesan sangsok kwa chonjae yangt'ae," [Inheritance of property by the children of *ch'ǒp* (secondary wives) in the Chosǒn period] *Taegu sahak* 39:95-128 (1990.8).

But before one can conclude that this decline matched the decline in the percentage of property given to daughters and to younger sons, and was offset by the increase in the adoption of agnatic nephews, we see a new resurgence of interest in protecting the privileges of the *sŏja*.

## The *Suyang Sŭngjŏk Ilgi*

This resurgence of interest in *sŏja* is seen in the initiation of a new register of adoptions titled the *Suyang sŭngjŏk ilgi* (The diary of adoptions by promotion to legitimacy) which was kept from 1843 to 1894.[41] In two volumes it recorded in outline form the name of the father, the name of the *sŏja* son, and the fact that he was being promoted to legitimate heir status. Why these men chose to promote their own *sŏja* to legitimate status[42] while others were supplanting their *sŏja* by adopting agnatic nephews is somewhat unclear. It could be that only those of less significant lineages and of minor sublineages were the ones who participated in the promotion of *sŏja*. Also, many of those lines, by that time, could have been lines that were already stigmatized as *sŏja* lines.

A greater question is whether the promoted *sŏja* was better accepted in society or not. A "promoted-to-legitimacy *sŏja*" was still a *sŏja* in many people's eyes and in most cases did not have an improved chance at obtaining a government position. There were those both in the early and late Chosŏn dynasty who chose to use *sŏja* as heirs. Early dynasty *sŏja* had some advantages on the basis of a tradition that allowed them to serve in government; late dynasty *sŏja* had the disadvantage of years of prejudice stacked against them but had the advantages of support from some powerful people and the institution of promotion to legitimacy. All in all, for the late dynasty *sŏja*, the disadvantages probably outweighed the advantages and therefore, when a choice was to be made, most chose to adopt.

## The Filter-down Effect

Most of the examples cited above have been drawn from the elite of society, the *yangban*. What of the commoner and slave?

---

[41]This register is also kept in the Kyujanggak collection, catalog no. 13038.

[42]There was cosmological justification for this point of view found in Neo-Confucian dogma. The male was equivalent to *ki* (Ch. *chi*); and only those of the same *ki* could participate in ancestor ceremonies. One who was not a descendant of the ancestor being honored at a *chesa* ceremony, could not benefit from the ceremony, neither could the spirit of the deceased enjoy the offering. See Deuchler, p. 133 quoting Chu Hsi, *Chu Tzu yü-lei* (Reprint, 1978), 3:6, 10, 18b, 20.

In the Chosŏn dynasty generally a social practice adopted by the elite came to be followed by the masses. This was certainly true of adoption. Although the record is sketchy for the non-elite, the evidence available points to the commoners and even the slaves following after the *yangban* elite. In fact, within the elite stratum, the social practices of adoption and inheritance seem to have begun with the upper levels of the *yangban* elite (high officials, merit subjects, and royal relatives), and filtered down, first through the layers of the elite stratum, and ultimately to the commoners and slaves. The *Kyehu tŭngnok* gives several examples. Beginning with the highest level of the elite, the importance of a royal family member having an heir is often stressed in the record. Entries in the *Kyehu tŭngnok* for royal relatives were often long, detailed entries, but those for other *yangban* elite are straightforward, simple entries. It was as if the officials knew the importance of the precedents they were setting.

Next in importance were matters of heirship for royal in-laws and merit subjects (*kongshin*) who were also seen in the documents. Many of the special entries and precedent-setting entries are those involving the upper level of the elite stratum of society. Other members of elite society, those with whom the above intermarried, followed suit. These patterns of what was appropriate for the elite became patterns for the lower classes. The filter-down effect is seen in a government register for non-agnatic adoptions.

## *The Suyang Shiyang Tŭngnok*

The lower strata imitating the elite is best seen in the adoption register called the *Suyang shiyang tŭngnok*, an adoption register that first records data in 1684 and ends in 1750.[43] It is primarily a record of non-elite adoptions, adoptions of commoners and slaves. The adoptions recorded therein were generally of children whose surnames were different from the parent(s). The difference between a *shiyang* adoptee and a *suyang* adoptee was a matter of age. A *shiyang* child was over three while a *suyang* adoptee was under the age of three years. The *shiyang* child could not have his/her name changed to that of the parent, but a *suyang* child could.[44]

The *Suyang shiyang tŭngnok* discloses its lower class composition not only by its contents, but by its very format—it is much more casual

---

[43]Kyujanggak catalog nos. 12960-1 and 12960-2, a two-volume register.

[44]*Taejŏn hoet'ong*, p. 715. See also Pak Pyŏng-ho, "Isŏnggyehu ŭi shilchŭngjŏk yŏn'gu" [A evidentiary study of non-agnatic adoption], *Pŏphak* (SNU Law Journal), no. 14-1, 1973. See also chapter one, page 22 and footnote 12.

appearing than its contemporary register for aristocrats, the *Kyehu tŭngnok*. Unlike the *Kyehu tŭngnok*, in which sons were adopted in the aristocratic or ideal form, i.e., sons of agnatic relatives in the proper generation level, the *Suyang shiyang tŭngnok* primarily recorded the adoptions that can be characterized as non-aristocratic or non-ideal adoptions. The child was very often an abandoned orphan, but there were also non-agnatic kinsmen (mother's and wife's relatives), one's slave by purchase, or one's slave's child found in the register. Cases of agnatic adoption are found, but more often the adopted child was either related through a female tie or was a non-relative. The adopting parent was not always a man, either; the record reveals several cases of single women adopting. And, perhaps the most surprising, at times the adopted child was female.

In addition to the contextual differences between the two adoption registers and practices, the individuals listed in the *Suyang shiyang tŭngnok* have titles or status designations which betray their non-elite standing. Some entrants were listed as public or private slaves. Craftsmen, eunuchs, palace women, widows, rural governmental clerks, military figures, and *sŏja* were among the more interesting status designations recorded in the *Suyang shiyang tŭngnok*.

The fact that the document begins its record late in the seventeenth century suggests that the commoners and slaves were becoming interested in mimicking lineage organization or attempting a kind of family continuity by means of adoption at that time. That the register ceased to record events after 1750 may indicate that the matter had become so mundane that there was no longer a necessity to record adoptions for commoners and slaves in a central government office. Reporting such matters, along with other changes in vital statistics, to the county officials at the time of the triennial census may have been sufficient; at any rate, we do not see any entries in the register kept by the Ministry of Rites after 1750.

Certain of the status categories are of particular interest. The eunuchs who served the Yi court married, adopted children, and maintained a family life. No eunuch adoptions are recorded in the *Kyehu tŭngnok*, but four can be found in the *Suyang shiyang tŭngnok*.[45]

Women, particularly palace women, provide an interesting counterpoint to the male-dominated sphere of son-giving and son-taking. The motivation for a woman to adopt appears to be the desire to have

---

[45]The entries can be found, as in the other registers by the date; there are no page numbers. The eunuch adoptions are found in the years 1685, 1687, and 1721.

someone to care for her in her declining years. Many of the women are indicated as being either former palace women or widows which indicates they were older, and they tended to adopt young girls although there were cases of women adopting boys. Here, too, however, the focus of the adoption is the benefit of the parent-generation, not the child.

The ages of the children in the *Suyang shiyang tŭngnok* were much younger than their counterparts in the *Kyehu tŭngnok*. As seen above, the adopted "child" in the aristocratic document tended to be a full-grown adult. In the cases of commoners and slaves, a great number of the children were listed as babies or abandoned orphans. Many of the adoptees were *suyang* adoptions, which by definition were under three years of age. From this we can draw the conclusion that the aristocrats were interested in having someone carry on the ceremonies after the demise of the father. The commoners were perhaps interested in having the experience of raising a child (like the practice in modern western society), but more likely they wanted someone to take care of them in their declining years.

An important trend is perceptible in the *Suyang shiyang tŭngnok* over the period of time it was kept. Initially, none of the entries mimicked the aristocratic format, but as time went by, more and more of the entries began to list adoptions of agnatic kinsmen in the proper generation. In 1693, we find the first usage of the phrase ". . . was without an heir by either wife or concubine," the quotation from the Code that was used formulaically throughout the *Kyehu tŭngnok*. Thereafter, it occurred more and more often. The simple, two-volume register is a tidy symbolic display of the commoner and slave attempting to emulate the elite tradition.

The Ideal Adoption

In this final chapter we have examined the ideal practice of agnatic adoption. The practice of petitioning the government for approval to make an adoption is preserved in the government registers. It is particularly useful to cross-reference data in the government registers with genealogies or sources. The *Kyehu tŭngnok* was the largest and oldest of the registers.

The *Pyŏl kyehu tŭngnok* contains exceptional cases which are sometimes long and complicated. Some are routine, such as those petitions from candidates whose parents are both dead; the law said that one or the other parent must apply. If both parents are deceased and another party petitions, then the adoption was recorded in the *Pyŏl kyehu tŭngnok*.

What was termed "long distance" adoption denotes the remote degree of kinship between the natal father and the biological father. In a tangible way, adoption is a measure of the breadth and depth of the lineage membership. The genealogy serves the purposes of keeping lineage mates in touch with each other, to keep track of ceremonies, to determine worthiness of potential marriage partners, and is a kind of map of lineage relationships. The *sŏja* continued to push for acceptance and recognition. Like early dynasty *sŏja*, some in the late dynasty were recognized, appointed to office, or were otherwise accomplished. But as we saw in chapters five and six, discrimination persisted. That they made some steps forward in the nineteenth century can be argued because of the emergence of the *Suyang sŭngjŏk ilgi*, yet their constant lament was that this kind of thing did not happen in China, why did it have to happen in Korea?

If the elite of society were encouraged to perform Confucian ancestor ceremonies at the beginning of the dynasty, but did so only with reluctance, and if under the Confucianization process gradually all *yangban* came to delight in ancestor ceremonies, did the process extend to the lower classes? The record of the *Suyang shiyang tŭngnok* shows something of the process. Initially, it is a record of mostly non-agnatic adoption, of sons and daughters, some of whom were related, matrilineally or affinally, and some were not. Later, incidents of agnatic adoption slip into even this document showing a mirroring of the upper class by the lower.

By the middle of the eighteenth century the ideal adoption, the adoption of an agnatic nephew, became the norm for all levels of society. Reinforced by the tenets of Neo-Confucianism and practiced by the pious elite of the society, adoption had become the solution for almost all of society, the solution to the problem of not having an heir, meaning a son. Daughters and their husbands lost the place they once held as heirs, and a man with only daughters was the same as a man without children. A few in the early, middle and late periods bravely supported their *sŏja* as heirs, but they were always a minority. The most acceptable alternative was to adopt an agnatic nephew.

The patrilineage as an institution grew in importance and in depth and breadth; as it did, nephews were transferred from one family to another within the lineage, often after the father died, to satisfy the needs of the ritual. Adoption, therefore, became an accurate measure of the functional boundaries of the lineage: one could adopt a distant kinsman only if he was recognized as a kinsman. The measuring stick, the institution of adoption, shows clearly that the lineages grew in depth and breadth after the mid Yi period.[46]

---

[46]The increase in publication of genealogies (*chokpo*) itself is another measure of the development of the patrilineal unilineal descent system in Korea. The numbers of printed genealogies increased dramatically in the seventeenth century and thereafter.

# CONCLUSIONS

Before we look back at the institutions of adoption and inheritance as they developed in the mid Chosŏn period of Korea, let us first look at what happened in two other countries with similar traditions influenced by similar philosophies and values. Both China and Japan give us remarkable comparisons; there are interesting differences amidst striking similarities.

Adoption and Inheritance in China
First China; the practice of adoption in China, on the one hand, bears striking similarities to what we have seen in Korea, especially during the T'ang period. After all, the lawmakers of both the Koryŏ and the Chosŏn periods used the Chinese legal code as their model. But after the T'ang period, which had a stratified and aristocratic society as did Chosŏn Korea, things changed. The code provided for the orthodox form of adoption, adoption of an agnatic nephew, which meant that the adopting father and son should not only have the same surname but they should be from the same lineage, and in the proper generational relationship. In the T'ang period, there was fairly close compliance with the standard, particularly among the upper class, but in subsequent dynasties, the law stayed the same but the practice varied. Several writers studying several regions of China concluded that China had a rich variety of adoption styles.[1]

The varieties of adoption permissible in China makes the orthodoxy of the practice in Korea stand out sharply. The Chinese made rules to punish those who made unorthodox adoptions,[2] they wrote proscriptions

---

[1] The most recent work is an excellent study by Ann Waltner, *Getting an Heir: Adoption and the Construction of Kinship in Late Imperial China* (Honolulu: University of Hawaii, 1990). Also see Arthur Wolf and Chieh-shan Huang, *Marriage and Adoption in China, 1845-1945* (Stanford: Stanford University Press, 1980); and James L. Watson, "Agnates and Outsiders: Adoption in Chinese Lineage," *Man* 10:2 (June 1975). In addition to these works centering on adoption, there are numerous anthropological field studies that contain information about adoption in China; notable among them are Maurice Freedman, *Chinese Lineage and Society: Fukien and Kwangtung* (London: Athlone Press, 1966) and Hugh Baker, *Chinese Family and Kinship* (New York: Columbia University Press, 1979).

[2] Waltner, *Getting an Heir*, p. 49.

191

against such adoptions in their genealogies,[3] and yet non-agnatic adoptions persisted, and even flourished. Those in the non-elite strata in Korea practiced non-agnatic adoption and the options exercised were probably of the same range as those in China, but the elite practice did not vary from the classic agnatic form. In China, however, even the elite practiced heterodox adoptions, even though such practice was not sanctioned by either law or ritual; their only sanction was custom, but custom is a powerful sanction.[4]

In spite of legal sanctions against adopting abandoned children (as one category of non-agnatic adoption), they succeeded as heirs and were responsible for the ancestor ceremonies as well.[5] Even Chu Hsi is quoted as showing a degree of flexibility that was not found among orthodox late-Chosŏn period Koreans:

> The setting up of heirs of different surname is indeed an abuse on the part of our contemporaries and is nowadays difficult to correct after it has happened. However, it is all right if, when participating in the sacrifices, the adopted man has a totally sincere attitude of respect and filial piety.[6]

Chinese folklore provided a fascinating model from nature that helped justify non-agnatic adoption. The *Shih Ching* tells us about the *ming-ling*, a variety of wasp (a sphex) that was believed to transform the silk caterpillar into its own offspring. Legge gives the following translation:

> The mulberry insect has young ones
> And the sphex carries them away.
> Teach and train your young ones
> And they will become as good as you are.[7]

In the biological world, the wasps carry off silkworm larvae and lay eggs in the carcass upon which their young feed until they emerge from the nest, but the ancient Chinese perceived the larvae as being *transformed* into wasps. The interpretation was that if, in nature, offspring can be adopted across species' lines, then surely humans can adopt those of different lineages or even different surnames. Because of the belief in the

---

[3]*Ibid*, p. 58; see also footnote nine below.

[4]Waltner, *Getting an Heir*, p. 4.

[5]*Ibid.*, p. 53.

[6]Quoted in Waltner, *Getting an Heir*, p. 74; and also I. J. McMullen, "Non-Agnatic Adoption" p. 141; both quoting *Chu-tzu ta-ch'üan, Ssu-pu pei-yao*, v. 1491, 58/31a-b.

[7]Legge, *Chinese Classics (Shih Ching)*, v. 4, p. 334.

transformation of the *ming-ling* insect, adopted heirs who originally had a different surname were sometimes called *ming-ling-tzu*.[8]

Chinese genealogies, while usually proscribing non-agnatic adoption on the one hand, some actually recorded cases of non-agnatic adoption.[9] Korean genealogies contain no entries indicating non-agnatic adoption, and in their prefaces, they do not even contain a prohibition against non-agnatic adoption, indicating that the practice is so far removed from the realm of possibility that it was not necessary to record such a proscription. Waltner cites examples of lineages using adoption the way they use marriage to forge alliances.[10] To that extent, many utilized non-agnatic adoption, and within that category there was a clear preference for the adoption of maternal line relatives (*wai-tsu*, K. *oejok*) in many cases.[11] China, although by ritual guidelines and by law, should have practiced agnatic adoption, in reality practiced a wide variety of options.

Inheritance in China does not appear to have undergone a transition; none is reported in the literature, except that which we can infer from the Confucian classics. The social order of ancient China, Confucius' time, was apparently one that featured primogeniture and a major role in ritual matters for the eldest son. Of course, during Confucius' time there were several states and each could have had a different system. When we come into the time of the unified empires, virtually the historical period, from Han to Ch'ing, the rule of inheritance has been equal division among brothers and no inheritance for daughters.

Although China did not have a transformation that saw the disinheritance of daughters, they did see the development of a lineage system. Patricia Ebrey has noted that in the Sung period there was a transformation from a family (*chia*) system to one where the lineage (*tsung*) was paramount. In that system, affinal ties were useful and provided social

---

[8]The varieties of options is reflected in terminology, and there are many more terms in China than in Korea. In China, in addition to the term *ming-ling-tzu*, there are the following terms, all of which mean one who is adopted: *chi-tzu, i-nan, i-nü, i-tzu, kuo-chi-tzu, lien-tzu, ssu-tzu, yang-tzu*. The Korean terms include: *kyeja, kyehuja, iphuja, yangja, suyangja, shiyangja*; and on rare occasion the term *myŏngnyŏngja* is also found.

[9]Waltner, *Getting an Heir*, p. 90; see also Patricia Ebrey, "The Early Stages in the Development of Descent Group Organization;" p. 55, footnote #23 provides a comment on her research on genealogies; she found that only one genealogy strongly condemned non-agnatic adoption, whereas others praised creative succession practices such as using a daughter or her children as ritual heirs. See also p. 49.

[10]Waltner, *Getting an Heir*, p. 95; and Jerry Dennerline, *The Chia-ting Loyalists: Confucian Leadership and Social Change in Seventeenth-Century China*. (New Haven: Yale University Press, 1981), p. 136-149.

[11]Waltner, *Getting an Heir*, p. 94.

connections.[12] She also notes that adoption highlighted the difference between the old order centered on the family, and the new order centered on the lineage. In the old order, a non-agnatic adoption was in order; but in the lineage system, an agnatic adoption of the proper generation was required[13]. Some authors have referred to a pre-Confucian period and the Confucianization process in China.[14]

## Inheritance and Adoption in Japan

Japan, on the other hand, experienced a transition similar to what we saw in Korea, from a partible inheritance system that included daughters to a unigeniture system. The system before, and the system after, were different in many ways from their counterparts in Korea, but there were similarities and indeed the transition was remarkably similar. The documents of medieval Japan that show partible inheritance look remarkably like those of Korea before the transition. A recent book by Jeffrey Maas chronicles the transition and also presents numerous documents in translation covering the period of the transition, the twelfth to fourteenth century, from the late Heian through the Kamakura period of Japan.[15] He writes of the profound social and economic changes in the late Kamakura period many of which were a result of the Mongol invasions and the warrior class's response to those attempted invasions.[16] Consolidation of assets was necessary to concentrate power in the hands of a few powerful warriors, and thus partible inheritance came under attack. In the transition to unigeniture, daughters were first discarded, and other sons followed.[17] But the old order died hard, and law suits by disinherited daughters were sometimes successful and prolonged the period of transition.[18] The era of partible inheritance, which

---

[12]Patricia Ebrey, "Conceptions of the Family in the Sung Dynasty," *Journal of Asian Studies* p. 229.

[13]*Ibid.*, p. 233.

[14]See Jack L.Dull, "Marriage and Divorce in Han China: A Glimpse of 'Pre-Confucian' Society," in *Chinese Family Law and Social Change* edited by David Buxbaum (Seattle: University of Washington Press, 1978); and Miyakawa, Hisayuki, "The Confucianization of South China," in *The Confucian Persuasion* (Stanford: Stanford University Press, 1960).

[15]Jeffrey P. Maas, *Lordship and Inheritance in Early Medieval Japan* (Stanford: Stanford University Press, 1989); and also see Akira Hayami who argues that partible inheritance continued into the seventeenth century Tokugawa period, "The Myth of Primogeniture and Impartible Inheritance in Tokugawa Japan," *Journal of Family History* 8:3-29 (Spring 1983).

[16]Maas, Lordship and Inheritance in Early Medieval Japan, p. 94.

[17]*Ibid.*, see pages 101, and 113, for examples.

[18]*Ibid.*, p. 105.

dated back to the beginning of the historical record, gave way to an era where ties were no longer based on kinship but on military ties.[19] In each of the points above, there are striking parallels as well as fascinating contrasts to the Korean case. The practice of adoption in Japan, however, was similar to that in China and unlike that in Korea. A wide variety of options were available including classic agnatic adoption, but also including several kinds of non-agnatic options. Adoption of daughters[20] and sons-in-law was practiced in Japan perhaps more than in China; indeed, many cases of succession to the controlling position in modern corporations are known to be handled by son-in-law adoption (*mukoyōshi*).[21] In ideal agnatic adoption, the proper generation level is one of the defining criterion; the adopted son must be a nephew, that is, in the generation below the father. The Chinese emphasized the *chao-mu* order (K. *sŏ-mok*), which was the system of alternating the spirit tablets of the ancestors in the ancestral hall; each ascending generation was honored on opposite sides of the hall in alternation. To adopt someone in the same generation, even if much younger, or to adopt someone in the grandson generation, even if of an appropriate age, was unacceptable. In Japan, however, adoptions in violation of the generational order were common. A younger brother was often adopted as a son.[22] Japan underwent a Confucian revival in the seventeenth and eighteenth centuries and non-agnatic adoption came to be criticized. Although the pro-Confucians tried to force the agnatic model onto Japanese society, they were only partially successful. Tradition persisted.[23]

The Japanese were torn by the issue of following the Chinese model. But they went beyond the debate of the Koreans, who saw value in the national tradition (*kuksok*) but eventually abandoned it for the perceived superiority of the Chinese way. The Japanese, in the manner of a pendulum, copied the Chinese T'ang code wholesale (the Taiho Code of the early eighth century), but thereafter retracted the code in favor of a domestic

---

[19]*Ibid.*, p. 94 & p. 114.

[20]*Ibid.*, p. 11.

[21]See Robert J. Smith, *Ancestor Worship in Contemporary Japan* (Stanford: Stanford University Press, 1974); and Two *Japanese Villages* (New York: Greenwood Press, 1969), p. 64-67; and Harumi Befu, "Corporate Emphasis and Patterns of Descent in the Japanese Family" in *Japanese Culture*, p. 35ff.

[22]*Ibid.*, p. 25, footnote 62.

[23]I.J. McMullen, "Non-Agnatic Adoption: A Confucian Controversy in Seventeenth and Eighteenth Century Japan."

model (the Yōrō Code of the late eighth century).[24] The Koreans, once they adopted the Chinese code, with the exception of a few court debates and some reluctance in compliance, did not look back—there was no retraction. Modeling on the Chinese pattern, although retaining unique Korean features, was straight-lined and unidirectional, whereas the Japanese pattern was pendular, cycling between emulating China and withdrawal for introspective modifications.[25]

## Korean Cases

The Korean cases are in some ways similar, and in some ways different from the Chinese and the Japanese cases. We have seen a remarkable transition in inheritance and adoption practices in the body of this book, and we have seen parties on each side of an issue in the transition argue for their side. Each side would cite precedents, codes, and texts that were complex and often contradictory, yet throughout the period, the result was consistent movement in one direction—that of the Confucianized patrilineal ideal espoused by Chu Hsi and the Korean Neo-Confucians.

The dramatic nature of the change can be summarized in a chart that shows the increase in the practice of adoption as the practice of equal inheritance declined. In table 10.1, we see the overlay of table 3.4 (the decline of daughter's inheritances) and table 9.1 (the rise of agnatic adoption). Clearly, the intersection of the two lines in the little-over-one-hundred years near the boundaries of the seventeenth century show what had happened. As daughters lost their standing as heirs, the role of the eldest son, and in his absente the adopted son, grew. Dramatically, the society had changed its basic value of how one generation should be succeeded by the next.

The institutions of inheritance and adoption were just two of those that were affected by Confucianization.[26] Other social changes included most notably marriage, ancestor rituals, lineage formation, *chokpo* compilation, and the movement toward single-surname villages which also underwent a similarly dramatic change in the early and mid Chosŏn. These

---

[24]Maas, *Lordship and Inheritance.*, p. 10.

[25]Edwin Reischauer often referred to the pendulum swings of Japanese history, swinging between borrowing from China (from earliest history) or the West (in recent history) on the one hand, and periods of isolation and indigenization, on the other.

[26]See footnote #12 above.

have been studied elsewhere and will be studied more in the future.[27]  Here, although this study has been limited to primarily two of these affected institutions, clearly they serve as symbolic representation of the wide range of changes that took place in family and society.

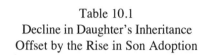

Table 10.1
Decline in Daughter's Inheritance
Offset by the Rise in Son Adoption

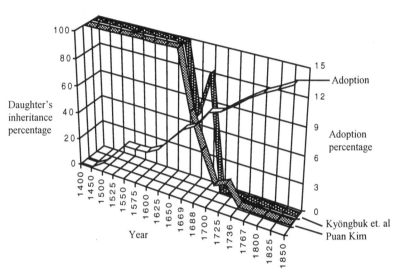

For table 10.1 above, I used examination rosters because of their clear linkage to a specific time, whereas genealogical records for the early period do not clearly indicate when an individual lived.[28]  Still, one of the most notable indicators of change is found in genealogies wherein one can easily observe numerous adoptions in later generations, but few adoptions in the earlier generations.  And when we look at the earliest editions of

[27]The most comprehensive study on the subject is *The Confucian Transformation of Korea*, by Martina Deuchler, which covers marriage and ancestor worship and many other aspects of the transformation.  See also Mutsuhiko Shima, "In Quest of Social Recognition" which covers the formation of the lineage.

[28]*Chokpo* do not start to give birth and death dates in a consistent fashion until the late seventeenth century.  Thereafter, they tend to give that data in the majority, but not in all, entries.

genealogies, indeed, there are few to no adoptions. Society had changed; the value placed on the line (*chong*), the lineage, was weak early on, but grew with the Chosŏn period.

In examining inheritance documents we find that one reason why early Chosŏn families did not adopt is that daughters could inherit property and perform ancestor ceremonies. Although there was an apparent preference for a male heir, a daughter's son could be assigned to carry on ancestor services. Yi Yulgok's assignment to be responsible for the ancestor ceremonies for his maternal grandparents is a good example.[29]

The *Shillok* reveals that discussions on the changes in the family and the development of the lineage were held at the court and the king played a conscious role in the process as he and his officials argued pros and cons and proposed laws designed to foster the development of a unilineal system, stressing ancestor worship and a patrilineal lineage organization.[30]

The result was a classic patrilineal descent system modeled on Neo-Confucian principles as espoused by Chu Hsi and other Sung dynasty Confucian authorities. But was the ideology alone responsible for the change? And if it was, or to the degree that it was, why did it take place when it did? Which brings us to the question of what caused these changes.

Causes—A Summary of Other Views

In examining the question of why this radical restructuring of the kinship system took place, my own initial views were like those of several others who early on began to look at this topic. The earliest after the Japanese period to write on this topic, Kim Il-mi, concluded that after adoption of the mostly Confucian marriage ceremony, two basic factors acting together account for the change and the timing of the change. The

---

[29]See chapter one, page 27.

[30]Deuchler's work on the specific texts used by the Neo-Confucian advocates is particularly useful. *The Confucian Transformation of Korea*, Chapter 2, "Neo-Confucianism: The Ideological Foundation of Social Legislation in Early Chosŏn." Certain kings also either added to or detracted from the Confucianization process, particularly in the early dynasty. As a general rule, the kings were less committed than were the bureaucrats; even King Sejong (r. 1418-1450), for example, maintained an interest in Buddhism that made the bureaucrats unhappy. Witness how the second royal publication in *han'gŭl*, after the epic poem in praise of the royal ancestors *Yongbi ŏch'ŏn'ga*, was a eulogistic biography of the Buddha. Myŏngjong (r. 1545-1567) kept a palace monk while his mother was alive, and made decisions concerning lineage succession that were less than Confucian. Yŏnsan-gun (r. 1494-1506), who was deposed for reasons of moral deficiency did not contribute to the development of Confucianism, but Chungjong (r. 1506-1544), however, coming to the throne after the ideological dispute accompanying Yŏnsan-gun's dethroning, was the first aggressively ideologically correct king (from the perspective of the Neo-Confucian consensus developed in the later dynasty).

first was the ideological factor expressed in terms of concern for proper ritual; the other can be termed either economic or demographic.[31] Later, Ch'oe Chae-sŏk had similar conclusions. In regard to the changes in property inheritance, the causes he outlined were: (1) to better carry out the ritual for the ancestors particularly as outlined in Chu Hsi's *karye* that led to (ritual) primogeniture; (2) the development of the lineage organization and with it the publication of genealogies and their focus on the ceremonies for the patrilineal ancestors; (3) the fragmentation of land holdings.[32] In regard to the development of the adoption system, he has four factors: (1) the spread of and popularization of the lineage concept of Confucianism; (2) the need to respond to the political turmoil of the time; (3) economic disorder after the *imjin* war necessitated consolidation and concentration of efforts, which meant primogeniture, which called for an eldest son, by adoption, if necessary; (4) preservation of elite privilege and status.[33]

The Taegu team of Kim Yong-man and Yi Su-gŏn have added several interesting dimensions to our understanding of the dynamics of the seventeenth century. Kim's first article (1983) offered the basic conclusions that the changes were caused by (1) intellectual factors, Neo-Confucianism, and (2) economic factors, fragmentation of land-holdings.[34] He argued that the lineage principle (*chongppŏp*) was the axle around which the changes turned. With the seventeenth century, the rotation around the axle was from a cognatic system to a patrilineal one, from partible inheritance to primogeniture, from uxorilocal marriage options to virilocal marriage; changes in the family system, the marriage system, the style of genealogical publication, the style of ceremonial offering, and social status system were all interrelated.[35]

---

[31]Kim Il-mi, "Chosŏn chŏn'gi ŭi namyŏ kyunbun sangsokche e taehayŏ [Concerning equal inheritance between men and women in early Chosŏn], concluded that there were changes in the mid-Chosŏn period that began to emerge first in the changes of the marriage customs that were debated in the Myŏngjong period and then modified in the Chungjong period. And that the changes in inheritance practices were linked to Confucian ideology together with the economic changes brought on by the changes in marriage and residence patterns. p. 65-66.

[32]Ch'oe Chae-sŏk, *Han'guk kajok chedosa yŏn'gu* [Research on the Korean Family System], p. 552f.

[33]*Ibid.*, p. 669.

[34]Kim Yong-man. "Chosŏn shidae kyunbun sangsokche-e kwanhan il yŏn'gu," [A study on the equal inheritance system of the Chosŏn period],p. 3, 25-37.

[35]*Ibid.*, p. 38f.

With Kim's second article (1985), more complicated issues were perceived.[36] Late seventeenth century changes in addition to primogeniture, virilocal marriage, and emergence of the patrilineage, he now included the increases in the practice of agnatic adoption, prohibitions against *oeson pongsa*, emergence of the single-surname village.

One key factor at the heart of the changes were the status considerations that emerged with the escaped slaves phenomena in the period after the wars when the government was weakened and unable to prevent slaves from running off. And in the field of economics he makes the remarkable claim that with the change to primogeniture, surplus capital was used for ancestor ceremonies and entertaining guests rather than for improvements in means of production, thus creating stagnation in economic and social conditions. Another economic side-effect was that the wealthy took advantage of small landholders in times of bad harvests and famine, (those who could not afford to pay their taxes) buying their land at depressed prices, in effect confiscating their land and creating rural day laborers and an urban work force, fracturing the farming class and leading to their impoverishment.

Kim's colleague, Yi Su-gŏn, added several more interesting conclusions and analyses of causal factors, including several in the political sphere.[37] He argues that partible inheritance was useful for early Yi kings, but primogeniture was useful for later Yi kings.[38] One factor leading to the seventeenth century changes was the mid-sixteenth century monarch's confidence in the throne (himself) and in the concepts of Neo-Confucianism. When Chungjong (r. 1506-1544) ascended the throne, replacing the first king deposed for reasons of immorality, he did so with more internal commitment to Neo-Confucianism than any king before him. Not only did Chungjong rate highest on the true believer scale, his court, filled with the faction that mustered the righteous zeal requisite to depose a ruling king was even more committed to Confucianism. Whereas earlier kings preferred partible inheritance because that would eventually lead to the fracturing of the power base of potential rivals to the throne from among the aristocracy, beginning in Chungjong's reign, they allowed the aristocracy to began to re-

[36]Kim Yong-man. "Chosŏn shidae chaeji sajok ŭi chaesan soyu hyŏngt'ae (I)," [The forms of property ownership of the landed aristocracy of the Chosŏn period].

[37]Yi Su-gŏn, "Chosŏnjŏn'gi ŭi sahoebyŏndong kwa sangsokchedo" [Social change and inheritance in the early Chosŏn period], in *Yŏksa hakpo* 129:23-76 (1991) or in *Han'guk ch'injok chedo yŏn'gu* [Studies on the Korean family system] (Seoul: Ilchogak, 1992).

[38]*Ibid.*, p. 76.

apportion property holdings in favor of the eldest son and in other ways assist the formation of patrilineages along the Chu Hsi model.[39] Later, under the Westerner faction's leadership, with the second deposition of a reigning monarch, Kwanghaegun (r. 1608-1623), and Injo's (r. 1623-1649) ascension, coupled with pro-Chinese, Ming loyalist initiatives, society was moving toward a strict interpretation of Confucian dogma with the dyads of king-subject, father-son, husband-wife, senior-junior upheld as cardinal values with the superior side of each set getting its due emphasis. And by extension, the legitimate versus *sŏja*, the slave owner versus slave, were also placed on even higher pedestals. The Westerner faction was austere in its adherence to orthodoxy and they retained power to the end of the dynasty.[40]

Yi makes a point that needs more attention from the Korean Studies community. Korea's long dynasties, five-hundred years for both Koryŏ and Chosŏn, is a feat unparalleled in world history, yet it is seldom held up for praise or analysis. Yi states that the remarkable longevity of the Chosŏn dynasty was a benefit of the internal changes of the inheritance and succession practices of the dynasty.[41]

Causes—A Mix of Factors

With several factors contributing to the transformation we have seen, which were essential in bringing about the changes and which were only contributing? Martina Deuchler's comprehensive study of the later Koryŏ-early Chosŏn period draws conclusions that are mostly centered on ideology alone. While it is true that ideology is a powerful social force, certain questions persist.[42] What of other social forces that were operating in the early Chosŏn period? She states that in the first century of the dynasty, the "ideological switches had been irreversibly thrown."[43] And in the second century of the dynasty, (1) internalization and application of lineage ideology developed momentum, (2) restrictive societal strategies were well-founded in the political realm, (3) these strategies gained added urgency by changing economic and demographic realities, (4) and that by the second

---

[39]*Ibid.,* p. 106 & 109.

[40]*Ibid.,* p. 111.

[41]Yi Su-gŏn, 1992, p. 64.

[42]Deucher's examination is thorough and convincing of the part the ideology played, particularly the ritual. But her consideration of other factors leaves some questions. She mentions economics in the development of commercial activities in the late seventeenth and eighteenth century (p. 298).

[43]*Ibid.,* p. 287.

century Korean aristocratic descent groups attained their full patrilineal structure.[44] My study comes to conclusions different from Deuchler's in these aspects of timing. I agree that each of these four points was achieved, but it was not until a century laterthat the process was completed. It is clear from the documents I studied that the achievement of the "full patrilineal structure" did not occur until the late third century, and in some aspects we do not see the "full" transition until the fourth century of the dynasty.

Another area of difference between my work and Deuchler's is in the interpretation of the causal factors, aside from the ideological, that contributed to the changes. What of the social forces of economics, demographics, politics and war? Below, we will briefly examine each of these.

Ideological Factors

Reading the documents themselves, one is impressed with the statements of concern for proper ritual. They wrote of high and lofty ideals, it cannot be denied, but there were undoubtedly financial motivations in all of these motivations as well. When the documents speak of giving more property to the eldest son, it is so that he can carry out the ancestor ceremonies. When there was a dispute about which son should inherit the eldest son's portion or which son should be adopted, the argument was over who was more suitable to perform the ceremonies. The argument was couched in terms of transcendental Neo-Confucian values, not in economic terms. Each party argued that it was his unsolicited duty or the obligation that he owed the ancestors, yet the ideological prerogative was intertwined with economic benefits. Property was essential for carrying out proper ritual obligations.

Confucianism entered Korea in its earliest form in the Three Kingdoms Period (third to seventh centuries A.D.) but reentered as the revitalized Sung dynasty philosophy called Neo-Confucianism in the late Koryŏ period (fourteenth century). Neo-Confucianism itself does not explain why the kinship system changed from one that sponsored equilateral inheritance within a cognatic kinship system to one of primogeniture (or near-primogeniture) within a unilineal, patrilineal lineage system. Confucianism in China, even after the Neo-Confucian revolution, using the same ritual texts used in Korea, taught the importance of the eldest son officiating at the ancestor ceremonies, yet property was divided equally among the sons (daughters were excluded). One must be careful not to make the common

---

[44]*Ibid.*

assumption that Confucian influence was always synonymous with Chinese influence.

Although authors of the documents written during the transitional period cited Confucian orthodoxy as the basis for the change, the question arises as to why the changes took place at that particular time. The philosophy was available centuries earlier. In a general sense it can be argued that it just took time. Neo-Confucianism entered Korea in the late fourteenth century, was adopted by the founders of the Yi dynasty as the basis for statecraft in the late fourteenth century, was adopted by the founders of the Chosŏn dynasty as the basis for statecraft in the fifteenth century, reached a high point of sophistication with the best Korean philosophers making commentaries and complex exegeses in the sixteenth century, and finally permeated to the level of the lineage and family in the seventeenth century.[45] One can argue that the changes in Korean society were simply a result of this straight line Confucian development, but what of other social forces and their impact on social developments, either to speed it along or impede it?

## The Changes in the Institution of Marriage

We see the influence of the newly adopted ideology in one of the first laws proclaimed in the dynasty—the marriage reform law of 1413. The law restricted men to one wife, but there were other aspects of marriage that were under review and revision. One such issue was where the wedding ceremony should take place. Koreans had been marrying at the bride's home whereas the ritual texts said the marriage should take place at the groom's home. The *Shillok* delineated the argument; to marry at the groom's home was the Chinese-style wedding, but to marry at the bride's home was *kuksok*, the "national practice." Nothing could be more contradictory. The conflict provided classic alternatives—one either chose the bride's home or the

---

[45]One can go on to include the eighteenth century as the point of high perfection of the Confucian social order, the nineteenth century as the beginning of the deterioration, and the twentieth century as the time of decline and cooptation with Western philosophies. For a moving account of the life of King Yŏngjo (r. 1724-1776) as one who felt the weight of the first three hundred years of the dynasty and who sought perfection in the Confucian order of the eighteenth century, see JaHyun Kim Haboush, *A Heritage of Kings*. (New York: Columbia University Press, 1988). For a view of the deterioration of the Confucian order in the nineteenth century, see Martina Deuchler, *Confucian Gentlemen and Barbarian Envoys* (Seattle: University of Washington Press, 1977) and Vipan Chandra, *Imperialism, Resistance, and Reform in Late Nineteenth-Century Korea: Enlightenment and the Independence Club*, (Berkeley: Institute of East Asian Studies, U.C. Berkeley, 1988). For perspectives on the way Confucianism functions in the twentieth century, see Roger and Dawnhee Janelli, *Ancestor Worship and Korean Society* (Palo Alto: Stanford University Press, 1982) and Vincent Brandt, *A Korean Village: Between Farm and Sea* (Cambridge: Harvard University Press, 1971).

groom's home; or one did as the early Chosŏn Koreans did, that is, chose a third alternative, a compromise. Part of the ceremony was performed at the bride's home and then the couple proceeded to the groom's.[46] The two phases of the ceremony are preserved in the language today although the marriage takes place at a neutral site. A man says he marries by saying he "goes to the wife's father's house," (*changga kanda*), and the bride says she "goes to the groom's father's house," (*shijip kanda*).

The location of the wedding was only part of the question; the greater question was the location of the residence for the new household. In Koryŏ times, most but not all marriages appear to have been at the bride's home, what is called matrilocal or uxorilocal marriage or residence. And although the wedding ceremony tried to adapt to the new Confucian order in the beginning of the Chosŏn period, there are numerous examples well into the sixteenth century, and some cases in the seventeenth century of uxorilocal residence. One does not see evidence for changing residence with each marriage in each subsequent generation. That fact, coupled with our knowledge of an equilateral inheritance system in the earlier period, leads one to the conclusion that the earlier marriage residence pattern was not uniformly uxorilocal, nor was it always patrilocal, but was a mixture. The new couple might live near either the bride's or the groom's parents depending on the availability of housing, proximity to farmland, need to assist aging parents, or other variables including perhaps factors of demography such as one partner in the marriage had no siblings whereas the other had many. The residence pattern was ambilocal, not consistently uxorilocal or patrilocal but containing elements of both. In addition, since traditional marriage alliances were drawn between people within quite a narrow geographic range, one partner was never too far from his or her own natal family.

Once the early Yi Koreans adopted the new marriage system, could the inheritance system and then the ritual system and then the institution of agnatic adoption be far behind? With the bride moving out of the natal home and into that of her husband, her claim on the natal home's resources diminished. As stated in the 1669 declaration of the Puan Kim lineage since the bride mourns for her natal father or mother only one year, she was given only one-third as much property (as one of the brothers who mourn for three years).[47] And the 1688 inheritance document from the Kyŏngsang area said:

---

[46]Martina Deuchler, "The Tradition: Women during the Yi Dynasty," *Virtues in Conflict*, p. 17.

[47]See chapter one, p. 40.

"The daughter will be given a little less since she lives in another county."[48] The reduction in the amount of property given to daughters was justified because of the ceremonies. The second son(s) (*ch'aja*), e.g., those sons other than the eldest, were soon to come under similar pressure. The system of taking turns (*yunhaeng*) in hosting or participating in the ceremonies came to be reevaluated in the light of the ceremonial texts which spoke of the eldest son as the primary officiant. And with daughters eliminated from the ceremonies, those couples who had no sons came to adopt so that a ritual heir could perform the ceremonies for them, particularly if the husband was himself a principal heir (lineage heir or ritual heir) to the lineage or sublineage.

Demographic Factors

The philosophical causes for the transformation seem wholly satisfactory if one does not ask the questions about the timing. Why did the transformation occur when it did? A look at the demographic conditions of the period will help to explain why these changes took place when they did.

In examining the demographic dimension, there have been several cleverly conceived articles that use sophisticated techniques to attempt an estimate of population dynamics of the Chosŏn period. Kwŏn T'ae-wŏn and Shin Yong-ha in 1977 and Tony Michell in 1979 made similar estimates of the entire Chosŏn period.[49] Their study was following in 1987 by a two part study by Yi Yŏng-gu and Yi Ho-ch'ŏl who show many of the same peaks and valleys in population over the course of the latter half of the dynasty, but who argue with the earlier studies on the size of Korea's population at the onset of the Chosŏn period.[50] All the researchers have indicated there was a gradual growth in population during the first two centuries, such that the total population likely doubled (from roughly over four million to nine million or from seven million to twelve), followed by a drop due to the Imjin invasions and the other warfare at the end of the

---

[48]See chapter one, p. 55-56.

[49]Kwŏn T'ae-wŏn and Shin Yong-ha, "Chosŏn wangjoshidae in'gu ch'ujŏng e kwanhan shiron" [Theories concerning estimates of population during the Chosŏn dynasty]. Seoul tae tonga munhwa v.14, 1977 and Tony Michell, "Fact and Hypothesis in Yi Dynasty Economic History: The Demographic Dimension," *Korean Studies Forum*, No. 6, Winter-Spring 1979-80, pp. 65-93.

[50]Yi Yŏng-gu and Yi Ho-ch'ŏl, "Chosŏn shidae e in'gu kyumo chipkye" [Collected estimates of the scale of population during the Chosŏn period], part 1 and part 2. Kyŏngyŏng sahak 2, 1987, and 3, 1988.

sixteenth and the beginning of the seventeenth centuries.[51] Within fifty or sixty years, the population had recovered to the point where it was before the wars. To this extent population growth increased dramatically in the late seventeenth century.[52] In the early Chosŏn dynasty, we see that growing population pressures were aleviated by settling in the northern frontiers. Both large landholders who wanted increase their holdings, and peasants who wanted to obtain a small piece of land to call their own found opportunities in opening new land. But after the late sixteenth century, and again after the late seventeenth recovery from the wars, a scarcity of land became the actual situation again.[53] After the first part of the dynasty, the continual increase in population put pressure on the environment. Actively claiming unused land for cultivation in the sixteenth century was a response to the pressures on the environment by population increase.[54] In this situation with pressures on the land, the crisis of the war served as the catalyst for the change in the inheritance system. In the later seventeenth century the pressures from population growth and other pressures on the environment combined to accelerate the changes that were already afoot.

Economic Factors

Population pressures also have impact on economic conditions. Was it coincidental that the changes in economic activity took place in the same time frame as the changes in the family and lineage? Here, rather than cite other secondary sources (and it is beyond the scope of this work to exam the primary sources) that argue there was an economic upturn in the seventeenth century, (many of those works are controversial and try to push back the horizons of "capitalist" market development to its earliest point) I will simply cite the dates of noteworthy innovations in technology or

---

[51]Estimates vary from two to four million dead. See also Han, Yŏng-u. "Chosŏn ch'ogi hogu ch'ongsu e taehayŏ" (Concerning the total number of households in the early Chosŏn period). Seoul taehakkyo in'gu mit palchŏn munje yŏn'guso (Seoul University population and development research center), 1977.

[52]*Ibid.*

[53]The Puan Kim documents provide a concrete example. The land held by the Yu lineage had been held for about six generations without being cultivated; it was only in 1621 that they began to farm the land. See page 44, footnote 37.

[54]Yi T'ae-jin, "Shimyuk segi Han'guksa ŭi ihaebanghyang" [Toward an understanding of sixteenth century Korean history], in *Han'guk sahoesa yŏn'gu* [Studies in Korean social history]," pp. 291-301.

government reforms to argue that there were many things happening in the seventeenth century. First, in the agricultural economy, transplantation of rice seedlings was developed in the seventeenth century. This innovation lead to double cropping and a tremendous increase in productivity. Such an increase in activity required a dependable system of irrigation, thus, the government instituted an new office, The Office of Embankment Works, in 1662, to oversee the management of reservoirs and irrigation canals. Maurice Freedman argues from his work on lineage formation in China, that intensive rice agriculture acts to create lineage organization[55] and that elaborate irrigation works, large-scale lineages, and high pro-portions of 'indivisible' estates all go together.[56] His examples from China are useful in examing the agricultural developments in Korea after the seventeenth century.

Second, the lineage ideal with its foundation in Neo-Confucianism was provided for by the establishment of the single-surname village and the great expansion in the numbers of private academies in the late seventeenth century. The wars acted a catalyst, and the institutions of inheritance and adoption began to change. We can suppose that with the development of primogeniture, there was tension surrounding the disinherited younger sons. But such economic inequality was believed to be compensated by allocating cultivation rights to the younger sons.[57] It is not unreasonable to suppose that the dramatic increase in escaped slaves was a by-product of the redistribution of cultivation rights to the poorer members of the lineage group, those who were excluded from ownership in the rising tide of primogeniture. Perhaps the formation of the sublineage (*munjung*) groups served the purpose of controlling the expressions of discontent that were likely to come from the disinherited members of the sublineage. The fact that the highest number of inheritance documents dates from this period indicates the severe tension surrounding the division of property. The potential for conflict should have been high, but the reason such conflict was limited is probably due to the development of the sublineage (*munjung*) system.

---

[55]*Chinese Lineage and Society: Fukien and Kwangtung*, p. 159.

[56]*Ibid.*, p.161.

[57]Chŏng Sŭng-mo, in "Tonghon'gwŏn kwa chiyŏk sahoe pon'gye yon'gu" [Study of Marriage Patterns and Rural Society], points out that the relationship between the landlord and the cultivators existed between the lineage members within the single-surname, lineage village. This relationship I believe can be interpreted as the product of compensation for loss of economic options for the younger brothers. Just how this worked has not yet been studied and awaits careful attention by future researchers.

Disadvantages of Partible Inheritance

The greatest impact of the economy on the inheritance system was simply the fact that great numbers of people on a finite unit of land led to smaller and smaller portions of land for each person—fragmentation of land holdings. If a family had a large estate in the early Chosŏn dynasty, the heirs could divide and expand, but after the mid Chosŏn point, they could only divide. As an analogy, if a couple had 1,000 units of land in a large estate and had ten children, five sons and five daughters, giving each one-tenth would destroy the estate, at least as a large concentrated entity of economic power. If, however, the father could send off the daughters to be taken care of by their husbands, give his eldest son 800 units of land and each of the other four sons 50 each, then he would have enabled his estate to last through time. Herein is the advantage of primogeniture over partible inheritance when resources are limited.

Both systems have advantages. In the earlier system membership in the lineage was based on cognatic kinship principles and presumably membership shifted in accordance with needs and activities. Resources did not impose limits on the system because resources were relatively abundant. In the later system, membership was fixed; a man was a member by birthright. By restricting the number of members a lineage group could better preserve its finite resources.

Political Factors

There is little question that Yi Sŏng-gye perceived the advantage of using the imported philosophy, Neo-Confucianism, to help him secure his nascent dynasty and he openly relied on the adherents of the new ideology. Although he relied on their advice as a means of retaining power for himself and his supporters and eliminating the power base of the remnant Koryŏ elite and the Buddhist monasteries, he unavoidably set the country on a course whereby it accepted not only the governmental aspects of the adopted philosophy but the other aspects as well. Charged with the responsibility of setting up a new dynasty, the official elite took the philosophical basis of their actions very seriously. Challenges to their legitimacy from China,[58] and undoubtedly from internal sources as well, caused the ruling elite of the

---

[58]Don Clark, "Chosŏn's Founding Fathers: A Study of Merit Subjects in the Early Yi Dynasty," *Korean Studies* 6:17-40 (1982); and John Duncan, "The Social Background to the Founding of the Chosŏn Dynasty: Change or Continuity?," *Journal of Korean Studies* 6:39-79 (1988-1989).

new dynasty to emphasize the orthodoxy that they claimed supported their rise to power.

Confucianism, perhaps more than any other philosophy or religion of traditional times, is tied to politics. A change in ritual or social behavior, based on ideology, can have consequences in the political sphere. Take the Neo-Confucian-inspired laws on marriage at the beginning of the dynasty. The laws were ideologically inspired, yet they had immediate political ramifications. Anyone violating the law paid dearly in the political arena. For example, the marriage law of 1413 stated that children of marriages in violation the law would not be able to take the government exams nor serve in governmental office.

An interesting aspect of the political ramifications of the transformation from partible inheritance to primogeniture is touched on by Prof. Yi Su-gŏn who has argued that the former helped the early dynasty kings, and the later, helped that late dynasty kings, as mentioned above.[59] Indeed, I agree that the transformation acted to support the monarchy on the one hand, and keep a balance between the monarchy and the bureaucracy/aristocracy on the other hand. If partible inheritance had continued throughout the dynasty, the weakening of the aristocracy could have lead to unchecked despotism on the part of the kings in the latter Chosŏn which could in turn have led to revolution and the demise of the ruling house. If, on the other hand, primogeniture could have taken hold earlier in the dynasty, the already powerful bureaucracy could well have produced a rival to the royal house, and in the turmoil of the times, either from external pressures or internal, cause an early end of the Yi house. Certainly the growth of the powerful lineages that came to dominate politics in the eighteenth century, and virtually take control of the court in the nineteenth century is evidence that had those lineages had an extra century or two to develop their power base, unfettered by the division of their holdings, they would have rivaled the court earlier than they did. The longevity of the Chosŏn dynasty, one of the longest found anywhere, is in part due to the changes within the dynasty over its 500 year history. The dynasty deserves more credit for both its flexibility as well as its longevity.

In the political arena, there is another area that needs comment. One of the dominant political themes of the middle and late Chosŏn period was factional strife (*tangjaeng*). The date for the split between the Easterners and the Westerners, the traditional starting date of the factional infighting, is 1575. It served the interests of various members of the elite who saw their

---

[59]See footnotes #37 through #41, above.

chances of success as linked to a factional affiliation to consolidate their wealth in the hands of those who could compete in the chase to obtain the highly coveted government appointment. The emergence of factionalism would serve to push society toward concentration of efforts (primogeniture), both for practical reasons as well as for purity of ideology (to be in line with the Confucian classics for the sake of solidifying one's position *viz-a-viz* ideological and political rivals), more than it would push society toward the lesser position of Korean practice (*kuksok*) and equilateral inheritance.

## Impact of the Wars

Finally, there is the issue of the Japanese invasion of 1592 (*imjin*) and the Manchu invasions of the early seventeenth century. Whereas there were already social forces in motion that propelled Korean toward the transformation herein documented, since the effect of the wars were catastrophic they should not be ignored. Anthropology tells us that one of the factors that causes an inheritance system to change is, indeed, war.[60] The argument is that loss of men in war causes change.

But the loss of life alone does not explain the complicated changes we have seen in Korea. The loss of life, estimated at about two million people, together with loss of productivity of the land during and after the wars created havoc for Korea. Tony Michell estimates, however, that the population levels quickly recovered in fifty or sixty years, only to level off in growth rates showing that the population had reached an optimum level given the technology and ecology of the day.[61] After the war, population continued to rise only a few more decades until it reached the point of stagnation, with peaks and valleys featuring the presence of famine at times, showing that population had grown to the edge of the technological limits of the ecology. Improvements in agriculture enabled increases in population but the setbacks in harvests resulted in drops in population.

The wars may have had their greatest impact on the inheritance system in an indirect way, that is, via the ideological system. Each victim in war is a hero. And heroes, particularly if they are members of one's family or lineage, must be remembered and honored. The first adoptions in many lineage genealogy (*chokpo*) were for those young men who lost their lives in the war before they sired a son.

Another aspect of the wars may have affected the already declining status of women. It would be difficult to determine how many women were

---

[60]Jack Goody, "Strategies of Heirship," p. 15.
[61]Michell, p. 77-78.

raped, and then to determine how many of them survived, but the *Shillok* recorded a few cases of men expelling wives from their households because they had once been captured by the invading armies. On balance, however, it is hard to believe that such cases were much of a factor in the disinheritance of daughters on a national scale in the following century, but the already declining status of women was not helped by the war.

Michell makes the point that societies that practice partible inheritance are much more vulnerable to crises of population and resources than are those which practice primogeniture.[62] Certainly those of the elite strata of society who held sizable property and who experienced the war were witnesses to this fact; and it gave them ready reason to advocate the way of the ancient sages. We can see evidence for this in the way the elite moved their households after the seventeenth century. In the early Chosŏn period, *yangban* would easily move to distant places; one of the interesting demarkations of the mid-Choson period is that when they would move at all it was to nearby counties.[63] Fujiya Kawashima concludes that the reason the pattern of relocation changed for elite class was a motivation to retain their status and preserve their privileges.[64] One affect of the war was for the elite to stay closer connected in their relationships and residential patterns. This manner of village organization was conducive to patrilineal kinship organization.

## The Cause and Effect

Which of all these various factors that were operating during the late sixteenth and seventeenth centuries were major factors, and which were minor? It is my view, that in the end Martina Deuchler's emphasis on the ideological and ritual, even though she does not treat other factors that were also is operation, is ultimately the most important. Although more factors were operating than the ideological, still, when the society changed, it did so along the lines of orthodox Neo-Confucianism. The analogy that works best to describe how these various forces worked to bring on the transformation of the kinship system, is to picture all the various forces pushing society through a funnel, much like a baker squeezes frosting through a tube as he decorates a cake. The shape of the funnel determines the form that appears on the cake. The shape of the funnel in Korea during

---

[62]Michell, p. 85.

[63]Fujiya Kawashima, "Bunka Ryu-shi ni mirareru ssizoku no idō to sono seikaku" (The characteristics of relocation patterns of lineage groups as seen in the Munhwa Yu lineage), pp. 61-63.

[64]*Ibid.*, p. 63.

the mid Chosŏn period was the shape of orthodox Neo-Confucianism. The forces that were squeezing the tube included the demographic, economic, political, and the forces of war; each may have had differing strengths, but each provide some force. And one of the most powerful of the forces was also that which gave it its shape — ideology. It was both a force and a formative agent; whereas the other forces did not have formative powers. Ideology, whether it is religion or some belief about capitalism, monarchy, or democracy, has the power to shape society and social action. And at the same time it is a driving force behind the change. Much of the reformulating of the social order was not complete until the late seventeenth century and even the early eighteenth century, still Deuchler's position is valid. Regardless of the causative factors and their relative strengths, in the end, all the forces were pushed through an opening that we call orthodox, Chu Hsi-style, Neo-Confucianism. Indeed, what we have seen was the Confucianization of Korea.

Periodization
    An historical point; one contribution of this work is in the area of periodization. Most authors write of early Chosŏn and late Chosŏn periods. Not only does one see that there was clearly an early Chosŏn system of lineage and family organization that was different from the late Chosŏn system, but we can justifiably argue for the recognition of an important transitional period in the mid Chosŏn dynasty. If it is true for the lineage system, adoption, women's status, and the system of inheritance including whatever economic or demographic phenomena came with it, then it is probably true of other aspects of society. This then is a call for a tripartite periodization of the Chosŏn dynasty. The first period, the early Chosŏn, covers the founding until the Imjin invasions (1392-1592). The second, the mid Chosŏn, covers the transitional period (1592-1700 [or 1720, the end of the Sukchong reign]). And the third, the late Chosŏn, covers the final two centuries of the dynasty (1700-1910) [or perhaps from the Yŏngjo period, 1724 to 1910].

The Family of the Future
    Recognition and understanding of the changes in the middle of the Chosŏn period would provide greater intellectual resources, on the one hand, and open options for application, on the other hand, for modern Koreans that face new dilemmas in a modern age. For example, in a day of intense population growth and policies for control of growth, families have fewer children. If all the children in a particular family are daughters, one need not look for agnatic adoptions or other means of finding an heir. The daughter,

as in the times before the mid Chosŏn period, can be the heir, perform the ceremonies, and in all ways satisfy the requisites of succession. The surname would not continue, but as with the case of Shin Saimdang's family, it would not necessarily be considered as a loss. As Shin Myŏnghwa must have been proud of his grandson, Yi Yulgok, modern Koreans need not place inordinate weight on having a grandchild of the same surname and in the process downgrade the daughter's children. A grandchild by a daughter should be recognized as fully as the grandchild by a son. It would be helpful, for example, to avoid the use of the term *oesonja* (literally the "outsider" grandchild); just *sonja* (grandchild) is sufficient. A grandchild is a grandchild.

The earliest extant printed genealogy, the 1476 *Andong Kwŏn-ssi sebo*, provides a worthy role model. Therein are listed the posterity by either son or daughter of the founder of the Kwŏn lineage. About 300 have the surname Kwŏn, and are thus "direct descendants" (*ch'inson*), but over 9000 have other surnames and are thus "outsider descendants" (*oeson*). In a new age, as Korea questions its traditional family and kinship system, it would do well to begin by extending full recognition to the daughter and her posterity. Modern science also argues for a return to equality of treatment; genetically, the daughter conveys as many genes and chromosomes as does the son. But in Korea and much of Asia since the late 1980's, modern science has provided the means of determining gender of infants before they are born. Armed with that knowledge, there is a growing number of mothers who terminate their pregnancies if they are carrying a female fetus. This is already recognized as a social problem, but it will become an even greater problem when the victims of the imbalance of gender, now so apparent in the grade school, reach marriagable age. There are many reasons that a society should not practice selective abortion of female fetuses, but as Korean society searches for alternatives, as Koreans search for a way to restructure the family and kinship system, they can find the best models, not in western societies, but within their own history.

# Definitions

Terms used in this study require careful definition. The difficulty is twofold: there is an inherent ambiguity in the use of many terms because as terms commonly used to describe family and kinship they have a popular and general meaning that is often different from, or too broad for, precise, scholarly application. For example, the term family in general usage can mean the nuclear family on the one hand, or as in the case of "the Rockefeller family" or "Kennedy family" meaning a multi-generational, extended family, something more akin to a clan, although that term is ambiguous at best. The second difficulty derives from the situation in Korea wherein there was one system in the late Koryŏ/early Chosŏn period, a system in transition in the mid Chosŏn period, and another for the late Chosŏn period. For example, the term "heir" in the early system, since it was a system marked by partable inheritance, meant one of many who inherited property or status; the term in the later system tended to mean one person, male, who inherited the majority of the property and the sole rights to perform ritual. Similarly, most of the terms below, to be understood correctly, must be viewed in the historic context in which the term appears.

adoption: The taking of a child or adult, usually male, but at times female, to be one's own child, for purposes of fostering and/or heirship (succession to a patriline and/or responsiblity for ancestor worship). In the early Chosŏn period, when the concept of the patrilineage was not yet developed, an adopted child was not adopted for the sake of carrying on a line, but rather for carrying on ceremonies for the parents only. Then the function of the agnatic adoptee (*kyehuja*) was not significantly different from that of the non-agnatic adoptee (*suyangja* or *shiyangja*). In the later Chosŏn period, under the system of patrilineal organization, the adopted child was an agnate of the proper generation who inherited the majority of the property and held responsibility for ancestral ceremonies for a long line of ancestors. In the later period, the Korean term for the adopted son was *kyehuja;* the process was known as *iphu.* After the seventeenth century, non-

215

agnatic adoptees (*suyangja* and *shiyangja*) were more properly cases of fostering rather than adopting.

adrogation: A phenomenon found in ancient Rome where a father adopts a mature son, often with children, into the new home. In most cases Korean classic agnatic adoption, after the seventeenth century, is adrogation, the adoption of an adult male, often with an heir already in place.

agnate: A man related to a man through a man; at the time of the patrilineal lineage organization, a member of the patrilineage. Prior to the formation of a patrilineage, an agnate was a relative on the father's side in distinction from two other groups, one's affines (*ch'ŏga*) and one's matri-filial relatives (*oega*). In Korean, there is a term for these two non-agnatic groups, *inch'ŏk*.

affine: One's spouses relatives; in the Korean context, (*ch'ŏga*) one's wife's relatives

bilateral kinship system: See cognatic kinship system.

ch'ŏga: The wife's family, one's affines. See *oega*, the mother's family or one's father's affines. See also *inch'ŏk*, collective term for both the *ch'ŏga* and the *oega*.

*chokpo*: The printed genealogy tables. In Korea, they followed what is called the T'ang dynasty format of either five or seven generations on a page. Early genealogies show the cognatic nature of early Chosŏn society; daughters lines were as complete as sons. Later genealogies, showing the impact of Confucianization, emphasized the patriline, carrying only scant data on the wives and daughters.

*chongppŏp*: The lineage principle; the term used by Neo-Confucianists to argue for the patrilineal system.

*chongja*: The lineage heir; the eldest son who inherits the rights to perform ceremonies for a line of ancestors. The concept was unclear at the beginning of the Chosŏn period, but became important after the transition.

*ch'ŏp*: A secondary or lesser wife of an aristocrat; a commoner woman was as a *yangch'ŏp*, and a slave woman, a *ch'ŏnch'ŏp*. Their children were discriminated against (see *sŏja*).

cognatic kinship system: A system of kinship that recons kinship on boththe father's side and the mother's side. Also called a bilateral kinship system. This was the system that prevailed in late Koryŏ and early Chosŏn.

epiklerate: A phenomenon found in ancient Greece where a male heir is selected by adopting one's son-in-law. In the Korean context this is often called matrilocal marriage, or more properly, uxorilocal marriage. Usually the location of the marriage is the location of the residence and son-in-law inherits of property from the wife's parents. Common in Japan (*mukoyōshi*), somewhat looked down upon but easily found in China (*term*), and rare in Korea (*teril sawi*).

foster: To foster a child is similar to adopting in that a child is raised, but is different from adoption in that there is not a transfer of rights such as the right to inherit property or the right to perform ceremonies. Generally, both the *suyangja* and *shiyangja*, after the seventeenth century were fostered not adopted. Technically, the *suyangja* was adopted, whereas the *shiyangja* was fostered, according to the legal definition of their status, but in actually practice, particularly after the seventeenth century, there was little difference between the two.

heir: (A) The sons and daughters, or adopted son or daughter, who divided property and shared rights to perform ceremonies, or (B) the *chongja*, lineage heir, eldest son or adopted son, who succeeds to property, and status (headship of a lineage or lineage segment) and holds the rights to perform the ancestor ritual. The former situation (A) prevailed prior to the seventeenth century, the latter (B), after.

*hŏyŏ mun'gi*: At times a special allocation, at times a general allocation. See *punjaegi*.

*hyŏngmang chegŭp*: "When the older son dies, the younger son is the successor"—the last remnant of lateral inheritance. This term marks the early transitional phase between equilateral inheritance and primogeniture. The practice of *hyŏngmang chegŭp* was mostly found in the late sixteenth through early seventeenth century, and contained elements of both the early ideology and that which was to come, orthodox Neo-Confucianism. It does not describe the situation in late Koryŏ and early Chosŏn, when property as well as rights were passed on equally to each one in the next generation, but rather fits the transitional situation and time frame when property was divided, but the ritual rights were given to the eldest son. In later times, both property and rights were given to the eldest son (primogeniture), in what can be vertical inheritance. Strictly speaking *hyŏngmang chegŭp* refers to the latter stages of "lateral inheritance;" the early stage, that of dividing all property and rights equally, can also be called "lateral inheritance."

*inch'ŏk*: One's relatives by marriage; in the patrilineage system, the wife's family (the affines, *ch'ŏga*) and the mother's family or matrifilial relatives (the *oega*). The opposite of one's agnates.

inheritance: Usually refers to succession to property. In the early Chosŏn period, property was divided equally between male and female offspring; in the later period, the eldest son received the largest share, with other sons receiving smaller shares and with daughters excluded from inheritances, although they may have received gifts and dowries. At times the term inheritance can refer to status, i.e., inheritance of rights to carry out ceremonies (headship of a lineage or lineage segment), and occasionally refers to office (commonly in Koryŏ period) or title (officially recognized in Koryŏ, but only occasionally and unofficially used in Chosŏn).

kindred: A kinship group based on blood relationships not on descent, found in the Koryŏ period and early Chosŏn.

kyehuja: An agnatically adopted son. The early Chosŏn code provided for a kyehuja to be the heir to the lineage although the code contained two provisions for adoption — the kyehuja and the suyangja. The kyehuja represented the Neo-Confucian ideal, the concept of the lineage, that had not yet taken hold in the society of the time. The suyangja, as an adopted heir, represented the pre-Confucianized society's argument in the code that a non-agnatic heir was also acceptable. As time went by, as the concept of the lineage developed, the kyehuja became preferred.

lineage: In Korea is tantamount to the patrilineage or the patrilineal descent group. Recruitment was by birth only, although expulsion from the lineage was possible. The lineage was in its embryonic stage at the outset of the Chosŏn period; the kinship organization of the early Chosŏn and late Koryŏ was not that of a lineage organization, but rather that of cognatic kinship groups that were flexible in structure, would change over time as needs arose, and would at times be organized around agnates, at times around affines and at times matrifilial kinsmen (relatives of one's mother, e.g. the affines of one's father). A lineage is distinquished from a clan by the factor that in a lineage one knows the founding ancestor and specific relationships among members, in a clan, there is an assump-tion of relationship, but a specific relationship, particularly with the founding ancestor, is not known.

oega: One's mother's family and relatives—"matrifilial" relatives, one's father's affines. Related terms included oeharabŏji, maternal grandfather.

patrilineage: See patrilineal descent group.

patrilineal descent group: Men related to men through men. The descent group, lineage, that recognizes descent from an apical ancestor (shijo) including all the male descendants who are members by birthright (K. pugye).

*pongsaja*: In general terms this is one who performs ceremonies. In the early Chosŏn period, several candidates could be the *pongsaja*; when ceremonies could be conducted on a rotational basis, each child would take a turn. In the late Chosŏn period, the *pongsaja* was the eldest son, the ritual heir.

primogeniture: In the Korean context, primogeniture meant inheritance of the majority, but not all, of the property, by the eldest son, who also would succeed to the ritual privileges held by the *chongja*, the lineage heir, the line of eldest son of eldest son.

*punjaegi*: A generic term for several kinds of inheritance documentswhich may include general divisions of property between all siblings made when a parent is still alive (in some cases, *hŏyŏ mun'gi*) or after both parents are deceased (*tongsaeng hwahoe mun'gi*); or special allocations usually to one heir (*pyŏlgŭp mun'gi* or at times called *hŏyŏ mun'gi*).

*pyŏlgŭp mun'gi*: A special allocation of inheritance. See *punjaegi*.

*shiyangja*: The *shiyangja* were over age three and could not change their surname to that of the parents. Both male and female candidates were possible. See also *suyangja*.

*sŏja*: The child of an aristocrat father and a commoner or slave mother who was classified as a *ch'ŏp* (secondary wife or lesser wife). They were discriminated against, by statute, after the founding of the Chosŏn court; they were not usually allowed to take the civil service examination and were limited in the kinds and levels of office they could hold.

succession: Inheritance of non-property, social position, usually the head of a lineage including the rights to perform ceremonies.

*sŭngjungja*: Depending on time frame and context, the term is used in the following ways: 1. One designated to carry on the line to the next generations. (Also called the *changja* or the *chŏkcha*.) 2. The agnatic adoptee (*kyehuja*). 3. A *sŏja* that is offically promoted to legitimate status (also called a *sŭngjŏkcha*). 4. And a grandson designated to perform the ceremonies for a grandfather.

*suyangja*: The *suyangja* was a non-agnatic adoptee under age three that was allowed to change the surname to that of the parents and had all the rights of a son born into the home. In the early Chosŏn period, some *suyangja* were regarded on the same footing as agnatic adoptees, but in the mid and later period, were considered less preferred and the practice is seen more in the lower classes of society. The term carried considerable ambiguity in certain contexts; for example, the terms *suyang kyehu*, and *suyang nobi* are found. The former would be nonsense if translated as non-agnatic, agnatic adoption; but would rather be the fostering of an agnatic adoptee—in the early period, this term was used meaning to make of a descendant who was not the eldest son the ritual heir. The latter is a "fostered slave," implying a foundling that is taken into the household to augment the servants' numbers not the family's.

*tongsaeng hwahoe mun'gi*: A general allocation of inheritance. See *punjaegi*.

uxorilocal marriage: The groom marries into the bride's home. The terms filiacentric union, matrilineal marriage and matrilocal marriage are also found. However, the term matrilineal implies a "line" or lineage, which was not the case in Korea, either before or after the seventeenth century. The term matrilocal refers to the residence pattern, which usually coincides with the location of the ceremony.

virilocal marriage: The bride marries into the groom's home; also called patrilineal marriage, a valid term in the post-transition era, but not accurate for the pre-seventeenth century since lineages had not yet been formed. The term patrilocal marriage refers to the residence pattern, irrespective of where the ceremony is held.

*yangja*: A generic term used to mean both the *kyehuja* (agnatic adoption to be a lineage heir), and the *suyangja* or *shiyangja* (non-agnatic adoptee, or more accurately, a foster child).

*yunhaeng*: The term meaning to take turns in hosting the rituals. Siblings, in rotation, would take turns hosting the ceremonies. The term describes early Chosŏn practice, is seen in documents advising that it be discontinued in the mid Chosŏn period, and is not seen in late Chosŏn.

# Glossary

Herein are Chinese characters for the terms introduced in the text, Korean (both Sino-Korean and pure Korean) and in a few cases of Chinese. Personal names are in the Glossary of Names, but names of lineage groups are included here. Place names can also be located on the map. Certain terms, key to the central themes, are also in the Definitions (page 215).

| | | | |
|---|---|---|---|
| Andong | 安東 | *chokson* | 族孫 |
| Andong Kwŏn-ssi | 安東 權氏 | Chŏlla province | 全羅道 |
| Anbyŏn | 安邊 | *-ch'on* | 寸 |
| An-ssi | 安氏 | *ch'ŏnch'ŏp* | 賤妾 |
| Chaeryŏng Yi-ssi | 載寧 李氏 | *chong* | 宗 |
| *ch'aja* | 次子 | *ch'ongbu* | 冢婦 |
| *changja* | 長子 | Chŏngdo Kim-ssi | 清道 金氏 |
| Changsŏgak | 藏書閣 | *chongga* | 宗家 |
| *chanyŏ* | 子女 | *chongja* | 宗子 |
| *chao-mu* (Ch.) | 昭穆 | *chongjason* | 宗子孫 |
| Cheju Island | 濟州道 | *chongjok* | 宗族 |
| *chesa* | 祭祀 | *chongppŏp* | 宗法 |
| *chewi* | 祭位 | *chongson* | 宗孫 |
| Cheng-te (Ch.) | 正德 （1506-1521） | *chŏnji* | 田地 |
| *ch'i* (Ch.) | 氣 | *chŏnmin* | 田民 |
| *chia* (Ch.) | 家 | *ch'ŏnmin* | 賤民 |
| Chia-ch'ing (Ch.) | 嘉靖 （1522-1566） | *ch'ŏnsogya* | 天屬也 |
| *Chia-li* (Ch.) | 家禮 | *chori* | 召史 |
| *chija* | 支子 | *ch'ŏp* | 妾 |
| *ch'ilgŏ chi ak* | 七去之惡 | *ch'ŏpcha* | 妾子 |
| *chinsa* | 進士 | Chosŏn | 朝鮮 |
| *ch'inson* | 親孫 | *ch'ulga oein* | 出嫁外人 |
| *chi-tzu* (Ch.) | 繼子 | Chung-chen (Ch.) | 崇禎 （1628-1644） |
| *chok* | 族 | *chungja* | 衆子 |
| *chŏkcha* | 嫡子 | Hahoe | 河回 |
| *chokpo* | 族譜 | Hahoe *t'aek* | 河回宅 |

# Glossary of Names

Herein are the Chinese characters for the names of Korean personalities mentioned in the text. Some Chinese names are also listed, using the Wade-Giles romanization system. There is one Japanese name.

| | | | |
|---|---|---|---|
| An Kyŏng-bin | 安敬賓 | Chŏng Kuk-saeng | 鄭菊生 |
| An Wi | 安瑋 | Chŏng Kwal | 鄭佸 |
| Chagŭnjoi | 자근 召史 | Chŏng Kwang-gyŏng | 鄭廣敬 |
| Chang Sŏn-jing | 張善徵 | Chŏng Kwang-jŏk | 鄭光績 |
| Cheng Hsŭn (Ch) | 成憲 | Chŏng Kwang-yang | 鄭光陽 |
| Chin | 陳 | Chŏng Kye-ju | 鄭繼胄 |
| Chinsagun | 進士君 | Chŏng Mun-ju | 鄭文周 |
| Cho Chŏng | 曹烶 | Chŏng Nan-jong | 鄭蘭宗 |
| Cho Chun | 趙浚 | Chŏng Ŏn-ho | 鄭彦浩 |
| Cho Hŏn | 趙憲 | Chŏng Pang-yŏl | 鄭邦悅 |
| Cho Kŭn | 趙瑾 | Chŏng P'il | 鄭泌 |
| Cho Mal-saeng | 趙末生 | Chŏng Se-ho | 鄭世虎 |
| Cho Min | 趙岷 | Chŏng Sŏk-ki | 鄭碩器 |
| Cho Pang-nim | 趙邦霖 | Chŏng Sŏng-myŏng | 鄭錫命 |
| Cho Pok-hae | 趙福海 | Chŏng Su | 鄭洙 |
| Cho Pu-rim | 趙傅霖 | Chŏng Tae-un | 鄭大雲 |
| Cho Sŏng-mun | 曹錫文 | Chŏng Tae-hwa | 鄭太和 |
| Cho Yŏng | 趙渶 | Chŏng To-jŏn | 鄭道傳 |
| Chŏn Ong | 田瀚 | Chŏng Tŏng-myŏng | 鄭德明 |
| Chŏn Sŏl | 田泄 | Chŏng T'ae-hwi | 鄭泰輝 |
| Chŏn Tŏg-yun | 田德胤 | Chŏng Uk | 鄭稶 |
| Chŏng Ch'ang-sŏ | 鄭昌瑞 | Chŏng Yak-yong | 丁若鏞 |
| Chŏng Ch'ang-son | 鄭昌孫 | Chu Hsi (Ch) | 朱熹 |
| Chŏng Hong-su | 鄭弘壽 | Chu-ke Liang (Ch) | 諸葛亮 |
| Chŏng Hyo-sang | 鄭孝常 | Ch'oe Chŏk | 崔適 |
| Chŏng Hyŏng | 鄭泂 | Ch'oe Chu | 崔澍 |
| Chŏng In-ji | 鄭麟趾 | Ch'oe Chun | 崔浚 |
| Chŏng In-gwang | 鄭寅光 | Ch'oe Han-jŏng | 崔漢禎 |

224

| | |
|---|---|
| Kim Hyŏn | 金 鉉 |
| Kim Hyŏn-dŭk | 金賢得 |
| Kim Hyŏng | 金 泂 |
| Kim Ik-su | 金益壽 |
| Kim Il-lyŏng | 金仁齡 |
| Kim Kae | 金 漑 |
| Kim Ki-myŏng | 金起溟 |
| Kim Ko | 金 顧 |
| Kim Kŭn-gong | 金謹恭 |
| Kim Kwang-jun | 金光準 |
| Kim Kwang-ok | 金光沃 |
| Kim Kyŏn-su | 金堅壽 |
| Kim Kyŏng-sang | 金景祥 |
| Kim Kyŏng-su | 金景壽 |
| Kim Kyŏng-su | 金慶壽 |
| Kim Kyŏng-sun | 金景順 |
| Kim Maeng-nyŏm | 金孟廉 |
| Kim Man-gil | 金萬吉 |
| Kim Man-jung | 金萬重 |
| Kim Mun | 金 璊 |
| Kim Myŏng-yŏl | 金命悅 |
| Kim Ok-kyun | 金玉均 |
| Kim Pang-bo | 金邦保 |
| Kim Pang-gil | 金邦佶 |
| Kim Pŏn | 金 璠 |
| Kim Pyŏk | 金 壁 |
| Kim Pyŏn | 金 變 |
| Kim Sang-hyŏn | 金尙賢 |
| Kim Shi-man | 金時萬 |
| Kim Shi-yang | 金時讓 |
| Kim So | 金 紹 |
| Kim Sŏk-ho | 金碩虎 |
| Kim Sŏk-p'il | 金錫弼 |
| Kim Sŏng-il | 金誠一 |
| Kim Su-ch'ang | 金守昌 |
| Kim Su-dong | 金守同 |
| Kim Su-gyŏng | 金守經 |
| Kim Su-hang | 金壽恒 |
| Kim Su-jong | 金守宗 |
| Kim Sŭng-jae | 金升才 |
| Kim Sŭng-sŏ | 金承緒 |
| Kim Tar-hyŏn | 金達賢 |
| Kim Tong-ŏn | 金東彦 |
| Kim Tŭg-i | 金得伊 |
| Kim Tŭng-mun | 金得文 |
| Kim U-jŏng | 金友正 |
| Kim Ŭng-p'yo | 金應豹 |
| Kim Yŏn-ji | 金用悅 |
| Kim Yŏng-su | 金連枝 |
| Kim Yong-yŏl | 金英秀 |
| Kim Yu-yŏl | 金有悅 |
| Ko Chun | 高 峻 |
| Ko T'ae-p'il | 高台弼 |
| Ko Tŭk-chong | 高得宗 |
| Kong Sŏ-rin | 孔瑞麟 |
| Kwŏn Ch'an | 權 纘 |
| Kwŏn Ch'ik | 權 侙 |
| Kwŏn Kam | 權 鋏 |
| Kwŏn Kan | 權 瑊 |
| Kwŏn Sang-gyŏng | 權 旰 |
| Kwŏn To | 權 霂 |
| Kwŏn Yun | 權 來 |
| Kwŏn Hyŏp | 權 澳 |
| Kwŏn Mok | 權尙經 |
| Kwŏn Nae | 權 蹈 |
| Kwŏn O | 權 衍 |
| Kwŏn Yŏn | 權 鈗 |
| Kyŏnyong | 見 龍 |
| Ma Chung-myŏng | 馬重鳴 |
| Ma Ch'ŏn-mok | 馬天牧 |
| Ma Sŏk-ki | 馬碩驥 |
| Ma Yŏ-ho | 馬汝虎 |
| Min Chŏngjung | 閔鼎重 |
| Min Kwang-suk | 閔光潚 |
| Min Sa-ryang | 閔思亮 |
| Min Yŏ-ik | 閔汝翼 |
| Mme An | 安 氏 |
| Mme Cho | 趙 氏 |
| Mme Ch'oe | 鄭 氏 |
| Mme Chŏng | 崔 氏 |
| Mme Ha | 河 氏 |
| Mme Hyŏn | 玄 氏 |

| Yi Kyŏng-yŏng | 李慶榮 | Yŏ Hŭi-nyŏng | 呂希寧 |
| Yi Man-nyŏn | 李萬年 | Yŏ Maeng-on | 呂孟溫 |
| Yi Mi | 李敉 | Yŏ Mun-mang | 呂文望 |
| Yi Mi-su | 李眉壽 | Yŏ Se-on | 呂世溫 |
| Yi Ŏn-gang | 李彦綱 | Yŏ Ŭi-nam | 呂義男 |
| Yi Pang-bŏn | 李芳蕃 | Yu Cha-gwang | 柳子光 |
| Yi Pang-sŏk | 李芳碩 | Yu Hwa | 柳和 |
| Yi Pang-wŏn | 李芳原 | Yu Il-sang | 柳日祥 |
| Yi Pa | 李坡 | Yu Myŏng | 柳溟 |
| Yi Pae | 李培 | Yu Myŏng-jŭng | 兪名曾 |
| Yi Paek-cha | 李伯孜 | Yu On | 柳溫 |
| Yi Pyŏng-ch'u | 李秉樞 | Yu Pi | 柳秠 |
| Yi Saek | 李穡 | Yu Pu | 柳溥 |
| Yi Shi-ch'un | 李時春 | Yu Sa-gi | 柳師琦 |
| Yi Shi-sŏng | 李時省 | Yu Sa-sang | 柳師商 |
| Yi Sŏ-jang | 李恕長 | Yu Sam-ik | 柳三益 |
| Yi Sŏk-su | 李碩壽 | Yu Sŏng-min | 柳成民 |
| Yi Sŏn | 李璵 | Yu Sŏng-yong | 柳成龍 |
| Yi Su-bang | 李秀芳 | Yu Tŭk-kong | 柳得恭 |
| Yi Su-dŭk | 李秀得 | Yun Am | 尹巖 |
| Yi Sun-nam | 李順男 | Yun Chi-nam | 尹芝男 |
| Yi Sung-mun | 李叔文 | Yun Ch'un-nyŏn | 尹春年 |
| Yi Tong-p'yo | 李東標 | Yun Ho | 尹瑚 |
| Yi Tŏng-mu | 李德懋 | Yun I-hong | 尹以弘 |
| Yi T'ae-gi | 李泰基 | Yun Kae | 尹漑 |
| Yi T'ae-nam | 李泰男 | Yun Kŭm-son | 尹金孫 |
| Yi T'ang-nam | 李擢男 | Yun Kyŏng-gyo | 尹敬敎 |
| Yi Yŏn | 李涎 | Yun Sa-ik | 尹思翼 |
| Yi Yŏng-bŏn | 李永蕃 | Yun Shi-shim | 尹時沈 |
| Yi Yu-gi | 李裕基 | Yun Shi-sŏng | 尹時省 |
| Yi Yu-hu | 李裕後 | Yun U | 尹遇 |
| Yŏ Chung-on | 呂仲溫 | Yun Wŏn-hyŏng | 尹元衡 |

# Appendix 1

# The Case of the Wanton Widow

*The following is a translation of an entry from the Yejong* Shillok *on a certain day in 1459. The case is presented without comment; there is no indication of its authorship, nor is there any statement by anyone in the court about the case, nor is it tied to any other issue. The usual situation in the* Shillok *is that each case presented is done so for the sake of arbitration by the king or discussion at court. Officials at court could bring issues before the King; inevitably the official who raised an issue advocated a position, for or against, as he argued the case before the king. This case sits alone. There is no tie to any person or issue at court. It stands on its own for whatever purpose, not the least likely of which was humor. It may have also had a moralistic purpose; an example of how not to behave.*

Mme Yi, the wife of the deceased magistrate of Tanyang, Nam Ŭi, was the granddaughter of Yi Ŭng, whose royal title was Yŏngyanggun. The husband, Nam Ŭi, died after having over ten children. He was not of a handsome countenance and his wife did not serve him well.

When Nam Ŭi died, Mme Yi survived as a widow. The Buddhist monks who sought contributions from her gathered around her gate like a cloud. The servants of the house were heard to say that it seemed that it was not that she like Buddhism, but rather, she liked the monks.

At that time there was a traveler who was residing at the home of an old widow. One day a monk came to visit. The monk whispered something in the ear of the old widow and left. The old woman turned to the traveler and said that a female guest was coming and that he ought to vacate the house for a while. The traveler was suspicious. When it came time to go, he bid farewell and feigned leaving but hid beside the gate to see who was going to visit.

The sun went down. Soon a monk arrived on horseback. He tied the horse, took off his shirt and sat down in a relaxed attitude. He asked the old woman, "Hasn't she come yet?" The old woman replied, "I am sure she will be here soon."

They lit the lanterns and set out some wine and waited. The first drum of evening sounded (there were five drums from sundown to sunrise). A woman wearing a red hood followed by a female servant entered the house. The three of them, the woman, the monk, and the old woman sat and cheerfully drank the wine. After a moment the old woman left, leaving the two of them sitting side-by-side. They were talking intimately. Then the traveler jumped out and shouted, "What kind of woman are you? What kind of monk are you? It appears to me that you are not a respectable woman. Why have you come here? I am going to take you to the police." The old woman reappeared and she and the monk nearly overcome by surprise begged the traveler not to go to the police. The traveler did not listen but acted as though he was going to drag the woman to the police.

Then the woman whispered to her servant to go home and bring several tens of bolts of silk. The old woman grabbed the traveler's jacket and implored him to stay his hand, offering him bolts of cloth and even the horse that the monk rode.

The traveler said, "This is not a small affair! It cannot go unreported. But since you have so implored, I cannot but stay my hand."

The monk and the woman fled. The traveler loaded the bolts of silk onto the horse and left.

Everyone wondered if the woman was Mme Yi.

Several years passed. Mme Yi wanted to remarry but could not say so directly. She went to her mother and said, "My slaves do not obey me. Is there some way of handling them?" Her mother knew what she meant, and said, "You must select your own husband! [don't expect me to do it for you]." Mme Yi sent her husband's spirit tablet to the home of her husband's older brother, Nam Yun.

She found a matchmaker through whom she heard about a military officer name Yu Kyun who was alleged to be well-equipped, both large and strong. She decided that he was the one for her.

She asked her own kinsman, Yi Chung-sŏk, for assistance and sent liquor and food to his house so that he could host an archery contest whereby she could meet the prospective husband. He invited several guests but could not identify which was Yu Kyun. He asked a female servant who the tall, well-built man over yonder was; she replied that it was Lieutenant Yu.

Mme Yi was delighted. She had made up her mind. Thereafter, every day she would look in the mirror and put on make-up. As it happened, one day while she was putting on her make-up, her husband's former wet nurse came by to visit. Mme Yi hurriedly discarded her mirror and before the wet nurse could say anything, Mme Yi said, "Don't try to dissuade me. I must marry again."

One day some of the servants lined up in the yard and asked Mme Yi, "Is it because you do not have sufficient property? Is it because you don't have enough servants? Why is it you have this plan to remarry?" One servant even began to cry. Mme Yi closed her door without responding.

After she married Yu Kyun, the slaves of Nam Ŭi had to go to other places (being inherited by relatives of Nam Ŭi). They were seen weeping as they walked down the road, but Mme Yi showed no remorse. Rather, she screamed at those lagging behind, "Why don't you go quickly; why stay here crying?"

Mme Yi loved Yu Kyun. She would always tell her friends, "My husband is a real man."

One time Yu Kyun became promoted. Some of his friends who liked to make fun, drew a picture of their wedding scene on the wall of the county magistracy and made fun of it. But Yu Kyun was not embarrassed by it.

Several years later, Yu Kyun died. Mme Yi once again intended to remarry. Several years earlier she had gone to a blind fortune teller who foresaw her entire life. He had said, "You will marry three times. You will live with the last one for one hundred years." At Yu Kyun's funeral she faced the corpse and said, "It is amazing that the blind fortune teller knew this would happen. You have died, too. Will I live with the last one for one hundred years?"

On the day of the burial, she put out liquor for guests and did not show an ounce of remorse. Later she called in the Buddhist monks to perform rituals for Yu Kyun. She was standing in front of the door watching when one monk who chanting and circling the courtyard passed in front of her and threw out his arm and caught her. She feigned anger and said, "You are strange. What kind of monk are you?" But she did not try to get away from him. Those who saw this suspected that this was not the first time he had put his arms around her.

Mme Yi had one bad eye. The neighbors used to call her "Mrs. One-Eye."

Yejong 1, 1459.6.*kapsul*, 6:16b (8:391).

# Appendix 2

## Decline in
## Inheritance Percentages for Daughters

The following figures support the graph on page 63. This is a sample of those of inheritance documents from the text that showed the decline of inheritance for daughters collected from the Puan Kim (p), Kyŏngbuk (k), or SNU Kyujanggak (s) or other (o) collections. Here, 100% represents a share equal to that of the son, smaller fractions are the percentage the daughter received compared to that of the eldest son. We could have selected many more showing 100%, and after the transition there were many more that showed 0%; it is those that show the transition that are interesting.

| Date | Case (p/k/s/o) | % | page in text |
|------|----------------|------|--------------|
| 1535 | Two daughters (s) | 100% | 29 |
| 1545 | Shin Saimdang (o) | 100% | 26 |
| 1581 | Kang Chu-shin (p) | 100% | 36 |
| 1609 | Kim Kae (p) | 100% | 36 |
| 1658 | Chŏng-ssi (o) | 100% | 24 |
| 1669 | Kim Myŏng-yŏl (p) | 67% | 39 |
| 1682 | Kwŏn Mok (k) | 50% | 57 |
| 1687 | Kwŏn Mok (k) | 90% | 57 |
| 1688 | Kim Su-jong (p) | 33% | 44 |
| 1688 | Yi Kae (k) | 80% | 55 |
| 1695 | Kwŏn Yun (k) | 10% | 55 |
| 1736 | Kim Pang-gil (p) | 33% | 48 |
| 1767 | Kim Chŏng-ha (p) | 0% | 49 |

# Appendix 3

# Adoption Rates Found in *Sama* Exam Rosters

Herein are the statistics for the graph found in table 9.1, page 164. We used the *sama* exam because, unlike the *munkwa* or *mukwa* exam, it had a constant number of successful candidates, 100 *saengwŏn* and 100 *chinsa*, and was given consistently every three years (and on the occasions of the *chŭnggwang* exams). Thus, calculations were both simple and likely to be representative. Other sources, *chokpo* and *hojŏk*, indicate that what was happening to those who passed the *sama* examination was also happening to others in the *yangban* sector of society, and eventually in other sectors of society as well. On the graph, the percentages were clustered in half-century groupings to better show the gradual rise rather than the peaks and valleys that would be depicted in a year-by-year graph.

| Year, %-age 50 yr ave | | Year, %-age 50 yr ave | | Year, %-age 50 yr ave | |
|---|---|---|---|---|---|
| 1469, 0 | | 1633, 1 | | 1765, 8 | |
| 1483, 0 | | <u>1648, 5.5</u> | 3% | 1774, 12 | |
| <u>1496, 0</u> | 0% | 1651, 8 | | <u>1798, 11.5</u> | 11.25% |
| 1507, 0 | | 1652, 3 | | 1803, 13 | |
| 1513, 0 | | 1660, 6 | | 1804, 13 | |
| 1528, 0 | | 1663, 1 | | 1828, 16 | |
| 1534, 1.5 | | 1681, 8 | | 1834, 11.5 | |
| 1540, 0 | | 1683, 8.5 | | <u>1835, 11</u> | 12.9% |
| <u>1546, 1.5</u> | .3% | 1693, 5.5 | | 1852, 17 | |
| 1552, 2.5 | | <u>1699, 6</u> | 5.75% | 1859, 12.2 | |
| 1558, 6.5 | | 1710, 9.5 | | 1861, 15 | |
| 1564, 2 | | 1714, 7 | | 1870, 15.6 | |
| 1573, 2 | | 1721, 10 | | 1882, 15.4 | |
| <u>1588, 6.5</u> | 3.9% | 1725, 6 | | 1888, 12 | |
| 1613, 3 | | 1735, 12 | | <u>1891, 13</u> | 14.3% |
| 1618, 2 | | <u>1740, 13.5</u> | 9.7% | | |
| 1624, 3.5 | | 1754, 13.5 | | | |

# Appendix 4

## Outline of Cases Presented

Cases, statements, and noteworthy documents covered in the narrative are listed here for handy reference and reminder.

238

# Appendix 5

# Documents and Sources

*The following is an overview of the major documents cited herein.*

*Chokpo*: Lineage genealogies, literally meaning clan or tribe charts, published in chart form with either five or seven generations on a page in a foremat borrowed from China. Also called *sebo* (literally, charts of the generations), or *p'abo* (literally, charts of a lineage segment).

*HIT*: *Han'guk Inmyŏng Taesajŏn,* the standard biographical dictionary of Korea.

*Kyehu tŭngnok*: The register of adoptions (21 out of 39 volumes exant) kept by the Ministry of Rites from 1618 to 1894. Most entries are simple abstracts, three or four lines long, of the basic facts of a case as approved by the King. Some entries are revocations of earlier authorizations, and some are applications denied. The companion register (11 out of 13 volumes exant), the *Pyŏl kyehu tŭngnok* (Register of Special Cases of Adoption) also known as the *Pŏboe kyehu tŭngnok* (Register of Extra-legal Adoptions) kept from 1637 to 1753 listed more complicated cases involving controversial methods of setting up an heir.

*Kyŏngbuk Chibang Komunsŏ Chipsŏng*: A collection of documents from the North Kyŏngsang province including 221 inheritance document from several lineages. Published in 1981.

*Kyusa*: A collections of essays favorable to *sŏja* together with petitions to the Kings from groups of *sŏja* and other documents. Published in 1859.

*MTP*: *Mansŏng Taedong Po* (The Genealogies of Myriad Lineages), a comprehensive genealogical table covering hundreds of lineages. Published in the early 1930's, it is a virtual who's who of Korea for the last six hundred years in genealogical table format.

*Pangmok*: Rosters of those who passed exam in a given year. *Munkwa pangmok* were rosters of those who passed the highest civil service

239

exam. *Sama pangmok* were those who passed the secondary level exam, either the *chinsa* or *saengwŏn* test. A given roster would list all who passed in that specific exam; the *munkwa* was given regularly every three years, but special exams were given almost yearly, and sometimes twice in a year. The *sama* exams were given every three years, with 100 in the *chinsa* section and 100 in the *saengwŏn* section each time.

*Puan Kim-ssi Uban komunsŏ*: a collection of documents including 29 inheritance documents covering ten generations over 228 years of the Kim lineage of Puan. Published in 1983.

*RZS*: *Richo no zaisan sozokuho* (Property Inheritance Patterns for the Chosŏn [Yi] dynasty), a Japanese period official publication, published by the Governor-General's office in 1936. It is a comprehensive collection of cases from the *Shillok* and a few other sources.

*Shillok*: The Annals of the Chosŏn period, the daily record of the dialogue of the Yi kings with their officials at court.

# Bibliography

Abbreviations for frequently cited sources:

*HIT Han'guk inmyŏng taesajŏn*
*KCKC Kyŏngbuk chibang komunsŏ chipsŏng*
*KHTN Kyehu tŭngnok*
*MTP Mansŏng taedong po*
*PPK Puan Kim-ssi Uban komunsŏ*
*PKHTN Pyŏl kyehu tŭngnok*
*RZS Richo no zaisan sozokuho*

English Sources:
*The Analects*. Translated by James Legge. Oxford: Oxford University Press, 1885.
Baker, Hugh. *Chinese Family and Kinship*. New York: Columbia University Press, 1979.
Beattie, Hilary. *Land and Lineage in China*. Cambridge: Cambridge University Press, 1979.
Befu, Harumi. "Corporate Emphasis and Patterns of Descent in the Japanese Family" in *Japanese Culture* edited by Robert J. Smith and Richard K. Beardsley. New York: Wenner-Gren Foundation for Anthropological Research, 1962.
Brandt, Vincent. *A Korean Village: Between Farm and Sea*. Cambridge: Harvard University Press, 1971.
Brook, Timothy. "Funerary Ritual and the Building of Lineages in Late Imperial China," *Harvard Journal of Asiatic Studies* 49.2:465-499 (1989).
Chandra, Vipan. *Imperialism, Resistance, and Reform in Late Nineteenth-Century Korea: Enlightenment and the Independence Club*, Berkeley: Institute of East Asian Studies, U.C. Berkeley, 1988.
Ch'oe Yŏng-ho. "The Civil Examinations and the Social Structure in Early Yi Dynasty Korea: 1392-1600." Ph.D. dissertation, University of Chicago, 1971.

241

Clark, Donald. "Chosŏn's Founding Fathers: A Study of Merit Subjects in the Early Yi Dynasty," *Korean Studies* 6:17-40 (1982).

Cook, Harold. *Korea's 1884 Incident: Its Background and Kim Okkyun's Elusive Dream*. Seoul: Royal Asiatic Society/Taewŏn Publishing Co., 1972.

Cornell, Laurel. "Retirement, Inheritance, and Intergenerational Conflict in Preindustrial Japan," *Journal of Family History* 8:55-69 (Spring 1983).

Davenport, William. "Nonunilinear Descent and Descent Groups," in *Readings in Kinship and Social Structure* edited by Nelson Graburn. New York: Harper and Row, 1971; originally published in *American Anthropologist* 61:557-569 (1959).

Dennerline, Jerry. *The Chia-ting Loyalists: Confucian Leadership and Social Change in Seventeenth-Century China*. New Haven: Yale University Press, 1981.

_____. "Marriage, Adoption, and Charity in the Development of Lineages in Wu-hsi from Sung to Ch'ing," in *Kinship Organization in Late Imperial China, 1000-1940*, edited by Patricia Buckley Ebrey and James L. Watson, University of California Press, 1986.

Deuchler, Martina. *Confucian Gentlemen and Barbarian Envoys: The Opening of Korea, 1875-1885*. Seattle: University of Washington Press, 1977.

_____. "The Tradition: Women duing the Yi Dynasty," in *Virtues in Conflict: Tradition and the Korean Woman Today*, edited by Sandra Mattielli Seoul: Royal Asiatic Society, 1977.

_____. "Neo-Confucianism: The Impulse for Social Action in Early Yi Korea," *Journal of Korean Studies*, 2:71-111 (1980).

_____. "Heaven Does Not Discriminate" *Journal of Korean Studies* 6:121-163 (1988-89).

_____. *The Confucian Transformation of Korea: A Study of Society and Ideology*. Cambridge: Harvard University Press, 1992.

Dull, Jack L. "Marriage and Divorce in Han China: A Glimpse of 'Pre-Confucian' Society," in *Chinese Family Law and Social Change* edited by David Buxbaum, Seattle: University of Washington Press, 1978.

Duncan, John. "The Social Background to the Founding of the Chosŏn Dynasty: Change or Continuity?," *Journal of Korean Studies* 6:39-79 (1988-1989).

Ebrey, Patricia Buckley. "The Early Stages in the Development of Descent Group Organization," in *Kinship Organization in Late Imperial*

*China, 1000-1940*, edited by Patricia Buckley Ebrey and James L. Watson, University of California Press, 1986.

_____ and James L. Watson. *Kinship Organization in Late Imperial China, 1000-1940*. University of California Press, 1986.

_____. "Women in the Kinship System of the Southern Song Upper Class," *Historical Reflections* 8:113-128 (1981); also appears in *Women in China: Current Directions in Historical Scholarship*; edited by Richard Guisso and Stanley Johannesen, Youngstown: Philo Press, 1981.

_____. "Conceptions of the Family in the Sung Dynasty," *Journal of Asian Studies* 43.2:219-243 (1984).

_____. "Concubines in Sung China," *Journal of Family History* 11:1-24 (1986).

Fabre, P. Alfred. "Avril au Pays des Aieux," *Catholic Church in China: Collectanea Commissionis Synodalis*, vol. 8 (1935).

Firth, Raymond. "A Note on Descent Groups in Polynesia," in *Readings in Kinship and Social Structure* edited by Nelson Graburn. New York: Harper and Row, 1971; originally published in *Man* 57:4-7 (1957).

Fox, Robin. *Kinship and Marriage*. Harmondsworth, England: Penguin Books, 1967.

Freedman, Maurice. *Chinese Lineage and Society: Fukien and Kwangtung*. London: Athlone Press, 1966.

_____. *Family and Kinship in Chinese Society*. Stanford: Stanford University Press, 1970.

Graburn, Nelson. *Readings in Kinship and Social Structure*. New York: Harper and Row, 1971.

Goodenough, Ward H. *Description and Comparison in Cultural Anthropology*. Chicago: Aldine, 1970.

Goody, Jack. "Sideways or Downward? Lateral and Vertical Succession, Inheritance and Descent in Africa and Eurasia," *Man* 5:627-638 (1970).

_____. "Strategies of Heirship," *Comparative Studies in Society and History* 15:3-20 (1973).

_____. *The Oriental, the Ancient, and the Primitive*. Cambridge: Cambridge University Press, 1990.

Haboush, JaHyun Kim. *A Heritage of Kings: One Man's Monarchy in the Confucian World*. New York: Columbia University Press, 1988.

Hayami, Akira. "The Myth of Primogeniture and Impartible Inheritance in Tokugawa Japan," *Journal of Family History* 8:3-29 (Spring 1983).

Janelli, Roger L. and Dawnhee. *Ancestor Worship and Korean Society*. Palo Alto: Stanford University Press, 1982.

Johnson, David G. *The Medieval Chinese Oligarchy*. Boulder: Westview Press, 1977.

————. "Chinese Kinship Reconsidered," *The China Quarterly* 94:362-365 (June, 1983).

Kawashima, Fujiya. "Clan Structure and Political Power in Yi Dynasty Korea—A Case Study of the Munhwa Yu Clan." Ph.D. dissertation, Harvard University, 1972.

————. "Lineage Elite and Bureaucracy in Early Yi to mid-Yi Dynasty Korea," *Occasional Papers on Korea* 5:8-19 (1977).

————. "Historiographic Development in South Korea: State and Society from the Mid-Koryŏ to the Mid-Yi Dynasty," *Korean Studies* 2:29-56 (1978).

————. "The Local Gentry Association in Mid-Yi Dynasty Korea: A Preliminary Study of the Ch'angyŏng Hyangan, 1600-1839," *The Journal of Korean Studies* 2:113-138 (1980).

Kendall, Laurel. "Korean Ancestors: From the Woman's Side" in *Korean Women: View from the Inner Room*, edited by Laurel Kendall and Mark Peterson. New Haven: East Rock Press, 1984.

————. Shamans, Housewifes, and Other Restless Spirits: Women in Korean Ritual Life. Honolulu: University of Hawaii Press, 1985.

————. *The Life and Hard Times of a Korean Shaman*. Honolulu: University of Hawaii Press, 1988.

———— and Griffin Dix, eds. *Religion and Ritual in Korean Society*. Berkeley: University of California Press, 1987.

———— and Mark Peterson, eds. *Korean Women: View from the Inner Room*. New Haven: East Rock Press, 1984.

Kim, Man-jung. "Kuunmong" [The nine cloud dream]. Translated and edited by Kim Chong-un and Richard Rutt. *Virtuous Women*. Seoul: Korean Commission for UNESCO, 1974.

Kim, Yung-Chung, ed. *Women of Korea: A History from Ancient Times to 1945*. Seoul: Ewha Women's University Press, 1977.

Lee, Ki-baik. *A New History of Korea*. Translated by Edward W. Wagner with Edward Shultz. Cambridge: Harvard University Press, 1984.

Maas, Jeffrey P. *Lordship and Inheritance in Early Medieval Japan* Palo Alto: Stanford University Press, 1989.

Matsumoto, Y. Scott. "Notes on Primogeniture in Postwar Japan," in *Japanese Culture* edited by Robert J. Smith and Richard K. Beardsley. New York: Wenner-Gren Foundation for Anthropological Research, 1962.

Mattielli, Sandra, ed. *Virtues in Conflict: Tradition and the Korean Woman Today*. Seoul: Royal Asiatic Society, 1977.

McMullen, I. J. "Non-Agnatic Adoption: A Confucian Controversy in Seventeenth- and Eighteenth-Century Japan." *Harvard Journal of Asiatic Studies* 35 (1975).

Michell, Tony. "Facts and Hypothesis in Yi Dynasty Economic History: The Demographic Dimension," *Korean Studies Forum* 6 (Winter-Spring 1979-80).

Miyakawa, Hisayuki. "The Confucianization of South China," in *The Confucian Persuasion*, Stanford: Stanford University Press, 1960.

Naquin, Susan. "Marriage in North China: the Role of Ritual," Paper presented at the Conference of Marriage and Inequality in China: January 1988, quoted in Jack Goody, *The Oriental, the Ancient, and the Primitive*. Cambridge: Cambridge University Press, 1990.

Palais, James. *Politics and Policy in Traditional Korea*. Cambridge: Harvard University Press, 1975.

Pehrson, Robert N. "Bilateral Kin Groupings as a Structural Type: A Preliminary Statement," in *Readings in Kinship and Social Structure* edited by Nelson Graburn. New York: Harper and Row, 1971.

Peterson, Mark. "Adoption in Korean Genealogies," *Korea Journal* 14:1 (January, 1974).

_____. "Some Korean Attitudes Toward Adoption" *Korea Journal* 17:12 (December, 1977).

_____. "Merchants and *Hyangban* in Kaesŏng," *Korea Journal* 18:10 (October, 1978).

_____. "A New Look at Old Korea," *Korea Quarterly*, 2:1 (1979).

Potter, Jack M. "Land and Lineage in Traditional China," in *Family and Kinship in Chinese Society*, edited by Maurice Freedman. Stanford: Stanford University Press, 1970.

Rawski, Evelyn S. "The Ma Landlords of Yang-chia-kou in Late Ch'ing and Republican China," in *Kinship Organization in Late Imperial China, 1000-1940*, edited by Patricia Buckley Ebrey and James L. Watson, University of California Press, 1986.

*Shih Ching*. Translated by James Legge. Oxford: Oxford University Press, 1885.

Shima, Mutsuhiko. "In Quest of Social Recognition: A Retrospective View on the Development of Korean Lineage Organization," *Harvard Journal of Asiatic Studies* 50.1:87-129 (June 1990).

Smith, Robert J. *Two Japanese Villages*. New York: Greenwood Press, 1969.

_____. *Ancestor Worship in Contemporary Japan*. Stanford: Stanford University Press, 1974.

Somerville, John. "Stability in Eighteenth Century Ulsan," *Korean Studies Forum* 1 (Autumn-Winter 1976/77).

Song June-ho. "The Government Examination Rosters of the Yi Dynasty," in *Studies in Asian Genealogy*, edited by Spencer J. Palmer. Provo, Utah: Brigham Young University Press, 1972.

Wagner, Edward W. *The Literati Purges*. Cambridge: Harvard University Press, 1974.

_____. "Social Stratification in Seventeenth-Century Korea: Some Observations from a 1663 Seoul Census Register," *Occasional Papers on Korea* 1:36-54 (1974).

Wagner-Song *Munkwa* Index. (Computer printout of data compiled from all known *Munkwa* examination rosters, by Edward W. Wagner, Harvard University and Song June-ho, Chŏnbuk National University/Wŏn'gwang University.)

Wakita, Haruko. "Marriage and Property in Premodern Japan from the Perspective of Women's History," *Journal of Japanese Studies*, 10:1 (1984).

Waltner, Ann. "Widows and Remarriage in Ming and Early Qing China" *Historical Reflections* 8:129-146 (1981); also appears in *Women in China: Current Directions in Historical Scholarship*; edited by Richard Guisso and Stanley Johannesen, Youngstown: Philo Press, 1981.

_____. *Getting an Heir: Adoption and the Construction of Kinship in Late Imperial China*. Honolulu: University of Hawaii, 1990.

Watson, James L. "Agnates and Outsiders: Adoption in Chinese Lineage," *Man* 10:2 (June 1975).

_____. "Chinese Kinship Reconsidered: Anthropological Perspectives on Historical Research," *The China Quarterly* 92:589-622 (December 1982).

_____. "Anthropological Overview: The Development of Chinese Descent Groups," in *Kinship Organization in Late Imperial China, 1000-1940*, edited by Patricia Buckley Ebrey and James L. Watson, University of California Press, 1986.

Watson, Rubie S. "The Creation of a Chinese Lineage: The Teng of Ha Tsuen, 1669-1751," *Modern Asian Studies*, 16.1:69-100.

_____. "Class Differences and Affinal Relations in South China," *Man* 16:593-615 (1981).

Wolf, Arthur and Robert Smith. "China, Korea, and Japan", in *Religion and Ritual in Korean Society*, Laurel Kendall and Griffin Dix eds., Berkeley: University of California Press, 1987.

Wolf, Arthur and Chieh-shan Huang. *Marriage and Adoption in China, 1845-1945*. Stanford: Stanford University Press, 1980.

Asian Language Sources:

Ch'oe Chae-sŏk. *Han'guk kajok chedosa yŏn'gu* [Research on the Korean Family System]. Seoul: Ilchisa, 1983.

Ch'oe Sun-hŭi. "Sangsan Kim-ssi punjaegi sogo" [A brief study of a Sangsan Kim-ssi inheritance document], *T'aedong kojŏn yŏn'gu* 10:907-931 (1993)

Ch'oe, Sŭng-hŭi. *Han'guk komunsŏ yŏn'gu* [Study of Old Documents of Korea]. Sŏngnam: Academy of Korean Studies, 1981.

Chŏng Sŭng-mo. "T'onghon'gwŏn kwa chiyŏk sahoe pon'gye yŏn'gu" [Study of Marriage Patterns and Rural Society], *Han'guk munhwa illyuhak* 15 (1983.12).

*Chŏnbuk chibang ŭi komunsŏ (1)* [Ancient documents from the North Chŏlla province, part one]. Chŏnju: Chŏnbuk hyangt'o munhwa yŏn'guhoe [The association for the study of North Chŏlla provincial culture], 1993.

*Chŏnju Yi-ssi Korim'gunp'a sŏnjo yumunjip* [Documents Left by the Ancestors of the Korim-gun Branch of the Chŏnju Yi Lineage]. Ch'ilsan'gunp'a chongch'inhoe publication, 1975.

*Chosŏn wangjo shillok* [Veritable records of the Chosŏn dynasty]. 48 vols. Seoul: Kuksa p'yŏnch'an wiwŏnhoe [National history compilation committee], 1955-58.

*Chu-tzu ta-ch'üan* [The complete works of Master Chu (Hsi)]. *Ssu-pu pei-yao*.

*Chu Tzu yü-lei* [Discussions with Master Chu (Hsi)] (Reprint, 1978).

*Han'guk ch'injok chedo yŏn'gu* [Studies on the Korean family system]. *Yŏksa hakhoe* [Korean Historical Society]. Seoul: Ilchogak, 1992.

*Han'guk inmyŏng taesajŏn (HIT)* [Biographical dictionary of Korea]. Seoul: Shin'gu munhwasa, 1976.

*Han'guk yŏsŏng-sa* [The history of Korean women]. Seoul: Ewha University Press, 1971.

Kawashima, Fujiya. "Bunka Ryu-shi ni mirareru ssizoku no idō to sono seikaku" (The characteristics of relocation patterns of lineage groups as seen in the Munhwa Yu lineage), *Chosen kakuho* 70:43-74 (1974).

Kim Il-mi. "Chosŏn chŏn'gi ŭi namyŏ kyunbun sangsokche e taehayŏ" [Concerning equal inheritance between men and women in early Chosŏn], *Idae sawŏn* 8:31-67 (1969).

Kim, Tong-uk. *Komunsŏ chipchin* [A collection of photocopies of ancient documents]. Seoul: Yŏnsei University Press, 1977.

Kim, Tu-hŏn. *Han'guk kajok chedo yŏn'gu* [Research on the Korean family system]. Seoul: Seoul National University Press, 1969.

Kim Yong-man. "Chosŏn shidae kyunbun sangsokche-e kwanhan ilyŏn'gu" [A study on the equal inheritance system of the Chosŏn period], *Taegu sahak* 23:1-47 (1983).

_____. "Chosŏn shidae chaeji sajok ŭi chaesan soyu hyŏngt'ae (I)" [The forms of property ownership of the landed aristocracy of the Chosŏn period], *Taegu sahak* 27:89-159 (1985.6).

Ko Yŏng-jin. "15/16 segi Chuja karye ŭi shihaeng kwa kŭ ŭiŭi" [The implementation of Chu Hsi's *karye* and its significance in the fifteenth and sixteenth century], *Han'guk saron* 21:73-171 (1989.8).

*Komunsŏ chipchin* [Collected photocopies of ancient documents]. Seoul: Seoul National University Library, 1972.

*Kwangsan Kim-ssi Och'ŏn komunsŏ* (Old documents of the Yean branch of the Kwangsan Kim lineage). Sŏngnam: Academy of Korean Studies, 1981.

*Kyehu tŭngnok (KHTN)* [The register of adoptions]. Kyujanggak collection, Seoul National University Library, catalog no. 12869.

*Kyusa* [The sunflower history, a collection of documents pertaining to *sŏja*]. Seoul: Ewha University Press, 1968.

*Mansŏng taedong po (MTP)* [The great genealogy of the myriad lineages]. Seoul: 1931-33.

Mun Suk-cha. "Chaeryŏng Yi-ssi nyŏnghaep'a kamun ŭi pun'chaegi punsok" [An analysis of the inheritance documents of the Nyŏnghae sublineage of the Chaeryŏng Yi lineage], *Ch'ŏnggye sahak* 9:69-137 (1992).

No Myŏng-ho. "Sanŭm changjŏk ŭl t'onghae pon 17 segich'o ch'ollak ŭi hyŏllyŏn yangsang" [The kinship aspect of the early seventeenth century village as seen in the Sanŭm census register], *Han'guk saron* 5:305-343 (1979.10).

_____. *Koryŏ sahoe ŭi yangjŭkchŏk ch'injok chojik yŏn'gu* (Research on the bilateral kindred of Koryŏ society). PhD dissertation, Seoul National University, 1988.

Pae Chae-hong. "Chosŏn shidae ch'ŏpchanyŏ ŭi chaesan sangsok kwa chonjae yangt'ae," [Inheritance of property by the children of *ch'ŏp* (secondary wives) in the Chosŏn period], *Taegu sahak* 39:95-128 (1990.8).

Pak, Pyŏng-ho. "Isŏnggyehu ŭi silchŭngjŏk yŏn'gu" [An evidentiary study of non-agnatic adoption]. *Pŏphak* [Seoul National University Law Journal] 14-1 (1973).

Pak Yong-suk. *Chosŏn hugi sahoesa yŏn'gu* (Research on late Chosŏn society). Seoul: Nŭlhamkke, 1994.

*Puan Kim-ssi Uban komunsŏ (PKK)* [Ancient documents of the Uban branch of the Puan Kim lineage]. Seoul: Chŏngshin munwha yŏn'guwŏn [Academy of Korean Studies], 1983.

*Pyŏl kyehu tŭngnok (PKHTN)* [Register of special adoptions]. Kyujanggak collection, Seoul National University Library, catalog no. 12903.

*Richo no zaisan sozokuho (RZS)* [Yi dynasty property inheritance practices]. Seoul: Chosen Shotokufu Chusuin, 1936.

*Sasong yuch'wi* [Various legal precedents]. (Originally published by Kim Paek-kan in 1585.) Seoul: Pŏpche chosa wiwŏnhoe, 1964.

*Soju yo o* [Collection of petitions from *sŏja*]. Yi Sang-baek collection, Kyujanggak, Seoul National University Library.

Song June-ho. *Chosŏn sahoesa yŏn'gu* [Studies on the Social History of Chosŏn]. Seoul: Ilchogak, 1987.

_____. "Chosŏn sidae ŭi kwagŏ wa yangban mit yangin (I)" [*Yangban* and commoners in the examinations of the Chosŏn period (I)], *Yŏksa hakpo*, no. 69 (1976).

_____. "Chosŏn yangban ko" [A Study of Yangban in Chosŏn], *Han'guk sahak* 4:27-357 (1983).

_____. "Han'guge issŏsŏ ŭi kagye kirok ŭi yŏksa wa kŭ haesŏk" [An Interpretive History of Family Records in Traditional Korea], *Yŏksa hakpo* 87:99-143 (1980).

_____. "Han'guk ŭi ssijokche e issŏsŏ ŭi pon'gwan mit shijo ŭi munje" [The origin and nature of *pon'gwan* (clan seat) and *shijo* (founding ancestor) in the Korean Lineage System], *Yŏksa hakpo* 109:91-136 (March 1986).

*Sugyo chimnok* [The collection of royal decrees]. Seoul: Chosen Sotokufu Chusuin, 1943.

*Suyang shiyang tŭngnok* [Register of *suyang* and *shiyang* adoptions]. Kyujanggak collection, Seoul National University Library, 2 vols., catalog nos. 12960-1 & 12960-2.

*Suyang sŭngjŏk ilgi* [Diary of adoptions by promotion to legitimacy]. Kyujanggak collection, Seoul National University Library, catalog no. 13038.

*Taejŏn hoet'ong* [The compiled codes]. Seoul: Kyŏngmunsa, 1978.

*Yŏksa hakhoe* (Korean Historical Society). *Han'guk ch'injok chedo yŏn'gu* [Studies on the Korean family system]. Seoul: Ilchogak, 1992.

Yang, Man-jŏng. *Hyangt'osa nonmunjip* [Collection of essays on local history of Hyŏn'gok Yang Man-jŏng]. Chŏnju, 1994.

Yi, Hŭi-sŭng. *Kugŏ taesajŏn* [Great dictionary of the national language]. Seoul: Minjungsŏgwan, 1961.

Yi, Kwang-gyu. *Han'guk kajok ŭi sajŏk yŏn'gu*, [Historical research on the Korean family]. Seoul: Ilchisa, 1977.

_____. *Han'guk kajok ŭi kujobunsok*, [A structural analysis of the Korean family]. Seoul: Ilchisa, 1975.

_____. *Han'guk ŭi kajok kwa chongjok* [The Korean family and lineage]. Seoul: Minŭmsa, 1990.

Yi Sang-baek. "Ch'ilsŏ chi ok" [The criminal case of the seven *sŏja*]. *Yi Pyŏng-do paksa hwan'gap kinyŏm nonch'ong* [*Festschrift for Professor Yi Pyŏng-do*]. Seoul: Ilchogak, 1956.

_____. "Sŏŏl ch'adae ŭi yŏnwŏn e taehan il munje" [One problem concerning the origins of discrimination against *sŏja*]. *Chindan hakpo* 1 (November, 1934).

Yi Su-gŏn. *Kyŏngbuk chibang komunsŏ chipsŏn* (KCKC) [A collection of ancient documents from the North Kyŏngsang area]. Kyŏngsan: Yŏngnam University Press, 1981.

_____. "T'oegye Yi Hwang kamun ŭi chaesan yurae wa kŭ soyu hyŏngt'ae" [The source of the property and the manner of its ownership in the household of Yi Hwang (T'oegye)] *Yŏksa kyoyuk nonjip* 13.14:641-680 (1990.2).

_____. "Chosŏnjŏn'gi ŭi sahoe pyŏndong kwa sangsokchedo" [Social change and inheritance in the early Chosŏn period], in *Yŏksa hakpo* 129:23-76 (1991); and also in *Han'guk ch'injok chedo yŏn'gu* [Studies on the Korean family system]. Seoul: Ilchogak, 1992.

Yi Sun-gu. "Chosŏn ch'ogi Chujahak ŭi pogŭp kwa yŏsŏng ŭi sahoejŏk chiwi" [The dissemination of the philosophy of Chu Hsi in early Chosŏn and the social position of women], *Ch'ŏnggye sahak* 3:53-95 (1986).

Yi T'ae-jin. "Shimyuk segi Han'guksa ŭi ihaebanghyang" [Toward an understanding of sixteenth century Korean history], in *Han'guk sahoesa yŏn'gu* [Studies in Korean social history]. Seoul: Chishik-sanŏpsa, 1986.

Yi Tae-yŏng. *Han'guk ihon chedo yŏn'gu* [Research on divorce in Korea].
   Seoul: Yŏsŏng munjae yŏn'guwŏn [The women's research center],
   1957.

Collected Writings (*Munjip*) and Essays:

Cho Hŏn. *Chungbongjip.*
Kim Chang-saeng. *Ŭirye munhae* [Answers and analysis of ritual
   questions].
Pak Mun-il. *Unamjip.*
Shin Kŭn. *Ŭirye yusŏl* [Discussion of propriety and ritual].
Sŏng Hon. *Ugyejip.*
Sŏng Man-jing. *Ch'udamjip.*
Yi I. *Yulgok chŏnsŏ.*
Yi Wŏn-bae. *Kwiamjip.*
Yun Chŭng. *Myŏngjae ŭirye mundap* [Questions and answers
   concerning propriety and ritual by Myŏngjae].

Genealogies (*Chokpo/Sebo*):

*Andong Kwŏn-ssi sebo.* 1476. Kyujanggak, Seoul National University
   Library.
*Chŏnju Yi-ssi murim-gun p'abo.*
   1961. Harvard-Yenching #K2290.5/4483.4.
*Hansan Yi-ssi yangdogongp'a sebo.*
   1963. Harvard-Yenching #K2290.5/4442.
*Kwangsan Kim-ssi sebo.*
   1957. Harvard-Yenching #K2290.5/8192.5.
*Kyŏngju Kim-ssi sebo.*
   1784. Harvard-Yenching #K2290.5/8103.2
*Kyŏngju Yi-ssi Kuktang-gong p'abo.*
   1931. Harvard-Yenching #K2290.5/4403.7.
*Kyŏngju Yi-ssi sagan sebo.*
   1934-35. Harvard-Yenching #K2290.5/4403.5.
*Munhwa Yu-ssi sebo (MYCP).*
   1535. (Reprint edition, Seoul: Kyŏnginmunhwasa, 1979.)
*Munhwa Yu-ssi sebo.*
   1803. Harvard-Yenching #K2290.5/4202.3.
*Puan Kim-ssi taebo.*
   Taejŏn: Hoesangsa, 1981.
*Sangju Hwang-ssi chokpo.*
   1969. Harvard-Yenching #K2290.5/4893.

*Taegu Sŏ-ssi sebo.*
   1852. Harvard-Yenching #K2290.5/2947.12 or FK544.
*Tŏksu Yi-ssi sebo.*
   1930. Harvard-Yenching #K2290.5/4421a.
*Yŏngil Chŏng-ssi soksu sojong sebo.*
   Central National Library, catalog no. *han* 58, *ka* 24-51.

Unbound Documents in Public Collections:
Chŏng-ssi inheritance document is held in the Central National Library,
   catalog no. *han* 58, *ka* 24-60.
Ma lineage document is held in the Kyujanggak collection, Seoul National
   University Library, catalog no. 11981.
Puan Kim documents are held by the lineage head in Puan, but copies of the
   originals are held at the Museum of Chŏnbuk National University.
   A reprint in a single bound volume was published by the Academy of
   Korean Studies. See *Puan Kim-ssi Uban komunsŏ* above.
Shin Saimdang inheritance document featuring Yulgok's mother and
   her siblings is held in the museum on the grounds of the Ojukhŏn
   shrine north of Kangnŭng.
Yulgok inheritance document featuring Yulgok and his siblings is held in
   the museum of Kŏn'guk University, Seoul.

Documents in Private Collections:
An adoption document of Ch'oe Kyŏng-yu held by the author; is seen in the
   underlay of the title page.
An adoption document of Chŏng Mun-ju held by his descendant Chŏng
   Chu-yŏng, a prominent member of the Confucian Association
   headquartered at the Sŏnggyun'gwan, Seoul. A photocopy is in
   the possession of the author.
Sungam [Sŏngam] Archive of Ancient Documents, the private
   collection of Cho Pyŏng-sun, an excellent collection of *Sama
   pangmok* (examination rosters).

# Index

# CORNELL EAST ASIA SERIES

FORTHCOMING

*Kojiki-den, Book 1,* by Motoori Norinaga, translated by Ann Wehmeyer
*Playing With Fire,* by Cho Chong-Rae, translated by Chun Kyung-Ja
*I Saw a Pale Horse and Selections from Diary of a Vagabond,* by Hayashi
        Fumiko, translated by Janice Brown
*Principles of Poetry (Shi no genri),* by Shagiwara Sakutaro, translated by
Chester Wang

To order, please contact the Cornell East Asia Series, East Asia Program,
Cornell University, 140 Uris Hall, Ithaca, NY 14853-7601, USA; phone
(607) 255-6222, fax (607) 255-1388, internet: kks3@cornell.edu.

---

# Korean Adoption and Inheritance
## *Case Studies in the Creation*
## *of a Classic Confucian Society*
### MARK PETERSON

The cases in Korean adoption and inheritance reveal steps in the transition called "Confucianization" that took place mostly in the seventeenth century. The transition from partible inheritance, equally divided between sons and daughters, to primogeniture; the attempt to use soja as heirs; the movement toward agnatic adoption as the way to provide an heir when there were no children, or when there were only daughters born into the household are all covered in numerous cases from the official history, from government records, and from private documents.

MARK PETERSON is Associate Professor of Korean Studies and Coordinator of the Asian Studies Program at Brigham Young University. Within Korean studies he researches and publishes in the areas of social history, contemporary Korean society, and classic Korean novels.

8-96/.5M paper/.2M cloth/TS